AF412118

The Frontiers of the European Union

Also by Malcolm Anderson

FRONTIERS: Territory and State Formation in the Contemporary World

THE FRONTIERS OF EUROPE (*co-editor with Eberhard Bort*)

THE IRISH BORDER: History, Politics and Culture (*with Eberhard Bort*)

POLICING THE EUROPEAN UNION (*co-author*)

Also by Eberhard Bort

BOUNDARIES AND IDENTITIES: The Eastern Frontier of the European Union

THE FRONTIERS OF EUROPE (*co-editor with Malcolm Anderson*)

THE IRISH BORDER: History, Politics and Culture (*with Malcolm Anderson*)

The Frontiers of the European Union

Malcolm Anderson
Professor Emeritus
University of Edinburgh

with

Eberhard Bort
Coordinator of Governance of Scotland Forum
Edinburgh

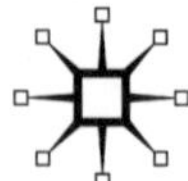

First published 2001 by
PALGRAVE
Houndmills, Basingstoke, Hampshire RG21 6XS and
175 Fifth Avenue, New York, N. Y. 10010
Companies and representatives throughout the world

PALGRAVE is the new global academic imprint of
St. Martin's Press LLC Scholarly and Reference Division and
Palgrave Publishers Ltd (formerly Macmillan Press Ltd).

ISBN 0–333–80435–X

This book is printed on paper suitable for recycling and made from fully managed and sustained forest sources.

A catalogue record for this book is available from the British Library.

Library of Congress Cataloging-in-Publication Data
Anderson, Malcolm.
    The frontiers of the European Union / Malcolm Anderson
    and Eberhard Bort.
        p. cm.
    Includes bibliographical references and index.
    ISBN 0–333–80435–X
     1. European Union countries—Boundaries. 2. European Union
    countries—Foreign economic relations—Europe, Eastern.
    3. Europe—Foreign relations. 4. Social integration—European
    Union countries. 5. International cooperation. 6. Europe, Eastern–
    –Foreign economic relations—European Union countries. I. Bort,
    Eberhard, 1954– II. Title.
    D1065.E852 A44 2000
    341.242'2—dc21
                                                          00–066884

10   9   8   7   6   5   4   3   2   1
10   09 08 07 06 05 04 03 02 01

Printed and bound in Great Britain by
Antony Rowe Ltd, Chippenham, Wiltshire

Contents

List of Maps

Acknowledgements

Essential financial support for the research on which this book is based was generously provided by an Economic and Social Research Council grant (ESRC No. R000 23 5602) and by a Nuffield Trust Fellowship which gave relief from teaching duties.

Edinburgh colleagues Anthony Cohen, Neil MacCormick, Tom Nairn, Peter Cullen (Trier), Jim Sheptycki (Durham) and Willie Paterson (Birmingham) helped in a variety of ways. A network of colleagues throughout Europe provided insights, information and material help. We particularly thank Didier Bigo (Paris) and Raimondo Strassoldo (Udine).

Conferences and meetings were facilitated with the help of Europa-Zentrum Baden-Württemberg (Sabine Leins), Europahaus Wien (Erich Wendl) and Accademia Europeistica Gorizia (Pio Baissero).

We are grateful to Anona Lyons (Department of Geography, University of Edinburgh) for drawing the maps in this book.

1
Introduction

Since the beginning of the turbulent twentieth century the changes, both in location and function, of European frontiers have been dramatic. The old multinational empires in Europe were showing signs of serious strain before 1914, and were already disintegrating in the Balkans. Even the multinational British state was on the verge of breaking up, threatened by Irish secession, because of the failure to establish a 'British Isles identity'. In the immediate aftermath of the First World War, radically new frontiers were drawn, influenced by the interests of the victors and by the principle of the self-determination of nations, in Central and Eastern Europe. The Second World War again resulted in boundary redrawing in Central and Eastern Europe as well as the partition of Germany. Transfer of populations on a massive scale accompanied this reallocation of territory, producing a greater coincidence of national and state frontiers. Territorial questions were then frozen for a 40-year period, during which time an 'Iron Curtain' separated two incompatible political and economic systems.

The frontiers of Europe returned, in the 1990s, to the centre of political debate, as the European Union (EU) member states took further steps towards closer co-operation and as radical transformation followed the collapse of Communism in Central and Eastern Europe. Within the EU, integration gained momentum through the 1986 Single European Act, creating the Single European Market (SEM) by 1 January 1993; at the same time, a 'border-free' Europe was envisaged in the 1985 Schengen Agreement and the 1990 Schengen Convention. Economic and political integration presaged a blurring of the distinction between international and sub-state boundaries within the EU, and particularly within 'Schengenland'. This raised the possibility that, as international frontiers lost the visible trappings of police, border check points and barriers, their importance as markers of identity would become more important. The effects of the abolition of controls at internal frontiers and parallel measures – the most important being the establishment of a new currency area – will be radical even though slow to take effect.

The collapse of Communism resulted in the drawing of approximately 20 000 kilometres of new international frontiers – a reconfiguration of the political map only witnessed before in Europe after major wars (Map 1.1). The end of the Soviet empire also allowed opening of the borders to East and Central Europe in 1989–90 and created the prospect of EU and NATO enlargement towards the east.

Map 1.1   New frontiers in Central and Eastern Europe after 1989

This cataclysm therefore created both new international frontiers as new states were established, and it altered the nature of these frontiers. The end of Communism and the opening of frontiers help to heal the 'wound' of the Iron Curtain and abolish the 'unnatural' division of the continent. The practices of the EU, including its mode of frontier management, have been extended to the East; EU programmes, INTERREG and PHARE, have supported the creation of Euroregions along the former Cold War border. But there is contradiction between the project for EU enlargement and the Schengen practices which entail hardened external frontiers. One of the most closed frontiers in recent history had been dismantled, but the EU countries still perceive threats coming from the east and their response has been to delay EU enlargement and engage in relative closure of frontiers. The response from the EU's eastern neighbours is a question. Why invest in improved border controls at a frontier which would become, in the relatively near future, part of the 'border-free' Europe?

I

Border-related issues which have surfaced during the main period of preparation of this book – April 1995 to September 1998 – have been particularly acute on the external frontier of the EU from the Finno-Russian frontier in the north to the Mediterranean in the south. Among the most discussed are:

- The gulf in socio-economic development with even the most developed of the East-Central European states lagging far behind even the poorest EU members in all indicators of economic activity.
- Differences of state organisation, federalised (Germany and Austria) or decentralised (Italy), confronted by centralised states (Poland, Czech Republic, Hungary and Slovenia) result in difficulty for transfrontier co-operation.
- Elites in the new democracies harbour worries about their identity and culture being overrun by global, usually American, imports, and regard frontiers as important for cultural defence.
- The Mediterranean states – Greece, Italy, France and Spain – are on a cultural frontier between countries of Christian tradition and Islam, an even deeper chasm in terms of economic developement. These southern EU states are faced with difficult problems of frontier control, and a lack of solidarity on the part of their EU partners in confronting their problems.

- The Finno-Russian frontier is set to remain, for the foreseeable future, the external limit of the EU. It is also the only border shared by an EU member state with Russia, and the contrast between a rich, developed, well-managed Western economy and a transitional mismanaged economy is nowhere more marked than along this frontier.
- The German–Polish border has had, as the eastern frontier of the EU in general, an explosion of transfrontier traffic. Euroregions cover the whole frontier zone, from Pomerania in the north to Neisse/Nysa in the south (Gerner 1997). Yet, this border has repeatedly been termed a 'crime zone' by the former German Minister for the Interior, and costly efforts have been undertaken by Germany to police it (Bort 1996).
- Sporadic Polish fears are voiced that Germans may return to reclaim property seized during the great expulsion of Germans from the territory annexed by Poland in 1945 (Gruchman and Walk 1997; Kennard 1997).
- The Czech–German border, although comprehensively covered by co-operative transfrontier Euroregions, still lives under the cloud of the Sudeten problem. The Sudeten Germans, supported by the Bavarian government as guardian of their interests (largely because it depends on the Sudeten vote), are dissatisfied with the January 1997 German–Czech Agreement.
- The 'velvet divorce' of Czechoslovakia in 1993 created a new frontier between the Czech Republic and Slovakia which was deemed to act as a filter for illegal immigrants and to relieve pressure at the Czech–German frontier (Bort 1996).
- Poland, the Czech Republic, Hungary and Slovenia have been, at least partially, successful in implementing Schengen-type controls at their eastern frontiers which has persuaded their western neighbours to keep their western EU borders as open as compatible with the Schengen restrictions.
- The Hungarians, having initiated the dismantling of the Iron Curtain in 1989, were offended when, in preparation for full implementation of Schengen, Austria started to control this frontier as the external EU border.
- Slovenia and Croatia have, since 1992 when they seceded from Yugoslavia, been engaged in establishing new international frontiers; the internal boundary-making in Bosnia-Hercegovina proved a nightmare for the EU. The Kosovo crisis of 1998, including a dirty border war, threatened larger conflict.

- Wave after wave of Albanian refugees tried to make their way into Italy, which – after having been until very recently a country of emigration – was confronted, on various sectors of its 8000 kilometres of sea frontiers, with intractable immigration problems.
- This influx of desperate Kurds, Albanians and African refugees raised the issue of an EU common responsibility for, and sharing the burden of, policing the external frontier (Anderson 1998).
- Greece has the peculiarity, shared with the United Kingdom[1] and Ireland, of having no common land frontier with another EU state. Its international land borders are 'under stress' in Macedonia, Thrace, Epirus and over the Aegean Sea border and over divided Cyprus. In 1996, the Aegean dispute came close to provoking war between Greece and Turkey over the uninhabited Imia/Kardak island.
- Spain and Portugal, traditionally countries of emigration are exposed to migratory pressures from the southern shores of the Mediterranean (Burke 1998). Ceuta and Melilla, the only land borders of the EU with Africa, are seen by African migrants as gateways to the EU.
- Spain is involved in the only territorial dispute between EU member states. Gibraltar has been a bone of contention between the UK and Spain for many years and has become, with Spain's participation in Schengen, an external Schengen border. This dispute is a potential hurdle for the UK wanting to opt in to parts or the whole of Schengen.

Within the EU, the issues raised by internal frontiers have received less publicity but crucial developments have taken place. Amongst these are the implementation of the Schengen agreements in 1995 and their integration into the 1997 Amsterdam Treaty, and the ratification of the Bayonne and Karlsruhe treaties giving the possibility of financial autonomy to transfrontier bodies set up by regional and local authorities. There have been persistent concerns that co-operation between law enforcement agencies was not sufficient to the task of combating certain forms of transfrontier crime, and the Treaty of Amsterdam and the 1999 Tampere Declaration were evidence of intent to tackle these problems. Romano Prodi, the President of the European Commission called, in October 1999, for a 'vast debate on frontiers'. Many difficult practical issues provide ample subject matter for such a debate. But there are also normative questions about the justification of frontiers, psychological questions about representation, and a range of views about the significance of territory.

The abolition of internal frontier controls and the issue of EU enlargement to the east revived an old question – what are frontiers for? Contemporary political arguments associated with frontiers touch on a wide range of fundamental matters – sovereignty, distribution of power, citizenship rights, the constitution of the EU, political identity, social cohesion, the protection of language and culture, the provision of services and many other things. But fundamentally, frontiers separate people and are intended to have this effect. Are the frontiers of European states, the external as well as the internal frontiers of the EU, ceasing to have the potential to have a uniformly separating effect? Are the shifts in territorial boundaries in Central and Eastern Europe symptoms of a new phase in history (Archibugi and Held 1995)? Are we witnessing, in Europe, the dissolving of frontiers and the 'end of territories' (Badie 1995)? If so, new forms of politics will emerge and creative politicians will find novel ways of solving problems. At the regional level, politicians already have political strategies transcending frontiers and actively participating into transnational networks (Brem and Bruno 1997).

II

The radical nature of the changes of recent years should not be exaggerated by comparison with what has happened in the past. For example, the closure and rigidity of the frontier between East and West during the Cold War have been surpassed in relatively recent history. It did not match that found, for example, by Freiherr von Richthofen (1984) on the China–Korea frontier in 1868.[2] The completeness of this deliberately created 'desert' frontier was not possible in the twentieth century, even under Stalinism. Nonetheless, as Roger Dion (1947) wrote, in the immediate aftermath of the Second World War:

> ... the war of 1939–45 conferred on political frontiers an efficacy which equals or surpasses those of natural phenomena. A frontier as artificial as the Franco-Belgian today separates economic regimes so different that we question a traveller coming from Belgium with as much curiosity as ten years ago one coming from Australia; and the line separating a democratic country from a totalitarian one can be in 1940 more difficult to cross than a formidable mountain barrier. Whether or not corresponding with natural frontiers, the linear frontiers of Europe have become terrible realities.

Unexpected and remarkable changes have taken place in European frontiers in the last 50 years. Recent developments have been misleadingly encapsulated by slogans concerning 'a Europe without frontiers' or the end of history or a new 'clash of civilisations' (replacing the competition of ideologies). The changes are profound because frontiers are no longer 'terrible realities', because no longer militarised. They nevertheless remain the focus of anxieties, even fears.

Some of these anxieties are linked to the future of the EU after enlargement and whether it will be able to maintain its present frontiers policy. Others are provoked by the great economic and technological transformations of the late twentieth century described as globalisation. These transformations supported and encouraged political change and, in particular, the development of global and European institutions. European institutions, in particular, have progressed far beyond the status of international meetings in which no authority was capable of holding states to the agreements made. Neither in its international dimension – states were not bound by any superior authority – nor in its internal dimension – states had absolute control over activities on their territory – is the doctrine of sovereignty reflected in contemporary European political practice.

Nonetheless, frontiers and territorial control remain of basic political importance. The international frontier remains the limit of criminal and civil law jurisdictions, police authorities, state administrations, educational systems, tax regimes, social security systems, as well as of many non-governmental organisations. In all these areas, tendencies towards transnationalisation are developing, which involve regular and systematic transfrontier co-operative relationships. If present trends continue in Europe, a slow integration of public institutions, characteristic of federal systems, and a more rapid integration of some social and economic organisations will take place. The degree of social integration will remain constrained by the important role of frontiers as the limit of official languages and the languages of everyday communication.

Whether further erosion of frontiers, and the end of the hypersensitivity about territorial questions, which characterised the high tide of the sovereign state, are close in Europe, depends on a continuing sense of military security and a relatively even spread of economic development. But it crucially depends on how large populations feel about homelands and their boundaries. Apart from a modest growth of a European identity and the strengthening of certain regional/minority national identities, the creation of new identities is not happening on any large scale. Sub-state frontiers have assumed greater importance, particularly in Belgium, Spain and the United Kingdom. Globalisation has created anxieties based on ill-defined threats to societies and their interests. But, as yet, there is no sign in the EU of the violent upheavals which, in the past, have been necessary to create new identities.

A liberal elitist consensus exists in favour of openness of frontiers, which denies the legitimacy as well as the feasibility of various reactions and objections to the lowering of frontiers. But frontier-maintaining mechanisms are important instruments in maintaining social cohesion – systematically destroying them may permanently weaken the ability of governments to fulfil some of their basic functions. Also, the liberal consensus stands in stark contrast to a variety of apprehensions, suspicions and even fantasies about the consequences of lowering the drawbridge to allow open access to territories previously guarded by the pervasive notion of an undivided sovereignty. The desire to make the EU external frontier as closed as practical to the inward movement of people and criminal activity can be regarded in part as a concession to these fears. It is also forms part of a project to create a European identity (the British and the Danes stand to one side) or citizenship – in which the insiders are all EU nationals and the outsiders are 'non-Europeans'. The notion of the foreigner as the non-European, or as the citizen of a non-EU state, is gaining ground at the expense of the traditional antagonism towards immediate neighbours. The non-Europeans are often perceived as a threat – the Americans as a cultural threat, the Russians and other East Europeans as a criminal threat, African and Middle Eastern immigrants as a social threat, and Asian tiger economies (until recently) as an economic threat.

III

Much variation was evidenced in interviews and visits to most of the frontier regions of the EU in elite attitudes towards frontiers and territory, and the significance of the control of territory. A total of 130 interviews were conducted in 14 European countries (Norway, Sweden, Finland, Poland, Germany, The Netherlands, Belgium, France, Luxembourg, Switzerland, Austria, Hungary, the Czech Republic, Slovenia, Italy and Spain). Those interviewed came from European institutions, central governments, regional and local authorities, and law enforcement agencies. This was neither a representative sample nor an opinion poll. The purpose of these interviews was to seek sources of information about frontiers and the methods used to overcome frontier problems. This information has been used sparingly in this book (written material has been referred to wherever possible) partly because it is too detailed for a general book of this kind and partly, by convention, certain categories of interviewees (for example, law enforcement officers) did not wish to be identified. Where no other identifiable source material has been found, the name of the informant has been included in the text, and a list of these informants is included in the bibliography.

The interviews, however, formed an essential background in identifying basic conceptions of frontiers and territory held by European elites. Four very broad conceptions of territory were expressed, and these have deep historical roots. The first is that territory is an attribute of a culture or a national group in the sense that it belongs to a people and the culture of that people is embedded in the land and in the landscape. When territory is regarded in this way, frontiers are inviolable and territory has a quasi-sacred significance.

The second attitude is territory as a frame within which differences and conflicts can be controlled and managed. According to this position, division of territory and the drawing of frontiers is always more or less arbitrary but nonetheless necessary in order to manage human affairs. This position is often associated with the view that the arbitrary division of territory is often the most important factor in the creation of identities (rather than that frontiers represent the limits of pre-existing identities).

The third conception is that territory is a tool of a political project. In this conception, when a new power centre emerges, a redefinition of territory is inevitable. The EU is a case in which territorial limits are relocated or their functions redefined to correspond with the development of the Union. Peripheral regions have asserted new claims to autonomy of decision making. According to this view, an ascendant political movement can conquer, symbolically or in practice, territory. Territory is reified, in the form of maps, to demonstrate the new distribution of power.[3]

Fourth, territory is conceived as a constraint on political action. The policy of governments, whether at the local, regional, national or European level is shaped by the nature of the territory, and its resources, which they control. This geopolitical vision assumes that the configuration of territory and frontiers are factors which influence or determine the form which political changes take.

These concepts form a crucial background to many political arguments taking place in contemporary Europe. They relate directly to the main focus in contemporary European debate on the openness of internal frontiers and the degree of closure of the external frontier of the EU. The four freedoms (free movement of goods, labour, capital and services) were enshrined in the 1957 Rome Treaty. But the fulfilment of this programme in the 1990s did not abolish frontiers, because many areas of public policy remain under the control of states and they continue to command physical force. Also EU internal frontiers remain in existence as language barriers, as technical and administrative obstacles, as imagined divisions based on historical memories, national stereotypes, and apprehensions about other societies and their mores.

IV

This book is not an encyclopaedia, still less is it an atlas. There is no attempt at a comprehensive coverage of all issues, arguments, policies and organisations bearing on European frontiers. It does not attempt to describe the topography, the physical geography, the human or economic geography of European frontiers. It is an attempt at a general political assessment of EU frontiers.[4]

In Chapter 2 we set out the range of theoretical concerns which relate to contemporary debates on frontiers. Notions of sovereignty, the nation, culture, language,[5] globalisation and the nature of European integration can trigger passionate disputes. The relationships between states and individuals, between states and localities, states and regions, regions and individuals are linked to the characteristics of frontiers (Breuilly 1998).

Aspects of these relationships are explored in Chapter 3, which is concerned with the variety of EU internal frontiers. Open internal frontiers (and the impact of EU policies) are a challenge to the constitutional order of member states. The sub-state regions are becoming international actors, and they now enjoy, in almost all countries of the EU, authority to co-operate with other regions across frontiers (Heberlein 1996; Brunn and Schmitt-Egner 1998; Beyerlin 1998). There is now a peculiarly fluid set of political relations between the EU, state, nation and region which must be taken into account (Loughlin 1993, 1995, 1996, 1997).

Chapter 4 is devoted to a more detailed examination of the diversity of changes on one set of frontiers, those of France. Local and regional perspectives on changing frontier functions are examined to see how frontiers are perceived. Certain towns close to the French frontier were chosen – Valenciennes, Longwy, Sarreguemines, Colmar, Menton, Perpignan and Bayonne – to explore the changing impact of frontiers.

Some issues, such as policing, where policy is made at the national level, have both local and national impacts. French governments and elites have strong reservations about the porousness of frontiers in cultural matters, and promote the idea of a national territory as a means of defence of a homogeneous culture.

The EU external frontier is the subject of Chapter 5. The external frontier is exhibiting some typical features of state frontiers, with common standards in place for the treatment of persons and goods checked at border crossing points. The frontier control regime established by the Schengen agreements is a significant step on the path towards a federalisation of Europe because, for certain policing purposes, the frontiers of the signatories of Schengen are treated as a single frontier.

Who is responsible for the external frontier is not, at the moment, a question which can be given a straightforward answer (Müller-Graff 1998). The location of the external frontier is also a focus of Chapter 5 because change in location affects the operation of frontier controls and, more important, alters the distribution of power within the EU.

The eastern frontier, the focus of Chapter 6, is a region of considerable variety and complexity and regions, within a broad band of territory adjacent to this frontier, have very different identities. In the past, the region was a locus of German expansionism, associated with the idea of *Mitteleuropa*. It is still difficult to envisage a dynamic development of the region without active German engagement. The shifting boundaries of internal and external security are most vividly exemplified on the eastern frontier. On this frontier, the EU countries have, whether consciously or unconsciously, attempted to establish a new imperial frontier, a *limes*, by drawing some of the neighbouring states into their orbit.

V

The conclusion of this book is an assessment of the importance of the location of the external frontier, and of the continuing role of internal frontiers. Unpredictable changes in the global environment have potentially uncontrollable effects in Europe but the increasing openness of all frontiers is probable. Their abolition, 'the end of territories' would represent a truly cataclysmic and improbable change. It is unlikely to happen because there remains in Europe a highly developed sense of territoriality, as defined by Glassner (1993) – 'a pattern of behaviour whereby living space is fragmented into more or less well-defined territories whose limits are viewed as inviolable by their occupants'. Prophecy is outside the scope of this book, as too are the gloomy forebodings, which find a ready audience,[6] such as: 'We stand on the brink, not of an era of plenty that free-marketeers project, but a tragic epoch, in which anarchic market forces and shrinking natural resources drag sovereign states into ever more dangerous rivalries' (Gray 1998). Doom-laden scenarios to the effect that the blind imperatives of new technologies, coupled with irresponsible capitalism, will emasculate political authorities, and result in an anarchic globalisation, is far removed from current European realities.

Also, closure of either internal or external frontiers because of external threats seems, except on a temporary basis, unlikely. Threats from across the EU external frontier exist but most, like organised crime and clandestine immigration, seem exaggerated. The lowering of frontiers within the EU has real benefits – it provides increased scope for collective action by member governments; it increases the area in which individuals and groups can exercise rights and engage in legitimate activities. The future can be moulded by deliberate decisions – the EU member states are not in the thrall of inexorable forces and can still make choices in frontier policy; also, regional and local governments can manoeuvre and make transfrontier alliances to promote their interests. Well-judged political choices on frontier policies by all levels of government are crucial if European societies are, to adapt one of Tom Nairn's colourful phrases, to lever themselves intact into an uncertain future (Nairn 1997).

2
Theory

Frontiers are linked to a number of complex arguments, discussed both by political theorists and, in different terms, by politicians. The purpose of this chapter is to identify some of the general features of these arguments. We are not proposing a grand new theory of frontiers which, in our view, is premature. Rather, it is designed to give an overview of the arguments, to show connections between them and give an orientation and theoretical background for the subsequent chapters of the book.

A general theory of frontiers has been a recurring intellectual temptation because boundary making seems to be a universal human activity. It is difficult to identify human groups completely lacking a sense of territory, and a frontier or boundary between what is 'ours' and 'theirs' is implicit in any sense of territory. How to theorise the activity of boundary making has presented an unresolved conundrum because frontiers have multiple, constantly changing, characteristics and functions. Attempts at scientific theories of human ecology and human territoriality, with explanatory value for all human attempts at boundary making, are still in their infancy and, as yet, cannot be applied convincingly.[1] They have not had a significant influence over the perceptions of policy makers, educated opinion or populations at large. Older theories, equally imperfect, like the geopolitical theorising of the late nineteenth and early twentieth centuries, had such an impact and are still relevant to any general analysis of frontiers.

Geographical theories

Geographical theories have provided politically influential arguments, particularly the doctrine of natural frontiers, the idea of *Lebensraum,* the struggle between the 'heartland' and the 'rimland', imagined by Mackinder. The prominent geopoliticians, who broadly thought that geography determined political action, of the later nineteenth and early twentieth centuries – Alfred Mahan (1840–1914), Sir Halford Mackinder (1861–1947), Rudolf Kjellén (1864–1922) and Karl Haushofer (1869–1946) – had genuine influence over educated opinion and over policy. Their views were vigorously opposed by a younger generation of French human geographers/historians – Lucien Febvre and Jacques Ancel – who contended that frontiers are inseparable from the entities which they enclose; human ambitions and imagination have created political entities and states which have, in turn, defined, usually in competition with others, the limits of their authority. This seems to be the assumption of most social contract philosophers – Hobbes, Locke, Rousseau – who have a fundamental impact on Western liberal democratic thinking.

The most persuasive position is a compromise between these two starting points. The effects on the nature of human societies of climate, resources available and defensibility of the territory have been a topic for writers from Aristotle to Montesquieu to modern political geographers. In the twentieth century, Jean Gottman and other geographers have been amongst the most prominent who have argued that there is a subtle interaction between environmental factors, human inventiveness and political ambition. Karl Marx, with his famous aphorism 'man makes his own history but he does not make it as he chooses', would have agreed with this position, although he went one step further. Marx proposed that the modes of production, a combination of economic organisation and technology, determined the class organisation of society; class interests were the basis of certain forms of territorial organisation. If the inevitability of class struggle is removed from the Marxist sequence of causality, this perspective is highly plausible. Technology and economic organisation, as well as geographical features, have influenced the location of frontiers and helped to shape their functions.

The various forms of this intermediary position are theoretical in the sense that they generate generalisations or broad interpretations, which take account of a wide range of evidence. But they are not characterised by theories which explain, in 'social scientific terms', the political boundaries within Europe. They rather provide suggestive observations or empirical generalisations on the relationship between physical geography, demography, economic development and political projects. Such relationships can only be briefly illustrated here. In terms of physical geography, Europe is a peninsula of the landmass of Eurasia. The long indented coastline of Europe, with three almost land-locked seas, hundreds of islands, and high mountain chains have facilitated communications and contacts in some places and made them difficult in others. In addition, different climate and soil conditions have helped to support the most obvious characteristic of Europe, variety.

This variety is manifest in the range of cultural and linguistic groups, patterns of settlement, social structures and political organisation. Political ambitions have also promoted variety in European societies and these have led to the rejection of imperial rule and, with the support of changes in military technology, the eventual establishment of sovereign 'nation' states. In turn, these states contributed to the sharply distinct linguistic, religious and political patterns found between European countries. A partitioned Europe was rendered almost inevitable by this combination of geography, technology and politics. Physical geography provided a framework in which certain possibilities were offered, but political and military action determined the location of frontiers.

In addition to frontiers between states, invisible frontiers, based on historical experiences and cultural values derived from or associated with religious differences, play a role in images of Europe. An east/west divide resulting in part from the great schism between Latin and Orthodox Christianity and a north/south divide in Europe between predominantly Catholic and predominantly Protestant Europe. The EU member states bordering the Mediterranean, sometimes to the irritation of their inhabitants, are stereotypically considered as having common characteristics, based on both cultural and geographical factors. Other groupings of countries are conceived as having a collective identity such as, dubiously, those of Central Europe or, more plausibly, Scandinavia. The Nordic countries have forged a Nordic social identity 'against' the rest of Europe, going far beyond the intergovernmental co-operation through the Nordic Union, just as the now fading British identity was constructed in the eighteenth and early nineteenth centuries, against the French (Colley 1992). These invisible frontiers are important parts of the 'mental maps' of individuals but they have no – or very weak (as in the Nordic Union) – legal, political or administrative expression. Nonetheless they play a role in the way in which identities are constructed.

Physical geography also influences the characteristics of political partition in contemporary Europe, although technological developments since the first industrial revolution, accelerating in the closing decades of the twentieth century, have tended to downgrade its importance. It has a continuing impact on the politics of frontiers in contemporary Europe, at three levels. First, physical geography may assist or inhibit the effective control of frontiers. Despite the development of sophisticated surveillance technologies, some frontiers remain hard to control. Even at the end of the twentieth century, difficult and long coastlines, sparsely populated mountain ranges, or hilly wooded country are expensive and difficult to police (often because of the social and moral, as much as the financial, costs involved). Second, physical characteristics encourage patterns of settlement, which separate or bring together the populations. These patterns of settlement are also influenced by economic and political factors, which either encourage attempts to overcome difficulties of the terrain or to a progressive depopulation. Thus, in recent years across the EU, hilly and mountainous country, areas of marginal agriculture and or poor communications, have tended to lose population, sometimes very rapidly. Third, physical features have encouraged or sustained beliefs in natural frontiers because physical features can become embedded in the imagination of large populations. Thus the crest-line of the Alps, the great wall of the Pyrenees and the 'moat' of the Channel have been invested with a mythic significance (see Chapter 3).

State sovereignty and national sovereignty

The debate on sovereignty, and the nature of the links between authority, population and territory, is a familiar one.[2] Whether the concept of sovereignty still has clear relevance in an interdependent world of open and permeable borders, is a controversial theoretical question. It is also an issue in political debate, especially in those EU countries where the idea of sovereignty has had most political resonance – the UK and France. 'Sovereignty of parliament', in the UK, and 'sovereignty of the people', in France, have been regarded as under threat in the process of European integration.

The history of the concept of sovereignty shows that it is not an immutable principle. Although alleged, particularly by neorealists, to be the stable principle on which modern international relations are founded, the exercise of sovereignty has, in practice, varied, in response to new situations. The original meaning, from Old French and transferred into medieval English, was supreme dominion, authority or rule. Although medieval rulers were occasionally called sovereigns, their authority was severely circumscribed – by the authority of the church, by customary laws, by the privileges of estates, and by the duties of the medieval kings towards their liegemen. They did not possess a monopoly of force to back what authority they had. Calling them sovereigns was a polite fiction, and the question now is whether describing the EU member states as sovereign is also a polite fiction.

In its classical expression from the Treaty of Westphalia in 1648 to the Second World War, sovereignty was territorial in character, with an internal and an external aspect. Within the territory of the state, the sovereign was the supreme authority and fount of law, with the ability to enforce that law. Externally, the sovereign had no superiors and could pursue unrestrained the sovereign interest of the state. This notion of the absolute quality of sovereignty always belonged to the realm of legal principle rather than political practice. But in international relations from the seventeenth to the mid-twentieth century, Europe approximated to an anarchical society in which states were in unrestrained competition with one another. Even those most committed to the view that sovereignty remains the basic feature of the international system accept that there are severe practical, economic, political and military–strategic, constraints on the ability of states to exercise independence of action. International jurisdictions and forms of co-operation have come to circumscribe more and more the effective liberty of action of states. This is particularly the case in military security, where European states are effectively locked into systems which prevent them taking military action against one another.

The exclusion of external influences from state territory has become impossible and the idea of the sovereignty of the UK Parliament, to use Dicey's celebrated nineteenth-century formulation, which could 'make or unmake any law whatsoever', has become absurd even as a legal fiction. There are evident legal and practical constraints within and outside state frontiers. Regional and local governments have become actors in the international system – a development contrary to the doctrine of sovereignty in its pure form, in which external relations are a monopoly of the state (Joenniemi 1997, Keating 1998). The new constitutional status and assertiveness of (at least some) sub-state authorities has led to concepts such as multi-level governance (Marks et al. 1994, Wallace 1983, Richardson 1996) – central governments remain powerful but, for certain purposes, other levels above and below central governments, have become essential. Nevertheless, the constitutional doctrine of sovereignty still has practical relevance because the final authority for particular categories of decisions must reside somewhere. Inherited concepts of state sovereignty make a difference in the way states approve (by referendum or constitutional assembly or parliamentary vote) major steps in relinquishing that sovereignty through European integration. Moreover, it is of political importance that the belief in the reality of state sovereignty remains widespread in sections of public opinion in the EU, despite evidence that the authority of the state is seriously eroded.

In practical political debate, the concept is often used in simple terms to mean political independence, self-rule and the avoidance of alien intrusion into domestic affairs. Politicians sometimes draw a distinction between 'practical' and 'theoretical' sovereignty, namely that real influence may be gained from pooling sovereignty and lost by insisting on retaining state sovereignty. Small countries often take a more pragmatic view of sovereignty than larger ones (Fitzgerald and Gillespie 1996, Bort 1997, Arthur 1999). The academic debate on sovereignty takes leave of these straightforward considerations and sometimes becomes esoteric, introducing discussions of feminism, individualism and postmodernism (e.g. Hoffman 1999). The scholarly literature on European integration largely avoids the term, partly because it is identified with the realist school of international relations which denies substance to the claim of supranationalism for European institutions.[3] Both the practical political and theoretical debates suggest that all is not well with sovereign national identities.

Nonetheless, the international frontier is almost universally regarded as different in kind from intra-state boundaries because of beliefs in state sovereignty. The limit of state is not yet regarded as the same as that between a local or a regional authority, even in highly decentralised systems such as the Swiss Confederation. However, the distinction cannot be as clear-cut as it was in the immediate post-Second World War period. Arguments are even being made that territorial units are no longer a basic factor in politics (Badie 1995, Ruggie 1993). International regimes, global markets and modern technologies have drastically reduced the importance of control of territory as a political resource. This is somewhat exaggerated, but the EU member states have undoubtedly lost legal autonomy to act in economic and social matters. They are more and more constrained politically to co-operate closely on a whole range of other policy matters. They are, therefore, in specific policy areas, more like governments below the state level, since they are restricted in law and in practice by a higher level (Wallace and Wallace 1996).

European Union member states have consented to the supreme judicial authority of the European Court of Justice in matters of European

Community law and to the European Court of Human Rights in matters affecting the treatment of individuals and their civil liberties. The International Criminal Tribunal at The Hague, along with international conventions on torture, genocide and crimes against humanity, now further limit the legal sovereignty of states. The immunity of heads of states and members of government from criminal prosecution is no longer accepted. Some will continue to argue that the consent to the authority of all these tribunals is voluntary and no executive arm exists to enforce their judgements. But the practical consequences of a state refusing to accept the authority of these jurisdictions are such that any action going beyond delay in implementing a judgement is not at the moment contemplated among the EU member states.

The clarity of legal frontiers, which characterised the high tide of the sovereign nation state, has been blurred, although legal frontiers still have crucial practical influence. The legal and executive authority of states does not extend beyond their frontiers (although the USA often tries to exert extraterritorial jurisdiction in commercial and criminal matters). In this negative but important sense, frontiers mark clear legal limits. Frontiers also have a basic role in legally defining nationality – the distinction between citizens and non-citizens – from which derive the crucial obligations and rights which affect the daily life of everyone. The tense political debates in Britain, France and Germany which have taken place on who is and who is not a citizen show that this is not a straightforward matter. A frontier, in this domain, may be a virtual rather than a geographical phenomenon because there have been cases of non-resident nationals having their nationality withdrawn and residents born in a country whose claim to nationality has been contested. The frontier is located where the states decide it should be drawn. One hundred thousand Hong Kong nationals of a British Dependency were, in the period before the 1997 handover to China, were deemed to be British nationals, the other five and a half million British Dependent nationals were considered Chinese.

Some now suggest that the benefits of sovereignty should be conferred on the sub-state level and on European institutions. According to this proposal, both these levels would acquire the right authoritatively to decide and to enforce decisions. The result is a layered, and not strictly hierarchical, system of government of a novel form. Those defenders of state sovereignty have three persuasive arguments for rejecting this. First, the system proposed would lead to constitutional and legal confusion which could only be remedied by a powerful European supreme court, leading to an undesirable 'government by judges'. Second, the lines of democratic accountability would be unclear in some areas, leading to a serious democratic deficit. Third, the system would lack the legitimacy which national sentiment gives to the sovereign state. This third objection is widely regarded as crucial because of the strength of national feeling and loyalty in Europe.

Indeed, from the time of the French Revolution, sovereignty became intertwined with the idea of nation, and with the political precepts known as nationalism. Nationalists assume that nations should be self-determining and that the boundaries of the state should, as far as practical, coincide with the boundaries of the nation. There have been endless controversies over the meaning of the terms 'nationalism' and the 'nation' and the relationship between nationalism and the state.[4] The arguments about the relationship of the nation to the state take two major forms. The first is that nation and state are two separate phenomena – that national identities emerged as a result of the solidarities built on language, culture and history and that these solidarities, if they do not have a state which represents them, will eventually demand one. The counter-argument is that a nation does not truly exist without a political project: nation and state formation are intertwined and, indeed, inseparable. Prior to the nineteenth century, a cluster of populations spoke German and had some cultural characteristics in common, but a German nation only came into existence when there was a political project for a state which included all, or as many as practicable, 'cultural' Germans.

Whatever meaning is attributed to nationalism and the nation, a very strong bond of loyalty to the state has been created because of the identification of the state with the nation. When life and death issues were at stake in the nineteenth and twentieth centuries, the identity of state and nation was crucial in maintaining a willingness to die for the country. National identities strengthened the frontiers between states both psychologically and politically. But nation states have seldom been culturally and ethnically homogeneous, and the identity of state and nation has never been complete. Citizens of states have also been linked with other states for reasons of ethnic, cultural or linguistic affinity.

In contemporary Europe, ethnic or national minorities abound. Even a country like Germany where *jus sanguinis* has, until the 1990s, been the sole basis of citizenship and where indigenous minorities are tiny (Danes and Sorbs), now has a visibly multicultural population as a result of immigration. In other countries, overarching identities, constructed at times of external danger, seem to be eroding. Reconstructed older identities are emerging – as in the UK, where the overarching British identity no longer has the binding force it had in the immediate post-1945 period. Scottish, Ulster and Welsh identities are re-emerging as countervailing loyalties to the British identity. In Spain, after the long winter of the Franco dictatorship, Catalan, Basque, Galician and Andalusian identities re-emerged in invigorated forms. Additionally, European micro-states, like their equivalents in other parts of the world, have flourished despite the absence of a national identity. They have been held in low regard but these states have, as Tom Nairn argues, a political legitimacy which make them as defensible as many larger nation states (Nairn 1998).

It is, however, clearer what frontiers are not than what they are in terms of sovereignty and effective authority. Until the last third of the twentieth century they were regarded as the map of effective power, they reified power, showing who had it and where it was located; this was always a vision, an imaginative construct or an ideal (Murphy 1996). Transnational firms and networks, and international institutions have assumed an importance to the degree that territorial limits are no longer plausible as a map of power. The doctrine of sovereignty, if still applicable, has substantially changed because of the existence of jurisdictions superior to the state. The notion of the nation state has changed because of the recognition of diverse identities within 'nation states' and the existence of transnational identities. This does not lead inexorably to the conclusion that sovereignty is no longer relevant or that there is a trend towards the 'abolition' of frontiers (Mann 1993).

Frontiers are changing their characteristics and are being redefined in popular and elite consciousness. The long retreat of the nation state means that the international frontier is losing some of its characteristics thought to be basic to it. But there is a strengthening of some frontiers in the sense of frontiers as 'us–them' divides, between the 'inside' and the 'outside'. This has been happening within states between minority ethno-national groups and dominant national groups (Caplan and Feffer 1996). Banal nationalism has elevated sporting competition as the arena in which our nation confronts the others (Billig 1995). Groups of 'like-minded' nations, such as the member states of the EU, are more and more conscious of an external frontier marking them off from the others. Fierce group loyalties, which require boundaries, are still all-pervasive in Europe. Sovereignty also remains an important idea because the desire for self-rule and the right to decide matters of public policy 'for ourselves' are very much bound up with it.

Frontiers of security communities

Although the term is of recent origin, the idea that frontiers marked the limits of security communities goes back to classical Greece, and probably beyond. Aristotle, for example, recommended that frontiers should be drawn in such a way that the configuration of the terrain allowed for effective defence. This link between the physical character of frontiers and security has been a basic consideration of policy makers until recent decades. In some places, such as Israel, this consideration remains a primary concern. The effective deployment of force has been both the guarantor of security and the arbiter of where frontiers have been located. Force has generally prevailed in drawing frontiers, and most contemporary European frontiers have their origins in peace settlements.

Frontiers were widely regarded, until the Second World War and perhaps even until the end of the Cold War, as an expression of balance of forces. Jacques Ancel wrote, summarising a widely held view: 'Geography concludes that the frontier is a political isobar which establishes for a specific period, the balance between two pressures: balance of [land] masses, and balance of forces' (Ancel 1938: 175). Strategic frontiers were sought to make the territory of states more defensible and to extend, if possible, the influence of states beyond the territory under their control. No principle of justice for delimiting territory had general currency in Europe, until the widespread acceptance of the principle of self-determination. However, the application of that principle for delimiting frontiers is usually fraught with problems because, as Ivor Jennings observed: 'On the surface [self-determination] seemed reasonable: let the people decide. It was in fact ridiculous because the people cannot decide until someone decides who are the people' (Jennings 1956: 56). Partly as a consequence, security interests continued to play a central role in the politics of frontiers.

How security interests are defined has changed in the course of recent history. As Waever has written: 'Security is a practice, a specific way of framing an issue. Security discourse is characterised by dramatising an issue and giving it absolute priority' (Waever 1996: 106). Security is what the outcome of political processes decides it should be. Since Thomas Hobbes, in the seventeenth century, made security the primary justification and purpose of the state, it has included an external element (defence against military attack) and an internal one (physical safety of people and preservation of their property against disorder and criminality). The state aspired to, and often achieved, the effective monopoly of physical force. The long-term consequences of this monopoly (the catastrophic wars of the twentieth century) and technological change have undermined the position of the state as sole provider of security. In turn, this has an impact on frontiers.

Frontiers of states are not, in contemporary Europe, military frontiers. Fortifications are no longer the omnipresent feature of the land and sea frontiers of EU member states because they no longer have any strategic value. Military threats are not posed by neighbouring states and, in the present stage of development of military technology, most individual states cannot pretend to defend their own territory, except through arrangements for collective security. The totality of the arrangements for collective security has an uncertain effect on frontiers but three generalisations may be suggested. First, states cannot 'go it alone' in defence of their territory unless, like Switzerland, they are embedded in an environment of neighbouring states which are both stable and themselves parties to systems of collective security. Second, international organisations now involve a dense web of commitments, often mutually supportive.[5] Third, states in Europe can no longer do what they like on their own territory if they infringe human rights. These represent a profound modification of political sovereignty and the security significance of state frontiers. In addition, the concept of security has been broadened – to include protection of human rights, and of the environment, as well as protection against criminality which are increasingly seen as part of 'societal security' (Buzan 1997, Wæver et al. 1993, Huysmans 1998, Bigo 1996, 1998).

The mixing of migration and crime issues is indicative of a 'culture of exclusion' (Ward 1996: 114) and of the new security discourse which no longer distinguishes between internal and external security. Migration control has become intricately linked with the discourses on crime and security in what Jef Huysmans and Didier Bigo have both called a process of 'securitisation' (Bigo 1999: 69; Huysmans 1995). Security has become a much broader concept, compared with the focus on military concerns which dominated the discourse until the changes of 1989–90, encompassing new risks and threats to society, the economy and the polity itself.[6] This constitution of a security continuum is, Bigo argues, 'not a natural response to the changes in criminality', but rather a proactive mixing of crime and immigration issues (Bigo 1999: 67–8).

Refining border controls as a means of exclusion can be seen as a response to the threat to societal security. Yet reinforced borders, a fortress mentality, often invoked when the Schengen system is criticised, are no longer practical solutions for internal security needs. The security of individuals has become deterritorialised (Bigo 1999: 73). Internal security now necessitates co-operation with foreign countries and is thus linked to foreign policy. The 1980s and 1990s were characterised by a debate in many EU member states on policing, coinciding with anxieties about urban insecurity and the city, and discourses on stopping immigration of unskilled workers.[7]

The impact of technological and political change on internal security is complex. The defence of life, limb and property of citizens still remains the responsibility of states and duly constituted authorities within them. The legitimacy of policing and criminal law enforcement depends on a democratic sanction provided by the representative institutions. But two developments undermine the traditional view of state sovereignty in this area. First, certain forms of criminality transcend frontiers and can only be combated by systematic co-operation between police and judicial authorities across frontiers (see Chapter 3). Second, both the police and the judicial authorities are under international surveillance and, in important respects, under European judicial control. The European Court of Human Rights has heard cases on penal policy, police methods and criminal procedure. The EU has integrated the fundamental rights of EU citizens, as guaranteed by the European Convention for the Protection of Human Rights and Fundamental Freedoms, in Article F (2) of the Treaty of European Union. The practical effects of this have not yet become clear. But it could lead eventually to cases involving police methods and judicial procedures coming before the European Court of Justice.

With the widening of the definition of security (to include problems of clandestine immigration, refugees, criminality, pollution, human rights abuses) the fields of internal and external security tend to merge. Threats, real or supposed, result in international agreements to co-ordinate efforts at repression in fields such as financial crime, money laundering, drug trafficking, trafficking in human beings and in body parts, dumping of noxious materials and other topics. New institutions for co-ordinating the 'fight' against these forms of criminality have been set up at the European and international levels. The repression of crime has become a European and international issue. For this to happen, an international consensus on what constitutes serious crime and on standards of justice is a precondition.

One unresolved question is when and how the regional European or the global level are the most appropriate level for considering issues of justice and establishing systems of adjudication and repression. Powerful arguments can be made that the great issues of justice are global.[8] Amongst these are that a more just world economy is not merely an ideal but a necessity for maintaining international stability. The social bond which underpinned the Westphalian state is dissolving in a globalising world and justice will not be seen to be done if the spheres of justice remain bounded by the frontiers of the state. Justice requires an equality of access to international regimes and institutions, and therefore the development of cosmopolitan citizenship (Hutchings and Dannreuther 1998).

Systems of redress are required to correct the abuses in the present international system which allow state and non-state actors to impose costs on others without their consent. A system of calling governments to account is essential in circumstances in which they or their agents are responsible for the most intolerable crimes (genocide, torture, human rights abuses of all kinds). Some progress has been made on these fronts, especially in the sense that these ideas are gaining influence, but the great problem is establishing courts whose authority and legitimacy are accepted throughout the world. As the example of Europe shows, the legitimacy of a tribunal such as the European Court of Human Rights and the establishment of effective co-operation in law enforcement are easier to achieve at the regional level. The sphere of justice can conceivably shift for some important purposes from the state to the European level, but the world is still too diverse for the shift, except in a few restricted cases, to the global level.[9]

Many citizens of European countries are uneasy about these shifts because their mental maps of the world are disrupted. The sense of security and of justice, provided for them by clearly defined frontiers and bounded communities, is undermined. Nationalist and 'sovereigntist' reactions against globalisation, against intervention in other states on human rights grounds, in favour of mutual assistance between states but against instrusions in internal affairs, are present in all EU member states. These reactions are sometimes related to communitarian political theory which holds that genuine self-government and the defence of values which people hold dear, require a sense of national identity and clearly defined frontiers. But they may also have a xenophobic nationalist basis – a dislike and rejection of foreigners, and nostalgia for an idealised past. Both represent a demand for clearly defined frontiers to provide a psychological sense of security.

Frontiers as factors in economic activity

Mainstream economic theory has hitherto contributed little to the analysis of political frontiers, except insofar as they are impediments to the efficient allocation of resources. Much economic analysis has implications for frontiers such as on the effects of tariff barriers, customs unions, optimal currency areas, industrial location, regional development and mobility in the labour market. The European Commission has commissioned a series of studies on barriers to trade, published in *The Single Market Review*, which attempts to identify the costs of the remaining non-tariff barriers to trade in the 1990s. Very little economic analysis is devoted to such questions as why frontiers are drawn, and the costs and benefits of particular frontiers.[10] These are not questions which governments have posed and hired economists to provide answers. Sometimes there is a political reluctance or intellectual inhibition to engage in cost–benefit analysis of frontiers.[11]

Two concepts not proposed by professional economists have direct relevance to the frontiers within the EU. These are globalisation (considered in the last section of this chapter) and 'economic culture' (Rohrlich 1987, Plaschke 1994). Concerning the second, the different economic cultures present in the EU are alleged to be a difficulty for particular policy proposals and for the further progress of integration. For example, a frequently expressed idea in the West European press about the 'crisis' over the single currency in May–June 1997 was that it was the manifestation of a clash of economic cultures. The outcome was interpreted as a balanced compromise between the French assumptions, envisaging a political input into the management of the single currency, and the Germans, wishing to have a completely independent European Central Bank. These economic cultures are, in the words of Kenneth Dyson, writing about industrial cultures, 'beliefs, values and attitudes by reference to which behaviour is evaluated and organisational structures acquire their meaning' (Dyson and Wilks 1983: 35). The frontiers between the member states protect the existence of different organisational structures and institutions, which are the essential underpinning of economic cultures.

Each EU member state has, it is argued, an economic culture which has been the outcome of a specific history, intellectual tradition, geographical situation, and economic and demographic structure. These have resulted in different systems of values and different habitual ways of doing things in the economic domain. These value systems have, until recently, been bounded to a great degree by the frontiers of the state because they are created and transmitted by institutions. In broad brush-stroke terms (which scarcely bear close historical scrutiny), Britain is imbued with a free trade ethos, associated with the first industrial revolution during which Britain emerged as the dominant industrial power. France has been marked by the imprint of Jean-Baptiste Colbert (1619–83) who gave a central role to the state in economic life. Germany, living with the legacy of the hyper-inflation of the 1920s which produced a political catastrophe, generally gives priority to a stable currency. Italy has, since the Middle Ages, weak political authority and a culture of the skilled craftsman and artisan, which encourages toleration of a large informal economy.

In the major EU countries, British, French, German and Italian citizens therefore vary in their attitudes to work, to financial rewards and to entrepreneurial activity. Majority preferences, in these countries, regarding the market, state intervention, regulation and contract, are different. Again in broad generalisations, in some countries, such as Britain, people are more individualist and ideologically liberal than others. By contrast, Germans, whether Christian Democrat or Social Democrat, value stability and seek social compromise; the Italians are anti-state libertarians, whilst the French remain convinced that political choices imposed through state action determine the shape of the economy. Citizens of each country, at least when their economies prosper, are convinced of the superiority over the others of its model, with all it implies for budgetary, fiscal, incomes, employment and monetary policies. However, none of these models has shown the capacity to cope with the challenges of globalisation, and the EU is therefore a necessary form of co-ordination between them.

These economic cultures can change. For example, France and Germany developed new economic cultures in the aftermath of the Second World War. For both, the war was an economic catastrophe, and the aftermath imposed a new set of constraints and choices. At the elite and popular level in the two countries, different conceptions and priorities emerged as a result of the war. People in the two countries drew on their historical experience, most usually in a negative sense – the firm rejection of Malthusianism in France and of intolerance of inflation in Germany. The results were new economic institutions and new attitudes towards economic activity. Although the French and German institutions and attitudes were very different, they shared the common belief that a high level of social protection for individuals is necessary to the stability and the dynamism of the economy. State provision of social protections, in both countries, is now under direct threat from changes in the global economy. A new shock is now emerging which is changing these cultures.

From the cultural perspective, the difficulty confronting the EU policy makers is to encourage a convergence of these different national economic cultures. The Maastricht Treaty gave preponderant weight to German values at a time when the Federal Republic, having just achieved German unification without serious economic difficulties, was dominant in the councils of the EU. The conditions for monetary union laid heavy emphasis on price and interest rate stability, which were translated into strict rules concerning public debt and budgetary discipline. This placed a burden on the other European economies but has made considerable progress in unlikely places – including the Italian ex-Communist ministers, in the UK (some independence for the Central Bank) and, more broadly, in public opinion across Europe.

But the main weakness in the development of a common European outlook is that German values were confronted with an apparently insoluble practical problem – persistent high levels of unemployment. The French therefore challenged the Germans and proposed a search for new instruments – 'a European economic government' and 'cooperative strategies' for combating unemployment. The Germans were more open to British ideas of labour market flexibility and reducing the tax burden on individuals and firms. In a striking phrase, Lionel Jospin, the new Socialist French Prime Minister, implicitly opposed this, saying that it was essential to build Europe without 'unmaking France' (in the sense of dismantling the French system of welfare and destroying specifically French cultural values).

Under the pressures of operating a common currency, a greater harmony of economic values and attitudes between Germany and France is a pressing issue. Both are now strongly influenced by Anglo-American practices in matters of takeover bids, shareholder value and global companies. International pressures may lead to a more homogeneous economic culture, but deeply embedded attitudes are likely to persist in populations at large. The frontiers of economic cultures remain, but with diminishing significance for economic elites. Since the argument suggests that different institutions sustain these economic cultures, greater approximation of institutional practices will erode frontiers between the cultures.

Cultural frontiers

In the last two centuries, as state sovereignty was translated into national sovereignty in a progressively democratised Europe, cultural homogeneity, in the sense of belonging to a national culture, replaced religious uniformity, as a perceived requirement for political stability. From the eighteenth century, a debate was initiated on whether the features which separated European countries culturally were more important than those which united them. In the nineteenth century, with the introduction of compulsory education associated with increasing nationalist sentiment, cultural differences were enhanced, sometimes deliberately. Cultural–linguistic characteristics came to have a crucially important function, legitimising states and political frontiers. The reaction against extreme forms of nationalism in the post-Second World War period has not effaced this legacy. As frontiers diminish as barriers to exchanges of all kinds between member states of the EU and, to a lesser extent, between the EU and non-member states, cultural difference still divides European peoples.

The notion of culture has an interesting history. Culture is etymologically connected to the notion of cultivation. In the seventeenth century, it gained a metaphorical meaning – human development, improvement or refinement by education and training. In the eighteenth century, it developed into a more general term, especially in German, as a group of people who shared these things, and eventually, in the plural, was used to suggest that humanity was divided into a number of separate cultures. In the nineteenth and early twentieth centuries, a variety of different and sometimes conflicting meanings emerged. A humanistic meaning became common – culture was something a person ought to acquire in order to become a fully rounded human being. Some people were considered 'more cultured' than others and some human products were more cultural than others. Culture, in this meaning, referred to 'high' culture – the music, literature, art and manners which appealed to the 'civilised' mind. This view of culture is eloquently expressed by Edward Said (1993: xii):

> ... culture means two things in particular. First of all it means all those practices, like the arts of description, communication, and representation, that have relative autonomy from the economic, social and political realms and that often exist in aesthetic forms, one of whose principal aims is pleasure... . Second... culture is a concept that includes a refining and elevating element, each society's reservoir of the best that has been known and thought... . You read Dante or Shakespeare in order to keep up with the best that was thought and known, and to see yourself, your people, society, and tradition in their best lights.

An influential contrasting usage emerged in the social sciences, particularly social anthropology. In Edward Burnett Tylor's classic text (Burnett

Tylor 1871), culture was defined as 'that complex whole which includes knowledge, belief, art, morals, law, custom, and any other capabilities and habits acquired by man as a member of society'. This was a relative and pluralistic view of culture in that the world was divided into different cultures, each having its own value. Anthropologists, in particular, were concerned to establish the notion of culture as central to the study of societies. Some broadened the concept of culture to include artefacts, technology and sciences. Within the two broadly different meanings outlined, specialised meanings proliferated.[12]

One of the specialised usages of culture which has been very influential is the idea of 'political culture' advanced by Almond and Verba (1963). They characterise political culture as 'attitudes toward the political system and its various parts, and attitudes towards the role of the self in the system' (1963: 13). They are employing culture in only one of its many meanings as 'the political system as internalised in cognitions, feelings and evaluations of its population'. When Gabriel Almond returned to the topic, almost 20 years later, he wrote that the 'concept stressed political knowledge and skill, and feelings and value orientations towards political objects and processes – toward the political system as a whole, toward self as a participant, toward political parties and elections, bureaucracy and the like' (Almond and Verba 1981: 27). In this meaning of the concept, culture can be divided vertically into a number of specialised, if overlapping, cultures.

Almond and Verba found that political cultures were very different from country to country. Some political cultures expressed and sustained democratic practices, whilst others did not. They identified three main types of political culture. First, the parochial political culture in which there are no specialised political roles, no separation of these from religious and social roles, and no expectation of change from the political system. This is a type of political culture present in primitive and tribal societies but it is also to be found in some larger ones such as the Ottoman Empire. The second is the subject political culture in which individuals are aware of the characteristics of the state and the policies of government; they may even approve of them but they do not think that there is anything effective they can do to affect political outcomes. Almond and Verba described Italy in the 1950s as falling into this category, but with an alienated political culture in which there was the virtually complete absence of trust between citizens and political authorities. Third is the participant political culture in which there is a good level of knowledge about the political system, the political authorities have a high degree of legitimacy, and citizens believe that they can affect political outcomes. This concept of culture has been very influential, even though highly controversial, in Western social science. According to the Almond and Verba analysis, European political culture cannot be considered as homogeneous. The re-establishment in the 1970s of democratic institutions in Greece, Spain and Portugal and the setting up of political institutions at the European level have, however, created conditions to spread similar political values across the continent.

Those who have regarded a common European culture as the basis and a support for European integration have usually been referring to the first meaning of culture as 'high' culture. This culture is usually thought to be derived from a common heritage in the Judaeo–Graeco–Roman–Christian tradition, supplemented by broad cultural movements which have affected the whole continent – the Renaissance, the Enlightenment and Romanticism. A set of very general shared assumptions about the nature of man and the worth of creative activity produced, particularly after the Renaissance and culminating in the eighteenth and early nineteenth centuries, a set of cultural products which were recognised as high art, from Saint Petersburg to Seville, from Edinburgh to Vienna. In other words, Shakespeare, Goethe, Cervantes, Hugo and Dostoevsky; Tchaikovsky, Handel, Purcell, Beethoven and Verdi; Velasquez, Turner, Poussin and Botticelli; Voltaire, Spinoza, Leibnitz, Rousseau, Hume, Burke and Marx did not merely belong to particular provinces, nations and kingdoms but to a European culture.

These remarkable figures – despite the fact, that many of them were hijacked as iconic figures by nationalists – were part of the European inheritance, shared by all educated people. Although nineteenth- and twentieth-century nationalism was deeply divisive, the European cultural inheritance produced, so it is argued, shared values which marked Europe off from the rest of the world. Encouraging the promotion of these values through the educational system at the expense of localism, sectarianism, provincialism and nationalism would produce mutual understanding, respect and harmonious relationships. Although Europeans spoke different languages (musical notation is the only common language), they shared a common vocabulary of concepts as a result of this common culture.

These assumptions were the basis of the first of the officially inspired works seeking to show what important things Europeans have in common. *The European Inheritance*, edited by E. Barker, G. Clark and P. Vaucher (1952), was commissioned in the latter stages of the Second

World War by the Allied Ministers of Education. This work was also intended to remove national bias from the writing of history through a scholarly collection of monographs to be used widely in the educational systems of Europe. The editors implied a unity of European high culture whilst admitting fault lines between northern and southern, western and eastern Europe, and described with some subtlety the variety of popular national cultures in Europe.

Subsequent attempts to write history from a European view have also adopted, often with less subtlety, the theme of the 'unity and diversity' of Europe. A recent example is J.-B. Duroselle's *Europe: a History of its Peoples* (1991) – which was simultaneously published in eight European Community languages. Duroselle put forward the view that: 'There are solid reasons for regarding Europe not only as a mosaic of cultures but as an organic whole.' Again, this work was intended to be widely used in the educational systems of Western Europe to encourage feelings of belonging to the European Community. He defined Europe as the member states of the European Community, with Austria, Switzerland and the Scandinavian states included, but with the implication that Finland, Poland, Hungary and Bohemia were on the fringe of Europe and anything further to the east was excluded. The book was conceived before the great events of 1989 but was published after them. Duroselle's approach was dismissed by one reviewer as 'half truths about half Europe' (Nicolas 1991). It was also characterised as 'Eurohistory' with an ideological purpose of justifying and promoting a particular form of political division. 'Non-Western' was, in the book, made equivalent to 'non-European'.

The controversy provoked by Duroselle's book demonstrates that the attempt to define 'Europe' by a common history and cultural values and mark it off from 'non-Europe' is fraught with intellectual and political difficulties. European culture is a malleable and shifting vision of images and references, which can be invoked to serve different political causes. Some cultural forms have originated in Europe and have been widely shared by Europeans. But any selection of them is bound to present a particular view of Europe – Duroselle's lack of attention to Greece and Byzantium raised such a storm of protest that the European Commission was compelled to distance itself from his work. The implied lack of 'Europeanness' of Central and Eastern Europe caused equal scandal. But the main consideration is not a flawed vision of Europe but the partial nature of any vision of Europe.[13] Any representation of European culture is necessarily a selection which will highlight some features and marginalise others; it will contain value judgements about what is worthwhile, beautiful and virtuous. Such representations serve some interests and are detrimental to others.

Some similar difficulties are confronted when cultures are treated as bounded by the frontiers of nation states. Indeed, attempts to invent a sense of a coherent European culture have some similarity with earlier attempts to present national cultures as homogeneous. There is one major difference – the sense of national identity has been, and remains, very strong by contrast with a weak sense of European identity. The term 'identity' in this context means the way in which a person wishes to be known by other people. Nation is not the only identity because individuals define their identity by their profession or activity, by their locality or region, and by gender (Cohen 1994, 1998). Occasionally they may wish to be known as Europeans. But national identity is usually conceived as a basic constituent of personal identity and, at present, a much more important one than European identity. The latter has emerged as a second identity but it is strongly felt only by an elite minority.

One recent trend in discussions of national cultures, as noted in the previous section, has been to stress the importance of institutions in transmitting culture. Thus Steffan Zetterholm has defined culture in a broad sense as the 'beliefs, norms, institutions' and 'traditional ways of doing things' in a society (Zetterholm 1994: 2). He emphasises that nation states in Europe have had very important homogenising effects through the educational systems and public policy. Whilst at one time this may have been a deliberate attempt to create what has been called 'the imagined community' of the nation (B. Anderson 1991) this is now 'on automatic pilot'. Cultures are reproduced without conscious or deliberate decision on the part of those who are performing this function. However, the substance of these cultures and the way they are reproduced vary considerably across the European countries. Basic nineteenth century features of the reproduction of national culture, as defined by Zetterholm, are still in place.

The pessimistic interpretation of cultural frontiers in Europe is that there are severe limits on the possibility of efficient intercultural communication. Europe is a mosaic of cultures, each of which has is 'its own story', making mutual understanding difficult. These cultures must always be exclusive, and have boundary-maintaining mechanisms, in order to retain their distinctiveness. There are variations in that some cultures are more open to the outside than others. For example, Edward Hall argues that some cultures are characterised by high context communications and others by low context communications:

A high context (HC) communication or message is one in which most of the information is either in the physical context or internalised in the person while very little is in the coded, explicit, transmitted part of the message. A low context (LC) communication is just the opposite, i.e., the mass of the information is in the explicit code (Hall 1977: 77).

The Finns and the English would in broad terms, according to this classification, be HC whereas the Irish or the French would be LC. If this is so, in addition to the barriers of language, there would be high non-verbal cultural barriers because of the form of communication (Eco 1987).

The issues concerning culture which confront us are theoretical questions, but with important practical implications. Frontiers between different cultural groups divide people within countries (in relation to immigrants and minorities), between countries of the EU and between the EU and its neighbours. These perceived cultural differences are the locus of misunderstanding and conflict. There is also broad support for the EU in public opinion in the member states, but this support is scarcely passionate because of a lack a common identity or focus of loyalty or a sense of a rich, shared culture (Bonnino and King 1997). The EU fails, therefore, to stir the emotions and attract strong loyalties. As the former President of the European Commission, Jacques Delors, memorably said: 'one cannot love a Single Market'.

The arrangements and policies of the EU are necessary because the problems facing European societies transcend the frontiers of the nation states; the problem-solving capacity of the larger system is necessary in changed global circumstances. But there is no automatic legitimacy transfer from the smaller (the state) to the larger unit (the EU), partly because the cultural we-group remains 'we-French, 'we-Germans', 'we Danes'. Language, national culture and nation remain the most important markers of identity. The attempt to create a 'Europe of the citizens', symbols – a European flag, anthem and holiday – and programmes such as the annual European city of culture have as yet failed to create an emotional bond between the EU and European peoples.

The varying and contrasting cultures and languages of the peoples of Europe are the most obvious characteristic of the continent. Yet substantial efforts are still made to define culture as a factor uniting the peoples of Europe (Koepke and Schmeltz 1999). This illustrates that different views exist, as they did in the eighteenth century, about the extent of cultural differences in Europe and where the frontiers between cultures are located. The confusion over culture is encouraged by government policies. These tend to be ambivalent, promoting greater internationalisation, Europeanisation and multiculturalism and, at the same time, engaging in cultural protectionism. Frontiers have been the essential instrument in creating and defining cultures, and imposing language use in Europe; whether they are going to continue to play this role in the same way is now uncertain.

The globalisation debate and images of frontiers

Globalisation is a vague concept but usually refers to a vast process of change with political, economic, strategic, social and cultural dimensions. Important connections exist between these: all of them, it is argued, point to major shifts in social, political and economic relationships. 'The world society created by globalisation cuts across national state boundaries', Ulrich Beck stated: 'not only economically, but through a multiplicity of social circles, communication networks, market relations and lifestyles, none of them specific to any particular locality' (Beck 1999). Global pressures challenge the independence or autonomy of states. Visual images of the world have been modified as a result of satellite technologies. The publication of brilliantly coloured photographs of the planet has given visual meaning to terms such as 'spaceship earth', the 'blue planet' and the 'biosphere'. This has promoted the idea of the common interest of human kind in protecting the planet as an ecosystem.

Globalisation also refers to an increasing range of problematic activities which have become global rather than limited to national or regional contexts. These include environmental damage, broadcasting, information dissemination and dominant ideology (particularly in human rights). International regimes, international organisations and the scope of multinational firms have greatly expanded. Technologies have shrunk distances both in terms of transport and information transfer. Industrial processes have become interdependent on a global scale. All this has altered the organisation of markets. Such changes and their implications are imperfectly understood and are interpreted in a variety of ways. Among large populations, they are not understood at all, and provoke feelings of anxiety and powerlessness. Globalisation is, as a consequence, sometimes demonised as the cause of social dislocation, cultural impoverishment, exploitation, unemployment and misery. Despite these widespread beliefs and fears, whether the concept of globalisation means anything precise is open to serious question, except as a shorthand term to refer to a variety of changes.

The extreme version of a globalisation hypothesis is expressed by Keniche Ohmae. He interprets the international economy as a 'borderless world', in which governments can interfere with market forces only at the cost of reducing the choice of their citizens and their standards of living. Governments cannot, for example, impose tax rates which are much out of line with world averages because to do so would result in capital flight. Ohmae writes that 'the global economy follows its own logic and develops its webs of interest, which rarely duplicate the historical borders between nations'. He assumes a sort of consumer sovereignty:

> ... as information about products and services becomes more universally available, consumers everywhere will be able to make better informed choices about what they want. It will matter less and less where it all comes from. Governments – and the national boundaries they represent – become invisible in this kind of search (Ohmae 1994: 183).

Thus consumer sovereignty is buttressed by increasing global information flows, made possible by new technologies, which allow market imperfections to be ironed out – prices of capital, labour, goods and services will tend to equalise across the globe.

To cater for the needs of this world economy, genuinely transnational corporations have developed which do not owe allegiance to particular states and locate wherever market advantage takes them. In this global perspective, 'the network' becomes more important than territory. Satellite communications and the World Wide Web become new loci of activities. Dense communications are created linking people without regard to territorial boundaries. Networks of people, spanning huge distances, grow spontaneously on all kinds of topics from scientific to sporting; these seem often more important to people than their neighbours or even the nation to which they belong. Access to networks, particularly in the 'knowledge-based' industries, becomes more significant for many activities than control of territory. This trend, according to Ohmae, is both irreversible and irresistible.

Ohmae deploys rhetorical assertion rather than empirical data to support his thesis. As Paul Hurst and Grahame Thompson (Hurst and Thompson 1996) point out, there are awkward historical facts to confront before giving credence to this version of globalisation. Many of the developments regarded as radically new were evident under the Gold Standard regime of the pre-1914 period. In that period, trade in merchandise, as a proportion of gross domestic product was, for leading trading nations, as much as it is in the 1990s. Labour mobility was also higher in the late nineteenth and early twentieth centuries than since the highly industrialised countries started to impose draconian restrictions on immigration. During the decade before the First World War, outward capital flow from the UK at 6.5 per cent of national income was greater than Japan's in the 1980s and 1990s. Capital is still far from being highly mobile.

Also, about three-quarters of the value added by multinational corporations is still located in their home countries. It is impossible to imagine the great names in international manufacturing – Toyota, Mitsubishi, Siemens, General Motors and Ford – cut entirely loose from their countries of origin.[14] In times of difficulty, they could, like the Hong Kong and Shanghai Bank in the 1990s, recentre their activities on their countries of origin. The fiscal and budgetary stance of governments and related economic indicators do not seem to have converged at a world level. The ratio of government revenue to gross domestic product is 60 per cent in Denmark as against 32 per cent in the USA, yet the Danish savings rate is higher than that of the USA, in 1995, and Danish acquisition of foreign assets was a mere 1.8 per cent of GDP. Despite these disparities, there has been no massive movement of labour or capital between Denmark and the USA.

France is the EU member country most attached to a voluntarist state economic policy, intervention in the labour market with minimum wages standards, job subsidy and limits on working time, generous state protection against illness, old age and unemployment, and protection of cultural goods. France resists many forms of deregulation of the economy and is regularly criticised by the OECD for doing so. Nonetheless, despite a relatively high unemployment rate, France remains the world's fourth economic power, with a highly successful record in the export of industrial and agricultural products. Across the world, governments still put up many effective barriers to the genuine globalisation of firms such as the use of government-sponsored R&D programmes from which foreign firms are excluded, technical standards, quota restrictions, limitations on foreign investment and export financing. Within the EU, such non-tariff barriers to trade are in principle outlawed but rigorous enforcement is very difficult. The World Trade Organisation lacks the authority to ban such practices on a global scale.

In terms of economic activity, economic organisation and economic policies, frontiers still seem to preserve important differences between countries, but there is no agreement about their importance. In broad terms, the disagreements range along a spectrum (Held et al. 1999). At one end are those who hold that the main actors in the international system remain the states, most economic transactions are local, frontiers remain a significant impediment to the movement of many goods and services, and changes in the global system are gradual. As Martin Wolf argues (*Financial Times*, 11 February 1996), 'Globalisation is, if not a myth, a huge exaggeration.' At the other end are those who consider that technological, economic and strategic changes have accelerated over the past ten years and have transformed global power relationships.

The historical origins of globalisation are directly relevant to how its contemporary impact on frontiers is assessed. The historians Fernand Braudel and Immanuel Wallerstein regard the sixteenth century as the period at which the world economy began to have a direct impact on the European political economy. At the beginning of that century, Europe was open to external trade via the Mediterranean but it had limited horizons and had access to distant markets only through Muslim intermediaries. By the end of the century, through a desire to control its own supplies and to explore the world, European seamen and merchants sought routes to America, Africa and Asia. The pioneering Spanish and Portuguese were followed by the Dutch, French and English. Europeans attempted to organise the world to their advantage and extended their control by conquest, settlement and treaty to most of the planet. By the end of the eighteenth century, the world was penetrated by the Europeans, with the exception of the interior of Africa and Asia, and the polar regions.

The globalisation of trade became a reality. Maritime commerce in cotton, spices, silk, tea, sugar, raw materials, gold and silver was the driving force. Europe, led by the United Kingdom, became the site of powerful new modes of production and manufactures, the product of the factory and capitalism dominated the world. The nineteenth century was a period of exponential growth in productivity and trade, accompanied by the development of transport and communications technologies – the railway, steamship, telegraph, telephone, the newspaper press. The large, and unanswerable question is whether developments in the last decade of the twentieth century are much more than a continuation of a process that commenced in the sixtenth century or even earlier (Buttsworth 1995).

The period from 1914 to 1945 can be represented as a temporary retreat from globalisation which had deep historical roots, and the process recommenced in the 1950s. The capitalist countries, under

American leadership, slowly recreated a zone of near free trade of industrial goods and free movement of capital. From 1960 to 1973 international trade as a consequence tripled. But two-thirds of this trade took place between three great trading blocs – Europe, the United States and Japan – and only 12 per cent of the goods produced in these countries were exported to other regions. Since the collapse of Communism, globalisation can be represented as the re-established world market, which existed before 1914. Communist regimes in China and Vietnam continue to exist, but even these are integrating into the capitalist economy. New technologies and products help the process of global integration, which is taking place faster than was previously possible.

Relations of power, although shifting, probably remain much as they were before. Rich, dynamic centres, although affected by the environment, have a degree of control over their own economic destiny and determine the fate of poorer and weaker regions. The current domination of the rich countries over the poorer ones has been represented as five monopolies – technological monopoly, financial control over worldwide markets, monopolistic access to the planet's natural resources, media and communications monopolies and control of weapons of mass destruction (Amin 1997). Those influenced by left-wing radicalism or Marxism argue that globalisation cannot properly be understood without taking account of the basic conflict of interest between capital and labour. In this account of globalisation the role of frontiers in preserving existing global balances is crucial.

The accounts of globalisation which stress its deep historical roots and which may produce serious social conflicts may be contrasted with a liberal and optimistic vision. This is that a rapid and recent transformation has taken place in the global relations which carries new hope of peace and prosperity.[15] As authors of a report commissioned by the European Commission state:

> ... it has only been in the late 1980s that a whole set of internationalisation processes have been integrated in a more systematic fashion covering a whole set of parameters including cross-country investment, production, marketing, trade and more general interfirm alliances and collaboration (Howells and Wood 1993: 3).

A belief in rapid and radical change is held by large sections of the educated public in many countries, business executives working in multinational corporations and influential politicians such as Raymond Barre, the former French Prime Minister. At the 1996 Davos economic 'summit' he explained his belief in the optimistic version of globalisation:

> The world has entered, from the beginning of the 1990s, in a new period of long growth – the ascendant phase of the Kondratieff cycle – an expansion sustained by technological innovation, price stability, the growth of trade and stimulated by global capital flows throughout the whole of the planet.

Barre, and most liberal economists, consider that economic globalisation brings economic benefits for all – the poorer countries will benefit from new opportunities offered by integration into the global market place, and winners will outnumber losers. They imply or suggest that a global system of economic governance is in place as governments, realising their loss of control over the domestic economy, work to defend their interests through international negotiation (Reinecke 1998).[16] The optimists also believe in the phenomenon, which the OECD refers to as 'techno-globalisation', in the fields of innovation, research and development; the pace of transfer of technology, they argue, is speeding up. They also reject the argument that globalisation increases unemployment and drives down wages in the industrialised countries. A report of the OECD Outlook for Employment (1997) argued that imports from countries with low wages had only a marginal impact on employment and wages.

The perception of a radical shift in the global system gathered strength as a result of the collapse of the Soviet Union and its satellites. This cataclysmic political change removed what some saw as a major alternative, or a challenge, to capitalism, the free market and liberal political ideology. Globalisation as an American-led process became a widespread belief among both critics and defenders of the idea of globalisation. The United States became the only superpower with the capability of military intervention anywhere in the world. The global military/political role of the USA was supported by the intellectual hegemony of American-led liberal neo-classical economics, with its concentration on the market where the consumer is king and markets should be transformed only by technological innovation. The late 1990s crisis of the Asian economies further enhanced this intellectual hegemony since heavily cartelised economies were shown to be fragile.

The different views of globalisation have important implications for perceptions of frontiers in contemporary Europe. If one takes the Ohmae view, what is happening to European frontiers is much the same as to frontiers elsewhere in the world. Recent economic changes mean that they are progressively being swept aside by market forces. The market is a neutral mechanism which results in the optimal allocation of resources, and frontiers are largely an irrelevance. If the market is now sovereign, states have lost the capacity to use policy instruments (tariffs, quotas, capital controls, devaluation, economic planning) which had been used to influence and to control economic decisions (a view taken by Kindelberger as early as 1966). It then follows that the allocation of resources is determined by the market, and these resources will include cultural goods which have the capacity to alter cultural values. Allegiance to the state will be weakened in favour of global networks.

If one takes the opposing view that internationalisation of the economy is a very long historical process and states are still basic units in the struggle to exploit the market, then control of territory and where frontiers are drawn are of fundamental importance. Frontiers may be open, but they remain an essential protection behind which firms, regulated and encouraged by governments, set out to conquer markets beyond the frontiers. There are non-economic factors which help to maintain frontiers – the need for security (in its changing forms), the need for bounded communities to organise government and administration, the attachment to a nation or a geographically based cultural–linguistic community. All these factors suggest that the global market place and new technologies can coexist with values which require, for their effective expression, some form of territorially bounded states.

The balance of the argument seems to be in favour of a moderate globalisation view. States cannot yet be consigned to the dustbin of history. They still have an influence over economic activity and over security. They represent and are the major agents which reproduce cultural difference. If they no longer exercise absolute control over activities on their territory they still have a decisive influence over movement of people (Joppke 1999). They are the focus of loyalty and political obligation for most Europeans. The attachment to the nation, which states claim to represent, is still strong. Territorial states are essential for the organisation of democratic institutions, the rule of law and the provision of highly valued services. For all these reasons, frontiers between them still matter.

But crucial changes are taking place in the international system. The transfrontier network, the region (in two senses – sub-state regions and regional groupings of states) and the international regime (in a wide variety of contexts – sea, space, airspace, Antarctica) are challenging the state as a sovereign entity (Guibernau 1999: 177). A range of issues and problems are recognised as global, in particular environmental problems, and international regimes have been established to confront them (Poalini et al. 1998). The global economy has been progressively integrating and becoming ever more interdependent. Non-state organisations and actors are assuming a greater role in international affairs and, like the environmental movements, Greenpeace and World Wildlife Watch, stimulate, challenge and publicise international regimes.[17] Tastes, consumer goods, cultural products, technologies, patterns of leisure are being disseminated worldwide, although the extent to which this is producing a homogenised, American-led world culture is open to question.[18]

But the treatment of globalisation confronts the same problem as assessment of arguments about geographical or cultural determinism. It is more or less convincing depending on what evidence is taken into account. None of these ideas can bear the critical scrutiny of careful historians, who inevitably find evidence to support quite different interpretations of social and political processes. But they are influential, if simplistic, ideas which affect perceptions of frontiers. They are short cuts, necessary for political action, to the understanding of a complex world.

Theory and practice

Theoretical arguments or statements about physical geography, sovereignty, security, culture and globalisation affect the way in which frontiers are perceived by political actors. Positive connections are made between these concepts, such as the belief that cultural homogeneity legitimises the exercise of sovereign authority, and negative associations, such as that globalisation undermines the ability of governments to maintain internal security or ensure distributive justice. These connections are present, in different terms, in political debate as well as in political theory. David Miller makes the link between sovereignty and national culture on national identity (Miller 1995) in an impressive philosophical contribution. But British conservatives and French *souverainistes*, defending national autonomy against 'encroachments from Brussels', also make it.

Such connections also exist between the explanations of the process of European integration and the various political strategies adopted by political actors in the member states. Realist, neo-functionalists, liberal intergovernmentalist, neo-institutionalist and federalist theories all have parallels in the political arena in the arguments made by politicians to promote certain strategies with regard to the EU. These various schools of thought about the EU have little to say about frontiers, when their jargon is stripped out, which cannot be said in the discussion of the concepts under review in this chapter. Their focus is on the processes and dynamics of the integration process (to the extent that they believe it is taking place). Implicit observations or recommendations about frontiers are frequently embedded in their work but it would unnecessarily complicate this discussion to tease them out.

Federalism is the one case where theorists and practicians accept the same label because the idea has a venerable and distinguished history (no politician would consider calling himself a 'liberal intergovernmentalist'). Federalism is a normative theory, a doctrine mainly derived from debate about the United States constitution, about how power should be distributed. It has the clearest implications for the EU internal and external frontiers. Leaving aside the idiosyncratic English eurosceptic view that federalism means centralisation of power, federalists hold that a division of authority between EU and the member states is taking place, as a result of the piecemeal construction of a federal constitution.

From the point of view of some economic policies and, except for Britain, Denmark and Sweden, for monetary policy, the analogy between the EU and the United States is close. Both have a common external tariff, the federal institutions regulate inter-state commerce, competition policy, external trade policy, and both have a central bank. In other respects, the EU is moving in a federalist direction, with free movement of citizens within the external frontier, elements of a European citizenship, common asylum and immigration policy, and an embryonic law enforcement capacity. Increased powers for the European Parliament and the inevitability of further extension of the qualified majority vote in the Council of Ministers at the current intergovernmental conference will further federalise the decision-making procedures.

For the federalist, the frontiers between EU member states are becoming, for some purposes, more like those between the states within a federation, and the external frontier of the EU is taking on state-like features. But the role of the member states has been and remains a determining one. The major steps in 'abolishing' European frontiers, from the four freedoms of the 1957 Treaty of Rome, through the 1986 Single Market agreement to the creation of the free movement area in the Schengen accords, have all been the result of the initiative of states and on their explicit authority.[19] The great puzzle is the extent to which states, or more precisely governments, are independent, free agents (Guibernau 1999: 160). Governments still believe that they have control over their own frontiers and, despite the principle of free movement and the various agreements associated with it, they can reimpose controls on people and, within more restrictive limits, on goods.[20] This raises doubts about the federalist position.

Many theorists adopting the neo-realist or liberal intergovernmentalist positions share the doubt. Politicians and social actors, it is argued, retain the possibility of choosing between options in frontier policy, subject to structural and environmental constraints. The EU has little autonomous authority, except that which is given to it by a coalition of states. A cacophony of theories and arguments about the dynamics of the EU is situated between the neo-realist position to the effect that the states retain the substance of authority and the federalists who hold that this substance is, in some areas, being drained to the European level. An examination of frontiers, as political and legal institutions, and the range of perceptions about them, makes a modest contribution to understanding the development of the EU. This book is not 'social scientific' in the sense of advancing a precise hypothesis which will demonstrate one of the theories to be correct – it does not seek to invent and test a model of the effects of frontiers or of frontier processes. It adopts a well-established, if rather unadventurous, alternative of comparisons which may suggest a new approach to the process of European integration.

3
Internal Frontier Issues

This chapter focuses on six topics; the first three are brief reviews of wide-ranging subjects, and the second three treat contemporary issues in more detail. The first topic is the general acceptance of the legitimacy of existing internal frontiers, although some of the factors which have encouraged past changes in the political map of Europe may support the emergence, in future, of new territorial identities. The second topic is the demography of frontiers and the intensity of exchanges across frontiers. The third theme is the effect of language use and cultural change on the significance of frontiers. The causes and nature of changes in this area (see Chapter 2) are long term, controversial and difficult to analyse. The fourth is the most publicised and significant change to the EU internal frontiers – the abolition of controls on movement of persons (with the exception of the UK and Ireland). The Schengen agreements, now integrated into the EU following the Treaty of Amsterdam, have brought about this change. The fifth theme is bilateral co-operation between neighbouring states to police and manage frontiers. The last theme is the development of transfrontier co-operation between local and regional authorities. The experience of transfrontier co-operation tends to show that internal frontiers will remain, for some time to come, important features of the political landscape.

'Natural' frontiers?

Some EU internal frontiers are etched deeply in the imagination of European peoples – the sea frontiers of Britain, the Pyrenean frontier, the Alpine crest for Italy and the Rhine–Danube where these rivers correspond to the old Roman *limes*. Physical features have, at various times in history, been regarded as 'natural frontiers' by governments and political elites and, in course of time, been accepted as such by large populations. But seas, rivers, marshes and mountains did not prevent, in the past, the movement and settlement of peoples across these topographical features. Migrations and displacement of peoples have punctuated European history. Radical changes in the location of frontiers, and also what those frontiers represented, have been commonplace.

Despite these changes, territorial stability has come to be more and more valued. Since the end of the Middle Ages, rulers have tried to legitimise their claim to particular territories by representing it as part of a divinely ordained or natural order, and so make it permanent. An example is the revival of the idea of 'natural' frontiers (the Pyrenees, the Alps, the Rhine and the seas) in late sixteenth-century France. Unfortunately, human settlement has never been tidily distributed according to such natural features. The consequence of this untidiness is that 'natural frontiers' have been interpreted differently according to the political interests involved. The Rhine has been a striking example of a natural frontier about which there have been very different kinds of discourse.

Whether the Rhine has historically separated or united the peoples on its right and left banks has been a subject of dispute between historians (Febvre 1997, Dion 1947), and this dispute has been of great political significance. On the one hand, since Roman times, it has been seen as a great line of defence, a physical feature to separate people, and to distinguish friend from foe. The drive of the expansionist French monarchy from the sixteenth to eighteenth centuries, followed by the temporary achievement of the goal of the Rhine as a French frontier by the Revolution and the First Empire, expressed this geopolitical image in aggressive political and military action. On the other hand, the Rhine has been a great trade route which brought peoples together in commercial exchanges, a route for the transmission of ideas and a locus of peaceful interaction of different language and cultural groups.

Lucien Febvre emphasised the latter role, in a book on the river published in the 1930s, of the Rhine as a unifier of peoples (Febvre 1935). His book was immediately denounced in Germany, particularly by an author determined to show that the Rhine had been a German river, at least since the Middle Ages (Schöttler 1997). The image offered by Febvre prevailed after the resolution of territorial conflict between France and Germany, and the 1955 reattachment of the Saarland to the German Federal Republic. The themes of the Rhine as a natural frontier, and a military defence line, have fallen into abeyance since the beginnings of the European integration process and Franco-German rapprochement. Building bridges across the Rhine between peoples separated by catastrophic wars was embarked on in the post-Second World War period.

The idea of natural frontiers has been widely dismissed, particularly since 1945, on the grounds that all frontiers are made by human beings and, in that sense, all are artificial. Some physical features are militarily useful at certain stages of technological development and irrelevant at others. But physical features can retain their hold on the imagination despite changes in strategic significance, technologies and political control. The Pyrenean mountain chain is an example. These mountains have represented a continuous wall, a great physical barrier, since the earliest references to them in antiquity. Since the sixteenth century, the failure of Spanish, French and German attempts to invade Britain has led to a sense of an inviolate sea frontier. The Channel remains of great psychological importance despite the construction of a fixed link (the tunnel) between the UK and France.

Internal EU frontiers, unlike the present eastern external frontier, are now considered, in a general sense, as 'natural'. Virtually all EU internal frontiers delimit, in the mind of the vast majority of EU citizens, the homelands of 'mature' nations. Where minorities exist, only small groups, sometimes politically troublesome, aspire to change these frontiers. However, important differences characterise these 'natural' frontiers because not all represent sharp breaks in the cultural landscape. In contemporary Europe, major languages, such as French and German, are spoken in other countries, and minority languages, such as Catalan, transcend these frontiers. Germans do not have the same sense of leaving Germany behind them, by comparison with regions with no linguistic German connections, when they travel to parts of Alsace-Lorraine and to South Tyrol. Peoples at the geographical core of the EU in the Rhineland, Flanders, Luxembourg and South Tyrol all bear obvious marks of intermingling and past migratory movement. Despite almost universal acceptance of them,[1] existing frontiers of the European nations are no more 'natural' than the belief that certain geographical features marked the natural limits of states.

Sparse and dense exchanges

Contemporary internal EU frontiers vary in terms of the densities of the population they divide and volumes of traffic which cross them.

Variations have complex effects and there are no consistent relationships between these factors and political effects. However, free access to the other side of the frontier and heavy cross-border traffic create an impression of effacement of frontiers and encourage a belief that frontiers are withering away.

Since ancient times some frontiers of Europe have been drawn through sparsely populated zones – forests, moorland or mountains. Others, such as those of the Low Countries, have divided densely populated regions, although as a general rule frontier zones are less populated than the heartland of the countries concerned. In sparsely populated areas, in some cases until the twentieth century, frontiers between peoples and states were often lawless zones, 'debatable lands', barely controlled by any political authority. In some cases where the principle of a frontier had long been agreed, such as the Franco-Spanish frontier agreed in the Treaty of the Pyrenees in 1659, many local problems had to be negotiated when the frontier was demarcated in the mid-nineteenth century.

These sparsely populated areas of Europe have sharply diminished in area and number since the eighteenth century, although some frontier zones like the *département* of Ariège in southern France, and northern Sweden, have been progressively depopulated in recent decades. Places where low density of population is an important factor in restricting contact, such as the central Pyrenees (see Chapter 4) are now rare. Scandinavian frontier regions are sparsely populated and, in the more northerly regions, population densities are the lowest in Europe. There is nonetheless an ease of transfrontier contacts in northern Scandinavia now, at the local level, even with the Russians of the Kola peninsula (Stokke and Tunander 1994). The conviction that fewer contacts meant fewer problems has, in the past, led rulers to favour 'desert' frontiers in the sense of either forbidding or discouraging settlement in the frontier regions. Also, these regions tended to be highly militarised, and this legacy still affects some frontier regions, such as the north-eastern frontier region of Italy (Strassoldo 1972, 1973). The Franco regime in Spain discouraged all activities in the Pyrenean frontier zone.

Intense economic activity plays a role in territorial politics in two main ways. First, it promotes a sense of a community of interest and of identity which historically has supported, as in the Netherlands, political independence, despite unfavourable geographical and political circumstances (Wils 1996). This indicates how, in future, the territorial organisation of Europe could change with emergence of new economic regions. Second, economically and technologically more advanced societies have both dominated and drawn population from less developed areas. The dominance of the French and German economies in the 1950s and 1960s drew labour from Italy, Portugal and Spain to the extent that, for example, Paris became the second Portuguese city in terms of numbers of Portuguese residents. The strengthening of the southern European economies has caused this migration to cease, and the EU as a whole is now a magnet for migrants from non-European countries. Intra-European migration is now much less important (with the exception of Luxembourg and the partial exception of Ireland) than immigration from outside the EU.

At the local level, transfrontier commuting is a general phenomenon where the opportunities for employment exist on the other side of the frontier. This is not confined within the EU: as Switzerland illustrates, a strong non-EU economy can exercise attraction over limited areas within the EU. All Swiss frontier localities draw frontier workers from neighbouring states, with Basel and Geneva having the role of regional economic poles of attraction over neighbouring districts in Germany and of France (Schuler et al. 1997: 118). Despite the political frontier, the very light controls on commuter traffic, which scarcely exist at all on the rail link between Mulhouse, Frick and Laufenburg via Basel inaugurated in 1997, help to create the impression of an integrated transfrontier region.

New territorial identities are being created in contemporary Europe on the basis of these changes. But the future is unlikely to follow the pattern of the past. The uncertain outcomes of military confrontations have forged the European nations. Essential elements in the development of national consciousness in modern European history – the use of military force, the spilling of blood, and frontiers closely guarded against neighbours – are absent. New territorial identities will not be nations, but a distinctive cosmopolitanism is likely to develop in certain transfrontier regions, encouraged both by absence of frontier controls and by high density of exchanges.

Linguistic and cultural divides

One of the principal fictions of the nation states of Europe is that they achieved linguistic, cultural and ethnic homogeneity (Wilson and Donnan 1998: 10). Some linguistic–cultural frontiers are more clearly defined than others, and some developments are eroding linguistic and cultural frontiers whilst others are having the contrary effect. There are borderlands, such as Alto Adige, Burgenland, the Pyrénées Orientales and Alsace, which form bridges between language and cultural groups divided by the state frontier. In other places, sharp breaks in the cultural landscape coincide with the frontier. Some are recent creations, such as the Oder–Neisse and the Franco-Italian borders between Menton and Ventimiglia. In general, in the realms of popular culture and of 'high' culture, barriers between people, symbolised by the international frontier, are eroding. But they are doing so in complex and uneven ways.

The language mosaic

National languages imposed on and spoken by the mass of the population are a relatively recent historical development, associated with universal literacy, mass education and the progressive intervention of the state in all areas of economic and social life. With the age of nationalism in the nineteenth and first half of the twentieth centuries, modern bureaucracies and universal military service, states achieved a linguistic uniformity which had not previously been imagined. But the linguistic map of Europe did not, and does not, coincide with the political map. The use of some languages does not stop at frontiers and the use of minority languages within states breaks the internal pattern of linguistic uniformity.

Cultural and linguistic frontiers have sometimes remained in place when the political frontier has shifted. A twentieth-century example is the predominantly German-speaking Alto Adige–South Tyrol, acquired by Italy at the end of the First World War. The attempted Italianisation by Mussolini's fascist regime failed and the majority remained German-speaking (Alcock 1970). The confrontation between two major language groups allowed the survival of a very small minority language group, Rhaeto-Romansch (Cole and Wolfe 1974).

Although linguistic diversity characterises the countries of the EU, the spread of English has been progressively breaking down language barriers. English is the most widely spoken international language (and the official language of states throughout the world), the dominant international language of diplomacy, international institutions, science, commerce, finance and transport. It is the second language in all countries of the European Union. This dominance of English is welcomed as a tool of communication but often feared for its cultural impact.

Other languages nonetheless retain a strong international position and transcend national boundaries. German is the most widely spoken language in the EU, it is the language of Austria, the Italian province of Alto Adige and the micro-state of Liechtenstein, the largest of the four official languages of Switzerland, and a minority language in Belgium and Denmark. French is spoken in Belgium, Switzerland and in the Italian province of Valle d'Aosta. It remains the second language of diplomacy and international institutions, and a language spoken by educated minorities throughout the world; 49 countries gathered in Hanoi in November 1997 for a conference of *Francophonie* (Barrat 1997). It has an equal role with English as a working language of the European Commission. Spanish is the world's fourth-largest language (after Chinese, English and Hindi) and thus, even though in Europe it is not spoken outside Spain, has an impregnable international position.

Because of the dominance of the teaching of English in schools, languages of neighbouring states tend to be spoken less, even in frontier regions, than in the immediate post-war period. For example, the proportion of schoolchildren studying German in the eastern (Nancy, Strasbourg) academic regions and Spanish in the south (Bordeaux and Toulouse academies) is greater than in the rest of France but, in all cases, they are far outdistanced by English. The spread of English has caused the relative failure of an aim of the 1963 Franco-German Treaty of Friendship to promote the mutual comprehension of each other's language. Throughout the EU, bilingualism in the language of the neighbouring state in frontier regions is in decline. Mutual comprehension is further diminished by the decline in local languages and patois, which was often mutually understood by people on both sides of the frontier. A common objective of transfrontier co-operation at local and regional levels is to try to reverse this trend by promoting bilingual nursery schools, the employment of native speakers from across the border to teach languages in schools, and frequent exchange visits of school pupils and cultural events.

Where transfrontier minority languages are spoken widely on one side of a frontier, a tendency has sometimes developed for the language on the other side of the frontier to diminish. There is, for example, a decline of Basque and Catalan in France, whereas there is an increase in the use of both in Spain. The command of French in the Spanish Basque country and Catalunya is in decline. The virtual disappearance of local dialects in the German and Belgian districts neighbouring Maastricht has resulted in a decline in mutual comprehension. This has been compounded by the decline in the teaching of second and third foreign languages in secondary schools. In the 1950s, it was common in the Netherlands for school pupils to learn French, German and English, with the result that they could understand people in the three neighbouring countries. In the last 30 years there has been a slow but inexorable decline in the teaching of French and German, with a consequent decline in social interaction with these peoples.

Language often represents a very sensitive psychological frontier. Language policy in some member states remains a potentially explosive issue. Deep divisions between language communities in Belgium leads to political and constitutional confrontation, and to local ill-feeling. Tensions occur when parents consider that the language policy pursued in schools is not useful for their children. Local languages often provoke bitter opposition. An example is the Catalan law of 30 December 1997 which caused a confrontation between the Popular Party (PP) of José Marie Azanar, in power in Madrid, and the Catalan government of Jordi Pujol, leader of the Catalan Autonomist Party. The new law extended the use of Catalan to public administration, firms, commerce, cinema, radio (with a quota of 25 per cent Catalan songs) and television. Penalties were envisaged for the non-use of Catalan. The law was characterised as a danger for the freedom of expression, a restraint on trade, and extremist by the Popular Party government in Madrid.

Sometimes language controversies concern very small populations such as Slovene in the frontier region of Carinthia in Austria (Knight 1997). But they can have wide political impact. In the Slovene case, Austrian protection of minorities (guaranteed by the 1955 State Treaty) was questioned and the national-populism of the Freedom Party, the majority party in Carinthia, was encouraged. The existence of a minority language can restrict the appeal of movements promoting autonomy for the region. This was the case, until recently, for the French Basque country, and for Wales where Plaid Cymru was too closely connected with the Welsh language interest to attract support in the Anglophone majority.

Even in these cases, where the numbers speaking the language are very small, an international network or association usually provides support for the survival of the language. Thus Rhaeto-Romansch, the fourth official language of Switzerland, spoken by tiny minorities in north-east Italy and western Austria, has an association to defend its interests. The Welsh gather with their fellow Gaels from Brittany, Galicia, Ireland and Scotland in pan-Celtic congresses. In France, representatives of minority languages, although they do not share common linguistic roots, meet on a regular basis to co-ordinate activities, and to exchange experiences about bilingualism. Transfrontier issues are sometimes involved. For example, the Basque autonomous regional government in Spain subsidises many of the materials and programmes for teaching Basque in France.

The protection of these languages has been supported by a modest EU programme for the protection of minority languages and by the 1993 European Charter for the protection of minority languages and cultures. This Charter accords to the minority languages an official standing in the educational system and public life of the signatory countries, although countries can choose which articles they adopt. Though the majority language group regards minority languages largely with indifference, language is widely seen as the most important transmitter of culture in its widest sense – the habitual ways of doing things, which distinguish human groups. Language frontiers, despite the often quoted example of multilingual Switzerland, are usually thought to mark the limits of a genuine sense of community. The speaking of the same language by all people in a country is regarded as making them, to use the title of Dominique Schnapper's book, 'a community of citizens' (Schnapper 1998).

The defence of cultures and languages is frequently couched in highly emotive terms. The French demand for a 'cultural exception' in the Uruguay Round of GATT negotiations and the Seattle World Trade Organisation Round in 2000 was invested with much emotional capital. This demand expressed fears of globalisation and of 'Anglo-Saxon' domination. Measures to protect languages, either through the European Charter of Minority Languages or through national measures such as the 1997 Toubon Law in France or positive support for Irish, have very uncertain effects. However, language is a basic marker of identity and protection of the language is a non-negotiable demand for any group which feels that its language is under threat. The translation of EU documents into all official languages of the member states reflects fears of the smaller nationalities that their languages would be permanently devalued if this was not done. The practice of all legal rules which have a direct effect in the member states is a functional necessity, whilst the translation of all documents is not (Usher 1998).

Nonetheless, people most exposed to different spoken languages are often the most relaxed about language difference. Where people co-operate in institutions requiring efficient communication, working languages are tacitly or explicitly agreed, without much difficulty.[2] In the Schengen system, a form of English, dubbed 'Schenglish', is used without creating national tensions. In the frontier regions, and in other contexts, where economic advantage is to be gained from efficient communication, a linguistic modus vivendi is quickly reached. The problems arise when relations of domination/subordination are perceived to lie behind language use or behind other kinds of cultural practice. Minority languages, languages of small nation states, and languages which feel particularly threatened by English fall into this category. Language frontiers (both geographical and virtual) will therefore change only as a consequence of long-term social processes.

High culture and popular culture

The contemporary importance of the frontier in the realm of artistic creation and 'high' culture is its role in separating patronage regimes. The spread of styles of architecture, music and painting in medieval Europe survived the establishment of national states, because of the cosmopolitanism of patrons. From the mid-nineteenth to the mid-twentieth centuries, some nationalist regimes made vigorous attempts to promote national styles of art which, in the case of Germany, went as far as banning foreign works from exhibition or performance (Burleigh and Wipperman 1991). But in the eighteenth century, patterns of the circulation of ideas, music and visual art were often maintained alongside the worst excesses of nationalism. In the post-1945 world, the international flow of ideas and cultural production has been almost completely free in non-Communist Europe, although the legacy of nationalism is present in state-based patronage and in protectionist regimes for works of art and cultural products.

The patronage systems of the different countries, the role played by ministries of culture, public bodies, organisations for commemorating and celebrating the national past, and private foundations have produced important national differences (Djian 1996: 215–52). The effect of these is uncertain, but they tie creative artists into their respective national systems more than would otherwise be the case. Two factors diminish national dominance – international dissemination of artistic production and the European-wide tendency to decentralise or regionalise the official support for the arts. Also, national differences are both taken into account, and attempts made to reduce their impact, in the increasingly dense network of cultural co-operation in Europe. This began with the establishment by the Council of Europe of the European Centre of Culture at Lausanne in 1949 and the European Cultural Foundation in Amsterdam in 1950.

Initially, the EEC had no direct competence in cultural affairs, although it intervened in this field from the early 1960s. The EU was given legal competence in culture by article 128 of the 1991 Treaty of European Union (to encourage and, if necessary, to support and complement the action of the member states in the improvement and diffusion of culture and of history of the European peoples; the restoration of the cultural patrimony; cultural co-operation and exchanges; artistic and literary creation; co-operation in the audio-visual media). The designation of European cities of culture is the EU's most successful venture because of the prestige attaching to the title and the economic spin-offs expected by the cities concerned. A sense of being part of a European cultural network has thus developed.

At the regional and local level, cultural exchanges have been one of the most dynamic forms of the transfrontier co-operation treated in the last section of this chapter. Visits from local theatre, dance and music ensembles, jointly sponsored tours of major international performers and companies, art festivals and exhibitions, joint promotion of, and publicity for, cultural events, co-operation between museums and art galleries have been initiated by local groups and sponsored by both public authorities and private interests. They have formed the basis of successful INTERREG proposals and have been regarded as an important stimulus for regional development.

Deliberate policies on 'high culture' at European, national and regional levels have had less all-pervasive effects on large populations than the changed market for popular cultural products. Popular culture has transcended frontiers on a grand scale since the Second World War. Before the First World War, and particularly in the inter-war period, the cinema, sport and popular music had an international audience, but the victory of the Allied coalition, led by the United States, aided by increased economic prosperity, had a dramatic effect on popular taste. The growing homogenisation of taste in clothes, leisure activities, music, films and television series (see Chapter 2), however, was balanced by the national dominance of television viewing and newspaper readership, which helps to support 'banal nationalism', analysed by Michael Billig as the persistent flagging of national allegiances (Billig 1995).

Mass tourism and European sporting competitions have both had the paradoxical effect of transcending frontiers and encouraging a narrow nationalism, or the new xenophobia, as it is sometimes termed. Foreign tourists have an impact on social behaviour of the receiving country but their numbers, lack of linguistic competence, inconsiderate, and sometimes rowdy, behaviour, and the facilities necessitated by mass tourism create antagonism. Sport played, and continues to play, an emblematic role in the development of transfrontier relations. The World Cup was established before the United Nations and the European Cup before the EEC. The internationalisation of soccer competition was accompanied by the increasing importance of the role of major teams as cementing or creating local identities (Giulianotti and Williams 1994). Sporting victories are consistently presented as national triumphs. Although Bourdieu has correctly called sporting entertainment one branch of show business (Bourdieu 1993), football in particular creates a sense of belonging and fierce 'tribal' loyalties. These promote a sense of territory and an aggressive rejection of intruders. The response to this is another form of integration in the increasing level of co-operation among European law enforcement agencies to control football hooligans and rowdy tourists (Anderson et al. 1995).

Frontier controls

The freedom of movement of labour, agreed in the Treaty of Rome, led to the eventual removal of all barriers to mobility of persons within the EU. The reticence and caution of national governments ensured that this was not done quickly. Until the mid-1980s controls remained in place on both persons and goods. Although tariffs had been abolished between member states in the 1960s, goods still had to clear Customs when entering a member state from another member state until the late 1980s. Following the signing of the 1986 Single European Act and the implementation of the '1992 programme', the removal of controls took place (excepting certain health, veterinary and phytosanitary controls). Systematic checks on persons were not abolished for most member states until the 1995 implementation of the Schengen agreements.

Abolition in the late 1980s of the remaining Customs formalities for goods at the internal frontiers caused little controversy because it was generally accepted, although not universally welcomed, that a common market meant the unimpeded circulation of goods. Firms dealing in internationally traded goods welcomed the change because their costs were considerably reduced.[3] At the local level, consequences were often serious, although usually temporary. Frontier towns were often specialised in activities dependent on the frontier – large parking areas for trucks with attendant hotel and restaurant services, the economically important presence of Customs and police personnel and their families, the sale of goods not easily available or differentially priced across the frontier. In Irun, in northern Spain, the end of Customs control had a direct impact on 800 people: over 70 small businesses closed, and unemployment rose from 18 per cent in 1991 to 30 per cent in 1993 (*El Diario Vasco* 13 December 1994, Raento 1997).

Many similar local problems occurred which were not large on a national scale, but they exacerbated the often depressed and marginalised local economies adjacent to the frontiers.

The more important, general consequences of abolition of Customs at internal frontiers were long term. Two major multilateral agreements for mutual administrative assistance in Customs matters, the Naples Convention (1967) and Naples II (now in process of ratification), exercise pressure to harmonise Customs legal powers and working methods. Naples II is mainly focused on strengthening Customs co-operation through measures such as transfrontier surveillance, hot pursuit across frontiers, controlled delivery, undercover operations and the temporary establishment of international teams to pursue particular investigations. The Treaties of Rome and Maastricht provide a basis for Europeanising Customs work. They impose on EU member states the obligation of combating fraud against the EU budget with the same methods and the same rigour as combating fraud against their own budgets. Much of this work falls on Customs, especially in the fields of the common external tariff, the Common Agricultural Policy and VAT.

Customs officials in all member states collect the external tariff, which forms part of the EU's 'own resources'. They apply identical rules for controlling goods at the external frontier. A programme for the exchange of Customs officers, the Mattheus programme, was instituted in the 1980s to promote mutual understanding of working practices in other member states and eventually to harmonise them. A central data base was set up to exchange Customs-related information. Criminal law enforcement[4] – the fight against counterfeit goods, child pornography, drugs, arms-trafficking, insurance fraud, and trade in endangered species – is an increasingly prominent Customs role, and the importance of European systems of co-operation in these areas is growing. Customs are therefore represented in Europol (as they have long been represented in Interpol), and they use the Schengen Information System as well as the specialised Customs information exchanges.

Characteristics of the Schengen system

The Schengen system was introduced in order to compensate for the security 'deficit' allegedly caused by the abolition of border controls. The system had discreet beginnings in the negotiations leading up to the 1985 Schengen Agreement and the 1990 Schengen Application Convention. These are now supplemented by, now voluminous, rules and practices (taken together they are now described, in the jargon of the EU, as the Schengen *acquis*[5]). All the other member states, with the exception of the UK and Ireland, eventually signed the Agreement and Convention.[6] The system is managed by an Executive Committee, which is now the EU Justice and Home Affairs Council of Ministers, a Central Control Group and a board for verifying that data protection rules are properly implemented.

The Schengen compensatory measures can be grouped under eight headings:

1. Strict control of the external frontier according to common rules, contained in the confidential Schengen manual for the external frontier,[7] and common visas.[8]
2. A co-ordinating committee and technical inspections of the external borders of all member states (and candidate members) to ensure that they meet the agreed standards.
3. Exchange of information on prohibited immigrants, wanted persons, stolen vehicles through the Schengen Information System (SIS), a computerised central data base (now with in excess of 8 million entries) in Strasbourg, which supplies information to and receives information from national data bases.
4. Data protection in the form of an independent control board with a uniform code of rules.
5. A task force to analyse intelligence about the role of organised gangs for smuggling illegal immigrants into the EU.
6. The establishment of national offices of SIRENE (*Supplément d'Information Requis à l'Entrée Nationale*) to deal with difficulties and emergencies.
7. Enhanced police co-operation and judicial co-operation between the participating states, particularly in the frontier regions.
8. Movement towards a common visa, asylum and immigration policy.

The entry into force of this system was delayed from 1990 to 1995 by international developments. These included the unification of Germany, the huge increase in the number of asylum seekers, and the spilling over, in 1995, of Algerian terrorism into France, and general doubts about the prudence of dropping systematic frontier controls.

Debate of the merits of the system was often submerged in wider, emotionally charged issues. Amongst these were the restriction of numbers of immigrants entering particular countries (to zero in the view of Charles Pasqua, the French Minister of the Interior in 1993), attempts to tighten rules on asylum seekers, links made between security, criminality and immigrants, and allegations concerning, on the one hand, the development of an alleged 'fortress Europe' (which, according to pro-immigrant groups, created a Europe which excludes non-Europeans) and a contradictory charge of a 'sieve Europe' (because the external frontier, according to the anti-immigration lobby, was highly porous).

Schengen also became a target for civil liberties organisations, and for pro-immigrant groups. The main criticisms are that Schengen represents a European-wide repressive system; it tends to criminalise clandestine immigrants and asylum seekers because they are entered in the same data base as drug dealers, arms traffickers and other 'real' criminals; it encourages racist attitudes, since most of the excluded immigrants are non-white; there are shortcomings in provisions for asylum seekers, compared with the standards laid down in the Geneva Convention; it lacks transparency because it is an intergovernmental system with weak arrangements for legal and political accountability; and the data protection guarantees are faulty (Curtin and Meijers 1995).[9] These charges were taken seriously by members of national parliaments, particularly in the Netherlands, the UK House of Lords and the French Senate, and by members of the European Parliament.[10]

The British position

The United Kingdom is isolated within the EU on Schengen. Sovereign control and use of frontiers remain, for the British government, an important issue, for symbolic and practical reasons. Britain and the Republic of Ireland were given a right to opt into the Schengen arrangements by the Amsterdam Treaty. The Irish are prepared to enter if it does not mean sacrificing the UK–Ireland free movement area. The UK government announced, on 12 March 1999, that it would accept virtually all of the *acquis*, except the abolition of border controls.[11]

The British government wished to retain frontier controls for law enforcement purposes, particularly in the fields of terrorism and drug trafficking and to control illegal immigration. The island position of Britain limited the number of points of entry to the country and, it was argued, made controls more effective than in other EU member states (House of Lords, 1998–99). The opt-out was supported by the lack of trust in some law enforcement systems in the EU. Additionally, the cost would be high of adapting Heathrow and other UK airports to Schengen norms, and there would be the associated cost of enforcing frontier controls on the very large transit traffic passing through

London to other European destinations. It would make the UK responsible for an important external port of entry to the EU as a whole.

Other reactions to Schengen

French governments, of both left and right, have considered Schengen as a necessary consequence of the completion of the Single Market. Yet, the French government hesitated about abolition of frontier controls. The last hesitations were the Juppé government's extension of the transition period of three months in 1996 because of alleged inadequacy of compensatory measures,[12] and the refusal to remove fixed frontier posts on the Belgian and Luxembourg frontiers because of Dutch drugs policy. Moderate parliamentary opinion both on the left and the right was cautious about Schengen, approving the principle of abolition of border controls but inclined to be critical about details.[13] This caution was encouraged by the electoral threat posed by the anti-immigrant, extreme right, Front National.

The dismantling of frontier controls met, in general, with negative reactions in law enforcement agencies. Giving up a method of control deemed useful for crime prevention and criminal investigation was unwelcome, but professional interests were also at stake. The Customs service and specialised frontier police, such as the Air and Frontier Police (PAF) in France, feared a severe reduction in personnel. This did not happen, with the partial exception of the German Customs service. German Customs has no role in the control of intra-EU traffic; unlike other Customs services, it did not have powers to stop and search traffic away from external ports of entry. The Italian Customs and Carabinieri responsible for frontier policing had increased resourcing because of the difficulty of maintaining the degree of control of the sea and air frontiers of Italy at a level which satisfied the Schengen partners. In France, many older Customs officers, who had spent their careers in the fixed frontier posts, took early retirement, but the total establishment of about 20 000 was maintained. Customs adapted, as far as possible, to a role of facilitating intra- and extra-EU trade, helping the competitivity of French companies and ports, and strengthening its criminal law enforcement role (Ministère de l'Economie, des Finances et de l'Industrie 1998).

Some local reactions to the implementation of Schengen differed from the national reactions. Local populations and interests reacted against the opening of the internal frontiers when, as at the eastern end of the Franco-Spanish frontier, Spanish contractors who evaded French regulations could no longer be stopped at the frontier. By contrast, complaints were made in the north-east of Italy about the hindrance to traffic due to strengthened controls at the Italian–Slovene frontier. Bavaria, with its own border police and its own specific position within the Federal Republic of Germany, has adopted its own perspective on frontier policies and continuously questioned Austrian competence as a full Schengen member state because more undocumented immigrants were reaching Bavaria. The German Federal government did not share this view. Generally, adverse reactions to Schengen, both within the law enforcement establishments and amongst private interests, were temporary.

Bilateral co-operation

Although the Schengen system modifies the practice of existing bilateral and multilateral arrangements for police and Customs co-operation, it does not replace them. Bilateral measures remain necessary because frontier surveillance, policing and control are the responsibilities of states and are regulated by national law. They are also necessary to take account of local circumstances and to ensure that the law enforcement agencies involved have a clear basis for co-operation. Schengen has also stimulated new forms of bilateral co-operation, such as joint police stations and new local protocols setting out the arrangements for transfrontier co-operation (see Chapter 4).

Bilateral agreements are often set within a complex network of multilateral agreements. Indeed, good bilateral co-operation is no longer sufficient to control busy frontier crossings. For example, the arrangements for policing the Channel tunnel are based on provisions of the Anglo-French Protocol of 1991, and include authority for a French police presence at Folkestone and a British police presence at Fréthun (*Protocol* 1991). Within the framework of the 1985 Channel tunnel treaty, there are letters of understanding between the Kent Constabulary and authorities in France, Belgium and the Netherlands for practical police co-operation. A broader network of multilateral co-ordination exists within the Cross Channel Intelligence Conference (see Chapter 4). In turn, this frontier comes within the area of competence of Europol and, for the continental partners, of Schengen. The frontier police also use the global system of Interpol. In addition, the police arrangements for co-ordination are sometimes integrated or co-ordinated with Customs systems.

This complexity of co-operative arrangements is confusing and lacks transparency. Effective systems of accountability and control are made more difficult, especially as each method of co-ordination and co-operation has its own lines of accountability and control. But these parallel and overlapping methods can be useful to law enforcement officials because if one channel of communication does not work, another can be tried. Not being a member of one of these overlapping systems of co-operation can be a disadvantage. The absence of the UK from Schengen denies English law enforcement officials access to the Schengen Information System. Although informally they can get information from it, this depends on the goodwill of individuals. The major element, which evades any control and any systematic evaluation, is informal co-operation which constitutes a large part of practical co-operation. Every formal system of transfrontier police co-operation creates the opportunity for individual law enforcement officers to become acquainted. When they know and trust one another, they will often communicate information outside the official channels.

The whole legal basis of frontier management and control, as well as the practical arrangements for law enforcement co-operation relating to frontiers, will eventually require rationalisation and reform, if the process of European integration continues. The integration of Schengen into the treaty system has resulted in a complex and unclear situation. A standard and simplified pattern across the territory of the EU may become a pressing necessity both to combat criminality and to ensure democratic and legal accountability of the law enforcement agencies (den Boer and Corrado forthcoming).

Transfrontier co-operation between local and regional authorities

Regular transfrontier co-operation between local and regional authorities has been established along all EU internal frontiers, including sea frontiers such as the Channel and the Baltic, and is now extended to the external frontier with the candidate states (Fitzmaurice 1993). It straddles state frontiers between EU member states and their neighbours, particularly Switzerland, Austria, Slovenia, Croatia, Poland and Hungary; three Euroregions (only two of which are fully functioning) have also been established across the sensitive German–Polish frontier (Bort 1997a).

Co-operation began in the 1950s, as a series of informal contacts which were gradually transformed into systematic institutionalised meetings of regional and local authorities.[14] The 1980 (Madrid) Outline Convention on Transfrontier Cooperation between Regional and Local Authorities provided a framework for co-operation; an annex to the convention provided a model agreement for these authorities. An additional protocol came into force in 1994, to allow the transfer of transfrontier agreements from public international law to the administrative law of the states concerned. In principle, this makes them more easily enforceable and allows obscurities in them to be clarified more quickly, for agreements on matters such as sewage and waste disposal, transfrontier industrial zones, water and gas supplies, and nature parks. The Convention has been very little used because most states entered a reservation to the effect that specific schemes had to be within the terms of bilateral treaties with neighbouring states.

Some moves have been made towards more harmonised legal bases, influenced by the EC/EU INTERREG programmes, the encouragement by the EU to establish Euroregions, and the realisation that this form of co-operation has spread to all EU frontiers. The main categories of transfrontier agreement are intergovernmental agreements or conventions or recommendations; treaties such as the Bonn Treaty of 5 March 1975, setting up the tripartite commission for the upper Rhine and the bipartite commission for the middle Rhine; private law agreements between local authorities (and perhaps other organisations); informal agreements between local authorities, sometimes including other organisations which result in de facto regular co-operation; and intermittent consultations about common problems.

The forms of co-operation range from fairly elaborate institutional structures, such as the Euroregion on the Dutch–German border,[15] to simple arrangements for regular meetings of executives of local or regional authorities such as the Working Committee for the Pyrenees.[16] Overlapping areas of transfrontier co-operation are common – for example there are now two Euroregions for the Pyrenees and a series of local associations, as well as the Working Committee for the Pyrenees. The regions involved in ARGE ALP (Working Community of the Eastern Alps) and the ALPE ADRIA (Working Community of the Eastern Alps) overlap, with four regions being members of both (Lombardy, South Tyrol-Trentino, Salzburg and Bavaria).[17]

Some publicly proclaimed intentions of transfrontier co-operation have remained fairly constant over the last four decades. These are to resolve the practical difficulties created by the frontier, to develop good neighbourly relations, to obtain remedies for harm and to gain information about decisions and developments which may affect the material interests of neighbouring regions. Less explicit intentions include dependent regions seeking access to influence decision-making processes of the economically stronger neighbouring region.

Dormitory towns in France are in this dependent relationship on the Swiss cities of Basel and Geneva; Barcelona exerts an economic attraction across the Catalan–French frontier; most regions in the Alpine arc in Switzerland and Austria, which have small populations, are exposed to overwhelming economic and social influences from densely populated and highly industrialised regions in the surrounding plains of Lombardy, Bavaria and Rhône-Alpes.

Other motives for co-operation have changed over the past four decades. The first forms of transfrontier co-operation between local governments across the Rhine originated in the early 1950s as part of a movement for Franco-German reconciliation. The enthusiasm for building bridges between people formerly separated by frontiers was evident elsewhere – on the French–Spanish frontier after the restoration of democracy in Spain and at the eastern frontier of the EU after the collapse of communism. Baltic Sea co-operation benefited from the enthusiasm for renewing contacts with parts of the former Soviet Union and additionally from an underlying serious concern about the security and stability of the region after the collapse of communism. The impetus provided by reconciliation of peoples tends to be relatively short-lived unless it is supported by other factors.

In the early 1960s, the focus changed from reconciliation to overcoming difficulties created by the frontier for economic development, particularly in the field of industrial location and land-use planning.[18] Many other examples in widely separated European frontier regions illustrate the interest in infrastructure planning, the development of transport facilities, the sharing of services such as sewage and waste disposal and similar matters. In the aftermath of the protest movements of the 1960s, a new concern about the environment emerged, leading to direct action campaigns, and the establishment of pressure groups and green parties. This affected the agenda of transfrontier co-operation and, in some places, created a popular basis for it.

The mobilisation of opposition to the concentration of nuclear power stations on the Rhine in the 1970s may not have altered the policy of states in the short term (with the possible exception of abandoning one projected nuclear power station at Wyhl). But it created new transfrontier networks of environmental campaigners and a radio station, Radio Dreyeckland, and the setting up of the Lake Constance Conference which saved the lake from environmental catastrophe. There were other successes in Saar-Lor-Lux, the Danube and the Alpine region. Transfrontier groupings of ecologists are to be found in other regions, for example on the Basque littoral.[19] This is 'bottom up' pressure to engage in transfrontier co-operation, contrasting with previous elite co-operation. Local elites have now adopted environmentalist programmes in transfrontier co-operation, partly to anticipate demands from the grass roots and partly because consensus building is sometimes easier on environmental than on other issues.[20]

In the second half of the 1970s and for part of the 1980s (a period described as one of 'euro-stagnation'), promoters of European integration took an interest in transfrontier co-operation. Some participants in transfrontier associations came to regard themselves as in the forefront of the European movement. This gave co-operation a new sense of purpose at a time when the standing and influence of land-use planners were in decline. Another phase was apparent after the 1986 Single European Act and the passage to the Single Market. Economic interests have come again to the fore – adaptation of local economies previously dependent on the frontier and frontier controls, new opportunities for joint ventures with the dismantling of frontier controls and, above all, the prospect of EU financial aid for frontier regions.

Political and constitutional difficulties

The constitutions and legislation of most European countries had to be modified to permit regional governments to enter treaty-like agreements with partners in other countries.[21] In France, although transfrontier co-operation happened in practice, it was not expressly authorised until 1982. It was, in principle, limited to consultations and discussions about matters of common interest. In 1992 a new law went further and provided a genuine basis for transfrontier co-operation. Regions were given authority to conclude conventions with foreign partners, provided that these do not conflict with the international agreements entered into by the French state. Regions and local authorities can also participate, with foreign partners, in *sociétés d'économie mixte* (semi-public firms) and *groupements d'intérêt public* (associations of public interest) – in other words, commit financial resources. This was partly to allow participation in the EC INTERREG programme and partly an aspect of decentralising authority away from Paris.

The situation in Italy was initially even more restrictive than that of France.[22] A 1977 Presidential decree gave regions the right to conclude agreements with foreign public authorities provided they were restricted to a 'promotional' character to develop the social, economic or cultural activities of the region. A 1982 law ratifying the Madrid convention permitted regional and local authorities to make agreements provided that these were expressly envisaged by a bilateral convention between Italy and the states concerned. In June 1990, local and regional authorities were allowed to conclude programme agreements (*accordi di programma*) with one another and with foreign territorial partners. Other EU member states have moved in a similar direction, with the exception of the UK which, despite the involvement in cross-Channel associations[23] with French authorities, does not see the need for enabling legislation.

The different constitutional and administrative structures of states, which also produces striking inequalities in budgetary powers and resources,[24] causes difficulties for transfrontier co-operation. The most obvious manifestation of differences is the varying extent of central government involvement in transfrontier co-operation. All the countries neighbouring France have more decentralised systems, and central governments play a much smaller role. The French central government, represented by the prefects, is always very much present. The contrast is most striking in the Franco-Swiss transfrontier – the Communauté de Travail des Alpes Occidentales (COTRAO – Provence-Alpes-Côte d'Azur, Rhône-Alpes, Liguria, Piedmont, Valle d'Aosta, cantons of Geneva, Valais, founded 1982); Conseil du Léman (*départements* of Ain, Haute Savoie, cantons of Geneva, Valais and Vaud, founded 1984); and the Communauté de Travail du Jura – Franche Comté and the cantons of Berne, Jura, Neuchâtel and Vaud, founded in 1985).

On the Swiss side, the Confederal government has some role, but the cantons are the dominant partners; on the French side the prefectures play the central co-ordinating and facilitating role. Services are administered by the central government in France but at the canton, the *Länder* or regional/provincial level in Switzerland, Germany and Belgium. The Italian and especially the Spanish regions also have greater legal powers and larger budgets than the French regions. These differences are usually accepted with good grace, but they can cause resentment when policy disputes arise.

Absence of compatible structures has encouraged informal agreements for joint projects (Risse, Ludwig interviews). However, when financial resources are involved, informal co-operation based on goodwill is not an adequate basis for projects. The existence of de facto joint projects was one consideration which led to the 1996 Treaty of Karlsruhe between France, Germany and Luxembourg (Ludwig interview; Heberlein 1997). This provided a new legal basis for jointly financed transfrontier projects and with other bilateral agreements such as the Franco-Spanish Treaty of Bayonne. It marked an important step forward, at least at the level of principle. Local agreements, involving a budget, can be arrived at with almost the same ease as with a neighbouring authority in the same country. These small agreements are the beginning of the transfer of sovereignty rights (Beyerlin 1998).

'Europe' and transfrontier co-operation

Three European organisations have influenced transfrontier co-operation – the OECD, mainly on the problem of externalities (transfrontier pollution and the costs of environmental protection) – a role which has disappeared as the EC/EU has become more active in environmental policy, the Council of Europe which promoted contacts between municipalities and local authorities and, now much the most important, the EC/EU.

The Council of Europe provided, since the 1950s, administrative support for meetings of local authorities, through the Congress of Local and Regional Authorities in Europe,[25] and a framework for consultation and the negotiation of conventions. The weakness of the Council of Europe's role is that it takes a considerable length of time (often decades) from the initiation of an idea to its implementation. The Council works through consensus and has no legal instruments to impose rules with direct effect in the member states, and has no resources to support projects. Co-operation between the CE and the EU, most recently through the EU Committee of the Regions, has been tried, with limited effect. Increased integration within the EU, encouraging all forms of transfrontier co-operation, could diminish the need for the kind of co-operation provided by the Council of Europe (Leresche and Levy 1995).

Since its inception, the EEC/EC provided indirect support for transfrontier co-operation. The European Commission promoted inter-regional networking (Leonardi 1992), the development of regional institutions and direct contact between the regions and the European Commission. The direct application of European law to the environmental and social spheres, direct contacts between the regions and the Commission since 1975 through the European Fund for Regional Development (FEDER), helped to give a European dimension to the activities of regional and local government and, therefore, to inter-regional co-operation. As the EC became increasingly important as a source of funds, permanent offices were established in Brussels by regional authorities, by their associations, and by various specialised associations of frontier regions, mountain regions, peripheral and maritime regions, and the Association of European Border Regions

(AEBR – founded in 1971). In 1996, AEBR jointly initiated, with the European Commission, LACE-TAP (Linkage Assistance and Co-operation for the European Border Regions – Technical Assistance Programme). This was to spread best practice and provide technical assistance (LACE – *Fiches Info* 1997–, LACE *Magazine* 1997–). The representation of local authorities in the Economic and Social Council and in the multitude of consultative committees of the EU, and representatives of the regions in the Regional Committee, all help to erode the previously clear distinction between the national and subnational levels of government.

Programmes aimed at joint transfrontier projects were introduced to help efface the effects of frontiers – INTERREG I (1990–94), INTERREG II (1995–99) and INTERREG III (2000–6) (Map 3.1). The less well-known RECITE I Programme (Regions and Cities for Europe) has financed 36 interregional co-operation projects in which 249 regional and local authorities are involved (European Commission 1997). The record of INTERREG I in promoting transfrontier co-operation between local and regional authorities was flawed because, amongst other factors, of the lack of co-ordination with other EC programmes and unclear guidelines. The distribution of funds was unbalanced – 63 per cent of the EU contribution went to the European periphery – improving communications infrastructure on the borders of Greece and between Spain and Portugal. INTERREG 1 was, in these cases, handled by representatives of the central governments (Covas 1995), contrary to the intention of the programme. Even in other places, the central government was the de facto initiator or co-ordinator or executor (or all three) of the programme, with only token local participation. On some frontiers, local politicians believed that the EC Commission did not understand what the real problems at the frontier were (Muñoa interview). Sometimes the negotiations which were supposed to arrive at joint proposals were a charade and it was difficult to get people involved in them to think in transfrontier terms (Ginderin interview).

INTERREG II took some of the criticisms into account. The regions were much better prepared and the programme succeeded in federating interests separated by the international frontier. A wide range of small-scale projects – environmental protection, tourism, transfrontier footpaths and footbridges, promotion of bilingualism, educational and cultural co-operation and many other projects were financed. The provision of full and reliable information about developments on the other side of the frontier was a frequent basis for successful projects. Information services have been set up, sometimes offices covering enquiries about employment issues, tax, how to build partnerships,

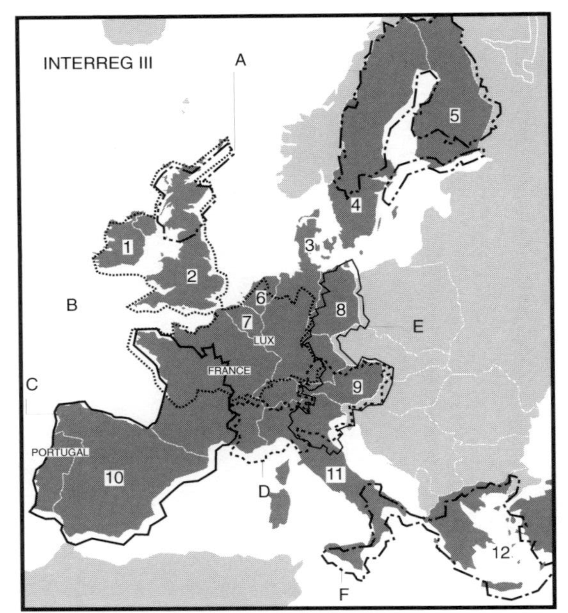

A	Baltic Region	4	Sweden
B	North Sea Region	5	Finland
C	Atlantic ARC	6	Netherlands
D	Western Mediterranean	7	Belgium
E	Adriatic and south-east Europe	8	Germany
		9	Austria
1	Ireland	10	Spain
2	United Kingdom	11	Italy
3	Denmark	12	Greece

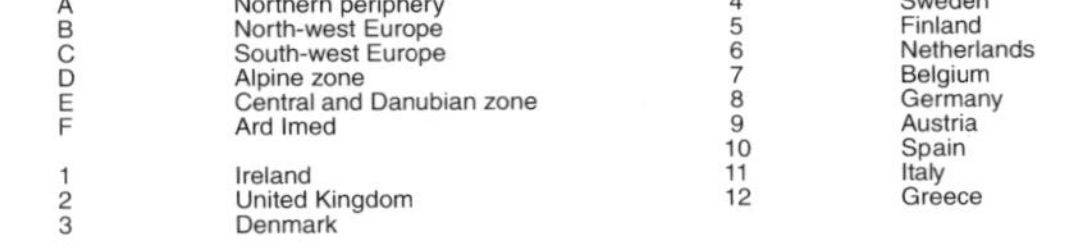

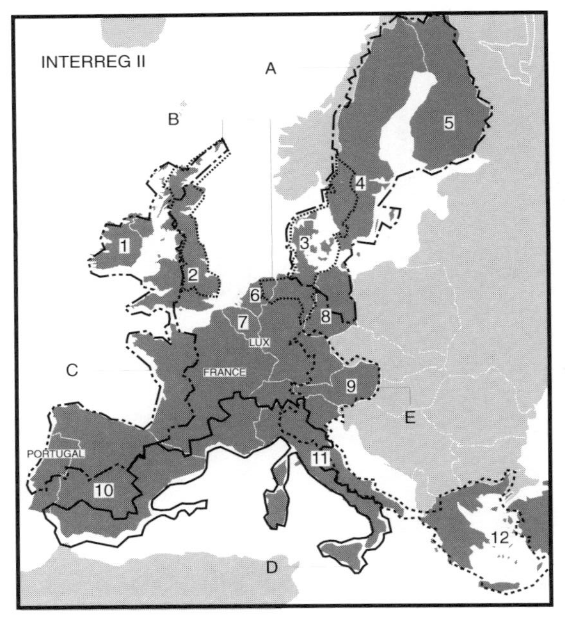

A	Northern periphery	4	Sweden
B	North-west Europe	5	Finland
C	South-west Europe	6	Netherlands
D	Alpine zone	7	Belgium
E	Central and Danubian zone	8	Germany
F	Ard Imed	9	Austria
		10	Spain
1	Ireland	11	Italy
2	United Kingdom	12	Greece
3	Denmark		

Map 3.1   Priority areas for INTERREG programmes

consumer rights, organisation of meetings and working groups and so on. Examples are the four INFOBEST offices (Kehl, Lauterbourg, Vogelgrun-Breisach, Weil-Huningue) on the frontier between France and Germany. Other initiatives include joint or co-operative tourist information services, transfrontier guides and hotel booking services,[26] transfrontier travel timetables and maps, and consumer rights bureaux.

The proposal in 1999 of the INTERREG III programme shows a commitment to continuing and developing co-operation between local and regional authorities across the internal frontiers. The late announcement of the programme (finally approved by the European Parliament and the Council of Ministers in early 2000) gave a short lead time for the preparation and negotiation of projects, the central governments were again to co-ordinate national bids, and the funds were insufficient for major projects. A new map of regional groupings and a new list of priority areas is intended to give the programme greater focus. The practice of working together, often on detailed matters, and the treatment of the whole of the EU as a single territory divided into large transnational regions, is intended to encourage the development of transfrontier communities of interest.

Although the EU has often played a central role in much of this co-operation, some has taken place independently of the EU framework. The most compelling examples of the relative unimportance of the EC/EU as the essential impetus of transfrontier co-operation are associations in the Alps–Adriatic triangle – ARGE ALP for the Alpine region stretching from Baden-Württemberg and Bavaria in the north to Lombardy in the south and Salzburg in the east and including the Swiss cantons of Graubünden, St Gallen and Tocino, and ALPE ADRIA, stretching from Bavaria to Slovenia and Croatia (Strassoldo 1998). These associations, unusually, have had, at certain times, a high political profile. Initially this was because they were interpreted, in certain Italian and Yugoslav circles, as evidence of a Bavarian/German attempt to regain influence towards the south-east. More recently, ALPE ADRIA was supportive, from the beginning, of the separatist aims of Slovenia and Croatia in the early 1990s, with the result that both remain members, even though they stand out as two sovereign states in an association of regional governments.

The Upper Rhine, comprising Alsace, Baden-Württemberg and Basel, has a dynamic independent of the EU. The setting up of the Tripartite Commission (France, Switzerland, Federal Republic of Germany) for the Upper Rhine by the 1975 Bonn Treaty was outside the EC framework and made no reference to it. This agreement was strengthened by the Karlsruhe agreement of 23 January 1996 to facilitate conventions between Swiss, German, Luxembourg and French regional local authorities, which again made no reference to the EU. In this region intensity of economic exchanges (see Chapter 4) – a transfrontier labour market, important direct investments, cultural closeness, an enterprising university and research community – have provided a basis for highly developed transfrontier co-operation.

Prospects for transfrontier co-operation

The scope of transfrontier co-operation is facilitated by the already mentioned intergovernmental agreements of Bayonne (1995) and Karlsruhe (1996) which permit them to create joint bodies, such as the Groupement Européen d'Intérêt Economique (GEIE), capable of assuming autonomous financial responsibilities. They also allow the financial participation of authorities on one side of the frontier as a junior partner in public utilities and development programmes on the other side. Local and regional govenments may use them as a way of increasing their own autonomy (Rizk 1997, Perrin 1996, Cambot 1998). Transfrontier co-operation has already proven its worth in sharing of services and, sometimes, joint investments – in emergency, hospital, waste disposal services and sewage disposal.

Practical problems in frontier regions create pressure for further reform of current arrangements. Sometimes problems are trivial, but they illustrate the imperfections of European integration so far. For example, the difficulties of frontier workers have not been solved by the dismantling of frontier controls and the reciprocal granting of social security rights within the EU – long-term sickness is an example, where incompatibilities between the two sets of regulations result in individuals having neither rights to sick pay nor unemployment benefit on either side of the frontier. Where people are supposed to go for benefits, especially when firms send workers across the frontier for extended periods of time, is sometimes unclear. Workers can lose benefits by being unaware of the procedures of the neighbouring state. These difficulties are resolved on an ad hoc basis by Infobest on the Alsace/Baden Württemberg frontier (Schneider interviews) and by exchange of officials once a fortnight in northern Lorraine (Festhauer and Mauchoffé interviews), but they create pressure for a general regime to cover all frontier regions.

The importance of the flow of information across frontiers has been shown in reports which are otherwise critical of the practice of transfrontier co-operation (Vernier 1993). The demand for information is likely to increase. Awareness of what is happening on the other side of the frontier is of paramount importance, particularly where a large and dynamic city is a transfrontier neighbour or a particularly dynamic activity, such as the technological park at Aachen, is located just across the border. Information about changes in economic activity, investment patterns, demand for labour, new local and central government policies, planning decisions, pollution and environmental measures, is of basic importance. Sometimes this information is publicly available, but local and regional policy makers on the other side of a frontier may not be aware of it in the absence of regular channels of communication and face-to-face contacts.

Despite the potential for development, transfrontier institutions or associations lack real political weight and influence. This is due to lack of impact among the populations in the frontier regions, political divisions, lack of resources, lack of a sense of transfrontier solidarity, constitutional obstacles and reticence or indifference of central governments. There is often very little public awareness of this form of co-operation. The practical achievements of transfrontier institutions are often mundane, and not especially newsworthy. They are usually given very modest coverage in the regional and the national press and by broadcasting services. The attempts to engage in ambitious transfrontier co-operation, such as an integrated land use or spatial plan, can be disrupted by sharp differences of view between different levels of government in the same country (van Ginderin interview). Regions trying to co-operate often have very different levels of resources at their disposal which constrains the size of projects to the level of the poorest partner.

There is little evidence that the frontier as a marker of the limits of political identity has been effaced from the mentality of the populations of the frontier regions (PAMINA 1995, Conseil du Léman 1997). Sometimes transfrontier ethnonational identities sustain institutional co-operation – for example in Euroregion Tirol (Luverà 1996) and in the Basque region – but this is rare and, where it occurs, tends to raise anxieties and opposition. For example, in January 1996 the Italian government opposed the opening of a joint office in Brussels representing the Euroregion Tirol. A record of lack of success of many transfrontier associations in promoting schemes tends to undermine their standing.

Transfrontier co-operative projects are not always welcome to the populations which they affect. They can attract opposition, enough to delay, if not prevent, their eventual implementation. The controversial Somport tunnel under the Pyrenees provoked a militant, and partially successful, environmentalist campaign against it. The mayors of the French communes affected rebelled in the 1980s against the solution for Rhine pollution – the dumping of saline waste in disused mine shafts – on the grounds that this would damage the water table. A similar case, which came to a head in the 1980s and early 1990s, was the pollution of the river Meuse with heavy metals from the old industrial area around Liège in Belgium which conflicted with the Dutch use of the Meuse to extract drinking water. The Liégeois wanted a slower clean-up timetable and lower eventual pollution standards to prevent economic damage to industry. This dispute tended to reinforce national stereotypes and traditional animosities.

It is a paradox of transfrontier co-operation (whether of an intergovernmental or interregional form) that, although the intention is to remove the source of conflicts, as transfrontier contacts become closer, it can trigger new conflicts. Sometimes popular sentiment is expressed against lowering the frontier as when Danes, in the early summer of 1997, formed a human chain on the German–Danish frontier under the slogan 'the frontier must stay'.

The most difficult issues of conflict in frontier regions cannot be resolved by existing transfrontier associations. Transfrontier associations have not yet succeeded in mobilising the necessary political support, control of resources and legal authority.[27] Potential sources of difficulty in frontier regions are cultural and linguistic conflicts, political subversion, economic dislocation or environmental damage resulting from transfrontier activities, and market dominance of the capital, labour and retail markets by a large centre on the other side of the frontier. Adequate resources, political legitimacy, executive authority and attention to the broader international context are necessary to resolve major conflicts. None can be solved without the intervention of the central governments – and the EU may also be an essential partner in a solution.[28]

Conclusion

Internal EU frontiers remain politically important because the states which they enclose are highly resilient political institutions. Most political activity remains confined within state boundaries, and nationals from other member states seldom effectively intervene in the electoral or party politics of another state. The exceptions are rare, such as the successful leadership of Daniel Cohn-Bendit of the Green list in France for the 1999 European elections. Such an intervention in a frontier region would, at the moment, be regarded as an affront to good neighbourliness. This was also the case in 1999 when the Bavarian Minister President Stoiber intervened in Austria to propose an outcome for the stalemate in forming a government coalition.

Highly distinctive national legal systems (which the EU is only slowly changing) and national administrations mean that there is a sharp break in structures and procedures at the frontier. Regulations governing everyday life differ within a few metres of one another in the frontier zones. What seems an easily comprehensible and 'natural' arrangement in one country is difficult to understand by citizens of the neighbouring state. Different expectations and understandings therefore rub awkwardly against one another at the internal frontiers. These differences will not easily be effaced because national sentiment, language and culture support them. These in turn are underpinned by national educational systems and a legacy of history which influences the nature of institutions and political values and attitudes.

Additionally, the state crucially retains the monopoly of coercive powers in the spheres of policing and the criminal law. In these domains, the state remains 'a security community'. The abolition of systematic frontier controls on persons has been a crucially important stimulus to co-operation in justice and home affairs. Institutions have been put in place – Europol and Schengen – which presage change, but these, at the moment, assist state agencies to fulfil their roles. Ideas of a European public prosecutor and limited harmonisation of the criminal law (a *Corpus Juris*) have been floated, and the European Council in 1999 at Tampere, more modestly, called for an approximation of criminal laws and procedures. Progress in these areas is likely to be slow, and the frontier remains intact as a legal barrier.

Co-ordination between public authorities across frontiers, where there is intense traffic and many economic and social exchanges, may in future reach levels equivalent to those between authorities within the territories of the states. The policy areas within the competence of regional and local governments may eventually be interlocked across the frontiers, in the sense that nothing major can be undertaken without a negotiation with partners in the other country. Attitudes of participants at this level of co-operation have already changed, and frontiers are no longer seen as walls across which co-operation is very difficult. However, the real test of whether frontiers are eroding is in terms of the everyday behaviour of people. Where transfrontier labour markets have developed and facilities (shopping, leisure, cultural, educational) across the frontier are frequently used, this is happening.

4
The Case of French Frontiers

No individual member state of the EU is representative of all of them, but France provides an illustration of key European issues. Ideas of national sovereignty, the unity of the national territory, and the bureaucratisation and centralisation of the state first made their appearance in France: these characteristics contribute to a sensitivity about the impact of greater openness and permeability of frontiers, shared to some degree by all EU member states. France also illustrates the complexity of the frontier of a modern state, set in landscapes and memories, the locus of various forms of unwelcome intrusion, an instrument of exclusion, and a limit of the power of the state to impose its will.

In the areas of frontier control and management of frontier issues, the French example shows that frontiers are always matters of negotiation. The issues for negotiation vary according to which section of the French frontier is examined.[1] The two major general issues are policing the frontier against unwelcome external intrusions and maintaining the integrity of the French nation by preserving its cultural independence.

Perceptions of territory

A clearly defined sense of French territory began with the emergence of the idea of 'natural' frontiers in the late sixteenth century and was deeply embedded from the end of the Napoleonic Wars. Two continuing characteristics of France are a strong administrative state and emphasis on the importance of territorial integrity. The Revolutionary slogan, 'the Republic One and Indivisible', had two territorial implications. The first was that any alienation of the territory of the Republic was inconceivable, an affront to the Republic and the French nation; the second was that there should be a uniformity of law, administration, rights and obligations across the whole territory. Certain important administrative institutions and their territorial organisation corresponded to these ideas – *départements*, prefectoral corps, administrative law and courts, a gendarmerie and *surveillance du territoire* to ensure public tranquillity and the security of the state.

The idea of France as a coherent, nationally homogeneous whole, with clear political, legal, cultural and linguistic frontiers, is now thought by some commentators to be under serious threat. Max Gallo, writer, historian and friend of President Mitterrand, sees the origins of a territorial crisis in a wide variety of factors – *inter alia* the fragmenting of the national community through unemployment and poverty, the alienation of the electorate from the political elite, the involvement in criminal investigations of the Mayor of Paris and the President of the Constitutional Council, the bankruptcy of financial institutions in the state sector, the dysfunction of the educational system, and the inability of the state to control corrupt practices. How, asks Gallo rhetorically:

> can one be surprised that, in Montpellier, some dream of being part of Catalunya, that a Basque département is proposed to ease the way for a merger with the rest of the Basque country, that in Savoy some wish to question the annexation of 1860, that an official report, following a European directive, proposes the encouragement of regional languages? (*Le Monde* 11 February 1998)

The disintegration of French territory, in the way suggested, is improbable, but a recurrent anxiety about a disintegration of the country, both socially and spatially, is evident. The frontiers are no longer perceived as clear lines or limits behind which people preserve a sense of community and of cultural and physical security.

Some issues in France are the place of frontiers in the perception of France as a historic 'community of citizens'; the importance of territory for the French language; the belief that some frontiers are sensitive because frontier regions are fragile economically and socially; the rapid growth of, and the issues posed by, transfrontier co-operation at the local and regional level; the new security problems of immigration and illegal trafficking; the degree to which frontier policy and political problems relating to frontiers are now shared with the EU; and the general anxiety about whether the state can defend the valuable aspects of French life and French interests when are frontiers increasingly permeable.

Sensitive frontiers – from military to economic vulnerability

Sensitive frontiers in France have, until recently, been those threatened by military invasion or those which sheltered unfriendly regimes with unacceptable ideologies, such as the Pyrenees for most of the period of the Franco dictatorship. Sensitive frontiers are now those perceived as presenting threats of crime and public order, particularly those across which drugs, arms, terrorists, child pornography and clandestine immigrants flow. A different kind of threat is discerned where important imbalances exist between the economic and demographic structure on the two sides of the frontier; these can trigger social dislocation, disorder and transfrontier crime.

The northern and north-eastern frontiers of France (Map 4.1) exemplify how perceptions of frontiers and frontier regions change. These frontier regions were regarded, at least from the Thirty Years War until the Cold War, as a major invasion route and the points of greatest vulnerability of France to military incursions. The impression of vulnerability began to fade from the 1950s, to be replaced by the time of the 1986 Single European Act by an image of the north as a privileged region at the heart of the European Community, with rapidly improving transport facilities – motorways and high-speed trains (from the mid-1990s) – linking the region with Paris, Belgium, the Netherlands, Luxembourg and Germany.

A depressed frontier region?

The northern administrative region (comprising the *départements* of Nord and Pas de Calais) was convenient for major markets, with a dynamic capital Lille, marketed by those promoting the region as an ideal location for industrial investment (with some notable successes). The jobs created in the region of the North by foreign firms in 1996 and 1997 were greater than in any other French region and, in the latter year, more than twice as many as in the second region – Paris. For example, in 1998 Toyota decided to build a major new factory at Valenciennes.[2]

But there was also a darker, less buoyant, image of the North. After the post-Second World War reconstruction phase, the great handicap of the northern region, shared with northern Lorraine and with neighbouring Belgian regions as well as the Saarland in Germany and parts

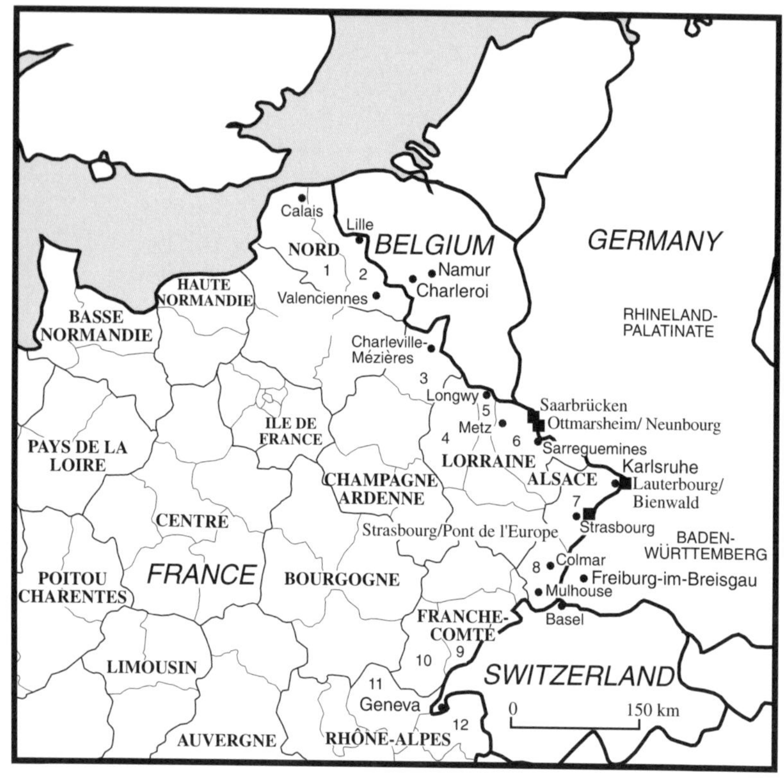

Départements

1	Pas de Calais	7	Bas-Rhin		
2	Nord	8	Haut-Rhin		
3	Ardennes	9	Doubs	■	Joint police stations
4	Meuse	10	Jura		
5	Meurthe et Moselle	11	Ain		
6	Moselle	12	Haute-Savoie		

Map 4.1   France: the north-eastern frontier

of Luxembourg, was the legacy of the first industrial revolution. The North was one of the great European nineteenth-century centres of coal, iron, engineering and textiles. This industrialisation was accompanied by the growth of regional banks, which now exist (if at all) in name only, and the establishment of great entrepreneurial families, which have either moved or have disappeared. The traditional strengths of the region led, in the post-Second World War period, successive French governments and the national planning authority to believe that the North had the indigenous capacity to carry out the necessary industrial conversion. By the 1960s this was obviously incorrect, because the old industrial firms, themselves often in terminal decline, were resistant to diversification and to new firms.

A serious social and economic crisis began in the 1950s, which also affected Wallonia, the French-speaking region of Belgium across the frontier. Industrial reconversion started to take root in the 1970s, but at considerable cost in social dislocation. From the late 1950s and 1960s, closure of coalmines, radical contraction of the textile industry and the relocation of steel production from inland sites to the coast resulted in a high level of male unemployment, deprived and difficult urban areas, the growth of part-time, often female, employment and a sense of insecurity created by the arrival and departure of footloose companies.

From being an area of heavy industry, the North diversified into services, mail order, white goods, electronics, motor manufacture and a range of other activities. The restructuring of the economy has, in general, favoured the regional capital Lille at the expense of smaller towns and centres, a trend with close parallels in other French regions. Large-scale and successful urban renewal of Lille, with a large university, research and service sectors, contrasts with unemployment and urban decay of towns, Roubaix and Tourcoing, in the same conurbation. The social problems included in the 1990s a transfrontier criminal problem of robberies by gangs from the Lille–Roubaix–Tourcoing conurbation into the richer adjacent region of Belgium. Drugs, usually from the Netherlands, also passed this frontier, en route for destinations elsewhere in France and in the United Kingdom.

Despite the closeness of Franco-Walloon social relationships, such as frequent intermarriage and friendly relations between employers' organisations and chambers of commerce, and a transfrontier labour market established from the nineteenth century (workers have commuted across the Belgian frontier in both directions depending on economic conditions and variations in the exchange rate), transfrontier co-operation has been relatively slow to develop. A medium-sized town, such as Valenciennes, was earlier and more enthusiastic about transfrontier contacts than a large city such as Lille. This changed in the 1990s, with the introduction of the INTERREG programmes. The northern region and the municipality of Lille then employed full-time officials specialising in transfrontier relations. With the increasing dynamism and ambition, together with its excellent road and rail links, Lille has the potential to fill the role of regional capital of a transfrontier region, similar to that of Basel and Geneva.

Between the North region and the Lorraine region lie the Ardennes, a *département* of the region of Champagne. The Ardennes remain embedded in historical memory as the invasion route of the German armies in 1940, bypassing the Maginot line and catching the French high command off guard. It is now a tranquil frontier zone and, on both sides of the frontier, is relatively thinly populated. The administrative centre of the *département*, Charleville-Mézières, is an old metal industry centre of relatively small size (just over 60 000 inhabitants) at some distance from centres of the same size with a similar industrial background – Charleroi and Namur – in Belgium. There is a rough equivalence between the French and Belgian sides of the frontier, a common cultural heritage and a common language. These factors provide the basis for amicable relaxed relationships and co-operation (the transfrontier region was been particularly successful in attracting funds from INTERREG II).[3] Nonetheless, the whole frontier zone from the Channel to Luxembourg has one of the highest levels of unemployment in France and in Belgium.

Lorraine and Alsace

In the last two decades, the most economically troubled area on the northern frontier was in the former steel-producing basin of northern Lorraine centred on Longwy (Meurthe et Moselle). In the early 1980s, the steel industry collapsed both in Longwy, and in the neighbouring districts of Luxembourg and Belgium. Serious public disorder took place in Longwy, with occupation of public buildings and violent confrontations with the police. The main solution proposed was the Pôle Européen de Développement (PED), based on a declaration by France, Luxembourg and Belgium (Déclaration 1995) supported by the European Community. The PED covered the transfrontier Longwy–Rodange–Athus basin and aimed at creating 8000 jobs in 10 years, of which 5500 were to be in France, through a balanced and co-ordinated programme of economic development.

The PED was called 'a laboratory of Europe' by Jacques Delors, and great efforts were made to ensure its success. DATAR (the French central spatial planning agency) drew up a development plan, and an interministerial mission was put in charge of the French sector of the PED. High priority was given to industrial retraining, and a European Technical College was established at the frontier, just outside Longwy (Convention Tripartite 1991) federating Luxembourg, Belgium and French facilities for training, with joint directors from these countries and supported by the EC since 1995 through the INTERREG II programme (Collège Européen 1997). A transfrontier network was established between the PED and other agencies or groups – trade unions and employers' organisations, employment exchanges, chambers of commerce, public transport companies, EURES (European Employment Service), Euroguichet (information service) and EUREFI (a partnership between public and private finance for transfrontier investment) (EUREFI 1996).

Ambitious plans have been made for a co-ordinating institution for a transfrontier conurbation centred on Longwy for infrastructure investments, joint services and economic development. This attempt to set up a transfrontier conurbation composed of 17 French communes, 3 Belgian and 3 Luxembourg communes was initiated in 1993, a steering committee of mayors of communes was set up, the preparatory work for it was financed in the INTERREG programme for the period 1995–99, and a management team was established in 1996 for making the project operational (*Résolution commune* 1993. Durieux, Thomas, Kunegel and Lauter interviews).

But, on the French side, less than half the crucial employment target was met. Internationally known firms – amongst them Panasonic, JVC, Daewoo – have come and gone. Longwy has also failed to attract large investments from the countries represented in the three partner countries. The only major French investment was Eurostamp (300 jobs) (Kunegel interview). The situation on the French side was alleviated by the buoyancy of the Luxembourg labour market – 6000 frontier workers cross daily from France into Luxembourg.[4] Various explanations have been offered for the relative failure of the French sector, *inter alia* that the arrangements for incoming investors were simpler and more straightforward in the other two countries, the French administrative structures were too cumbersome, taxes were too high (taxes on firms are 15 per cent lower in Luxembourg).

These explanations suggest that the frontier location of Longwy is a disadvantage. But this does not seem to be confirmed by other evidence – German firms represent about 60 per cent of the new start-ups in Lorraine, mainly in Moselle close to Metz (Prétat interview), and Mercedes-Benz chose a site near Sarreguemines for manufacturing its new small car. The character of Longwy as an old decayed industrial area seems a more plausible explanation for its relative unattractiveness to investors. The local industrial culture, long dependent on a small number of steelmasters, is not conducive to local entrepreneurial initiative. According to the Mayor of Longwy, the most important local political figure, an effort to democratise the PED and the transfer of the responsibilities of central governments to the proposed transfrontier conurbation are essential preconditions to encourage a more self-reliant entrepreneurial outlook (Durieux interview).

The rest of the northern and the eastern frontier region, from Moselle to the Swiss frontier, consists of formerly German-speaking Lorraine and Alsace. This section of the frontier is diverse in character, but traces of a troubled history remain – an experience of four changes of national allegiance in 75 years.[5] The Second World War finally settled the Alsace–Lorraine question because, as Frédéric Hoffet remarked, Hitler and Nazi atrocities promoted the cause of France among the population at large more than all previous attempts to inculcate a sense of French patriotism (Hoffet 1951). There is no discernible nostalgia for Germany, although the legacy of German sovereignty in labour law, social security, the religious regime and the hunting regime are still appreciated among local elites (interviews chambers of commerce). The strong support in Alsace for the Front National in the French 1997 parliamentary elections was not an expression of anti-German feeling but reflected 'a very German desire of order and respect for authority'. Regionalism was also forcefully expressed in the 1998 regional electoral campaign by the FN candidate Robert Speiler who demanded a status similar to 'Swiss cantons or German *Länder*' for Alsace.

Some complexes about Germany remain; beliefs persist that German management practices are better and that German firms are more efficient – although these beliefs are frequently not supported by evidence (Director of ANPE, Sarreguemines). Germans are sometimes suspected of seeking a dominant position and to be uninterested in co-operation with French counterparts on an equal basis. Some express the view that transfrontier co-operation is a charade. The hesitation of the two *Länder*, Rhineland-Palatinate and Baden-Württemberg, about the Council of the Rhine (established in April 1998) is an alleged illustration of lack of enthusiasm by Germans for working with their

French neighbours. There are also nationalist attitudes expressed by French elected representatives. The RPR (Gaullist) Senator for Haut-Rhin, Hubert Haenel, considered in 1998 that French interests would be better served by co-operating with neighbouring French regions, rather than Basel and Baden and that transfrontier co-operation could become the basis of an, in his view, undesirable 'Europe of the Regions'.

A certain lack of equality is a potential source of tension – the great majority of frontier workers cross from France to Germany, whereas the leisure traffic for shopping and tourism is, in most sectors of the frontier, predominantly in the opposite direction; Germans persistently refuse to use the French language and, to do business, Alsatians have to speak German; there are pockets of German residents on the French side of the frontier, because of lower housing costs, but they work and send their children to school in Germany, and they neither learn French nor integrate in French society (Gantz interview). Since the majority of the population of Alsace do not now speak German, the linguistic habits of the Germans may eventually cause irritation. Feelings of dependency and even inferiority are expressed in particular frontier zones – around Sarreguemines, Wissembourg, Haut-Rhin south of Mulhouse – where large numbers of workers cross the frontier to work in dynamic towns such as Saarbrücken, Karlsruhe and Basel.[6] In large centres, such as Mulhouse, Strasbourg and Metz, which dominate a sizeable hinterland, sentiments of dependency and inferiority are largely absent.

Reactions of frontier workers to their experience is mixed because, although they are generally appreciated by their employers, according to the Director of the Sarreguemines Employment Exchange (APNE), there is a marked difference between those employed by large and those by small firms in Germany – the small firms have much greater freedom in labour law which results in misunderstandings and conflicts. Workers in Alsace and Lorraine are also employed by the many foreign firms established in France. About 48 000 jobs in Lorraine (a quarter of the industrial workforce) in 1997 were in non-French companies, with a third of them, 15 457, in German firms (Apeilor 1997). Some of the best-known German names are present, such as Mercedes, Continental and Krupp.

The Lorraine–Alsace frontier, from Longwy to the Swiss frontier, has an intensity of transfrontier interaction unequalled in the EU. According to the chambers of commerce, the proximity of the frontier was, for a long time, a negative factor both because of a perceived risk of invasion (which persisted until the 1960s) and because the frontier hampered trade. By the 1980s, the negative impact of the frontier had largely disappeared, partly due to very active transfrontier co-operation. Chamber of commerce representatives suggest that the frontier still represents a knowledge barrier for tradesmen and small firms (administrative, tendering, invoicing, etc. practices differ on the other side of the frontier). This disadvantage is countered by the *Chambres des métiers*, in association with the chambers of commerce, which provide information services and support for networking in specialised sectors.[7]

Density of transfrontier co-operation

The Upper Rhine network of co-operative institutions includes the Regio founded in 1963, renamed, and given a strengthened transfrontier structure in 1995, the Regio TriRhena, in which the socio-economic elites of the region meet and which, according to testimony, is more influential than ever in arriving at a consensus on common problems. Since 1988, a series of major 'Three Countries Conferences' have been organised, each attracting between 300 and 400 participants. Themes have been transport (1988), culture (1989), environment (1991), economy (1993), youth and education (1995), commerce, trade and crafts (1997). The aim of these conferences has been to stimulate initiatives, to create a common consciousness, and to influence regional decision-making processes. A joint tourist office, and a ten-year climate study which has just been concluded, are other factors of growing co-operation on the Upper Rhine. In 1989, a confederation of seven universities was set up – the European Confederation of Upper Rhine Universities – comprising the universities of Basel, Freiburg, Strasbourg 3, Karlsruhe and Kaiserslautern. Aiming at integrated study courses, it allows for the common use of libraries, laboratories and other research facilities. In addition, the Euro-Institute at Kehl was set up for the training for civil servants, with a research speciality of environmentally sustainable land use (Schneider interviews).

Economic forces have a major role in stimulating transfrontier co-operation and encouraging belief in its value. Chamber of Commerce estimates show, in the district of Germany immediately adjacent to the frontier, as much as 80 per cent of the direct investment is Swiss. The transfrontier labour market has also developed strongly. In the early 1990s, about 53 000 French workers commuted daily to Switzerland and Germany to work in administrative and research jobs as well as in manufacturing. In some firms, transfrontier labour plays a crucial role;

in the early 1990s, the Basel firm of Sandoz employed 1700 Alsatians and 500 Germans out of a total workforce of 7400. In tourism and leisure there now are mutual advantages from transfrontier business – the Black Forest is visited by large numbers of French and Swiss every year, and Germans and Swiss are also very important for the Alsatian restaurant, hotel, food and wine industries. In the 1970s, the buying into hunting syndicates in Alsace by Germans and Swiss caused considerable bad feeling, demonstrating that although transfrontier business has economic advantages it may attract hostility (Anderson 1982).

For reasons of geography, Basel industrialists look across the frontier because of the scarcity of development opportunities in the Swiss hinterland of Basel. The supply of labour in Switzerland is limited, and Basel attracts large numbers of frontier workers from France and Germany. The great majority of French *frontaliers* in the Haut-Rhin work in Switzerland (in 1998, 30 739 as opposed to 5300 who work in Germany) – 200 Germans work in France (Moschberger interview). Also there is not enough room on Swiss territory for an international airport, which Basel as a major industrial and financial centre requires. The airport is therefore located on French territory at Mulhouse with, since the early 1950s, an extraterritorial, toll-free road corridor connecting the city with the airport. The airport itself is constructed as a double airport, all facilities duplicated (Swiss/French). In the 1970s, a third (German) partner was added because, by the 1990s, one-third of the users were heading for German destinations. The retitling of the airport, Euro-Airport Basel-Mulhouse-Freiburg, reflects this. This airport, with a trinational management board, is unique in the world. Attempts at establishing binational airports in the region and elsewhere on the French frontier have not been successful.[8] Traffic tripled in 20 years between 1975 and 1995, and the airport fulfils an important hub function in European air traffic. (Schneider interview)

Geographical considerations could also have provided a pressure for Geneva to engage in transfrontier co-operation, since the canton of Geneva has 102.5 km of frontier with France and only 4.5 km with Switzerland. But Geneva was a relative latecomer to the intensity of co-operation, which has been a feature of the Basel frontier. Nonetheless, this frontier had a regime – a free zone – which other frontier regions, separated by tariff barriers, would welcome. This zone was established in 1815–16 and has been maintained despite French attempts to abolish it. Also, Geneva has two major facilities which are partly in Switzerland and partly in France – the airport of Geneva-Cointrin and CERN, the European Centre for Nuclear Research. Like Basel, in the

1970s Geneva entered into an arrangement to transfer some of the tax revenues derived from frontier workers to the neighbouring French communes.

An intergovernmental co-operation committee was set up in the 1970s but an effective regional committee, the Conseil du Léman, only came into existence in 1987. This late mobilisation can be explained partly because of the individualistic nature of the transfrontier workers (either professionals or workers in the tertiary sector) and the tendency, since the nineteenth century, of communities on both sides of the frontier to turn their backs on one another. The desire by the leaders of government in Geneva not to be left out of general European developments is a motive behind the establishment of the Conseil du Léman – a consideration which was shared by other frontier communes in Switzerland (Leresche 1995).[9] A burst of activity took place in the Geneva region after the refusal by referendum of Swiss participation in the European Economic Area, with more than 20 conventions, agreements and arrangements for transfrontier co-operation signed in 1993–95 (Baettig and Ricci 1995).

Scale and transfrontier co-operation

Differences of perception and attitudes exist towards transfrontier co-operation, relating to the size of the centres involved in it. The larger and more secure the dominant cities are, the more local elites are disposed to regard transfrontier co-operation as useful economically, but of marginal value politically – partners, allies and networks to defend interests are less important to them than to the smaller centres. There is a contrast between Colmar, a medium-sized town (about 65 000 inhabitants), the *Préfecture* of the *département* of Haut-Rhin, and Strasbourg (with over 400 000 inhabitants in its conurbation), the regional capital. Strasbourg has a high profile as a European city – the site of the Council of Europe and the European Court of Human Rights, and one of the meeting places of the European Parliament. It is at the apex of the urban hierarchy of Alsace, a major cultural centre, with international standing and attractiveness to investors. The smaller urban centres of Alsace and the neighbouring German town of Kehl are dependent on Strasbourg as the locus of political power, cultural influence, an important administrative and financial centre, and the hub of a communications network.

Colmar has none of these advantages, and the transfrontier networks have assumed a much greater importance to it. Joseph Rey, Mayor of Colmar for 30 years, developed transfrontier relations in the aftermath of the Second World War. Co-operation was formalised in CIMAB (Community of Interests of Middle Alsace-Breisgau) which still exists (Colmar 1998). Mayor Meyer, in office since 1996, has developed transfrontier co-operation and used it as a base to bid for European and transfrontier projects. Relations between the Chambers of Commerce and the municipalities of Colmar and Freiburg im Breisgau are close (Meyer interview). In Colmar there are varying degrees of enthusiasm for transfrontier co-operation. Most of those who are strongly in favour are personally involved in some aspect of co-operation (Masson interview) – particularly in universities, schools and museums, and among musicians and organisers of art exhibitions.

The adaptation of the north and north-eastern frontier regions to the open frontiers of the end of the twentieth century is far from complete. The legacy of the past remains in the perception and reality of peripheral location, structural economic problems, mentalities moulded by past conflicts, and partially or ill-adapted political and administrative structures. But the instruments of renegotiating the frontier are now in place and there are few reservations about making use of them.

The French–Italian frontier

The French–Italian frontier (Map 4.2), which runs through difficult mountainous terrain, is of recent origin. It dates from the transfer to France in 1859 of Nice and Savoie, in recognition of the assistance given by Napoleon III to the House of Piedmont in the war against Austria to achieve Italian unification. The delimitation of the frontier has been the focus of intermittent but temporary problems. Mussolini had designs on French territory during the Second World War, and occupied part of the Maritime Alps, but was rebuffed by Hitler. Three communes, on the French side of the Col de Tende (the crest-line of the Alps) were annexed by France in 1947. There was some discussion in 1945–47 of annexing the partially francophone province of the Valle d'Aosta but this project was dropped. None of the difficulties of the Second World War and the immediate post-war period have left enduring conflicts.

Although there remain attitudes of superiority towards Italians among the French population, the acceptance of Italy as a democratic state and founder member of the European Communities has removed all major obstacles to good relations between the two countries. In the 1990s, some policing issues created temporary tensions. The appearance, in the middle of the decade, of encampments of Kurds and

Départements

1	Ain
2	Haute-Savoie
3	Savoie
4	Hautes-Alpes
5	Alpes de Hautes Provence
6	Alpes Maritimes
7	Pyrénées Orientales

■ Joint police stations

Map 4.2   France: the eastern frontier

Albanians in the Italian frontier zone waiting for the opportunity of slipping into France led to accusations of Italian 'laxism' in controlling illegal immigrants. The allegations (Aubert 1993) of investments by Italian organised crime in hotels, restaurants and leisure facilities on the Cóte d'Azur created a suspicion of Italians. The crime statistics seem to indicate that the Italians resident, or frontier workers, in the *département* of Alpes Maritimes have a very low crime rate. Italian funds of dubious origin are supposed to be held in Monaco banks, although valid information about these funds is difficult to obtain.

The Italian and French governments signed a limited agreement on transfrontier co-operation in 1993 (République Française 1993),[10] but the physical and human geography of the area is a major barrier to effective co-operation. The narrow coastal littoral is the only location where a large volume of traffic can cross the frontier. The Maritime Alps make the construction of new rail and motorway links further north costly and difficult. Current plans for a tunnel under the massif of Mercantour and for improvement of the road and rail links via Tende are unlikely to happen because they are too costly. The population in the interior is of low density and does not exercise any significant pressure for new transfrontier transport links or for transfrontier co-operation in general. This empty interior creates a psychological distance between the main urban centres of Marseilles, Nice, Turin and Milan. Turin, the capital of Piedmont (the Italian frontier region), has good transport connections but orientated, as its economic interests, towards Lyon and the Italian interior, not towards the French frontier region of Provence–Alpes–Côte d'Azur (PACA). This is even more the case for Milan which, as capital of Lombardy, has transfrontier links with the 'four motors' of Baden-Württemberg, Rhône-Alpes, Catalunya (and Lombardy), as well as other European and global economic connections.

The immediate frontier zone on the littoral – particularly the towns of Menton and Ventimiglia – is the only promising site for extensive transfrontier co-operation. Based on a comprehensive 1991 agreement with Ventimiglia (Ville de Menton 1991), the Mayor of Menton, Jean Claude Guibal, is firmly committed to this co-operation and has an able small team of officials supporting him. There are political obstacles – the municipality of Ventimiglia has been very unstable, with five administrations succeeding one another in quick succession. Moreover, the way of conducting business and negotiations varies between the two municipalities. Menton is a retirement town, and the older generation is either indifferent or hostile to co-operation with Italians.

Nationalist sentiments are prevalent amongst them (dating from the Second World War when Menton was occupied by Italy). These attitudes affect the members of the municipal council and the majority do not support the strategy of the Mayor (Botteghi and Satore interviews).

The characteristics of recent transfrontier co-operation on the Franco-Italian border are diversity, lack of institutionalisation and relative weakness compared with, for example, the Rhine frontier. It now covers a wide range of activity – transport, water supply, environmental protection, waste disposal, hospital services, education at the school, university and professional levels, and research. There are various co-operative arrangements – a transfrontier development commission, the Working Community of the Western Alps (CTAO), a land-use planning co-ordinating committee, inter-university agreements,[11] local authority agreements between the *département* of Alpes Maritimes and the provinces of Imperia and Cuneo, and between the municipalities of Nice, Menton and Ventimiglia as well as between the regions of Provence–Alpes–Côte d'Azur (PACA) and Liguria[12] and some specialised territorial agencies.

The INTERREG programme marked the beginning of real transfrontier co-operation (Botteghi interview) – but a major difficulty, on the French side of the frontier, is the lack of an effective leader of, or co-ordinator for, co-operation. This leads to a lack of coherence between the various transfrontier initiatives. The weakest legal formulae for co-operation are chosen to engage in co-operation – non-binding agreements on common actions with partners across the frontier. There is no agreement allowing joint bodies with financial responsibility, and, as yet, there is no demand for such an agreement. A major obstacle to co-operation is lack of harmony between legal, economic, fiscal, economic and administrative systems on each side of the frontier. In addition, social practices and customary behaviour are also markedly different on the two sides of the frontier.

An experienced participant in transfrontier co-operation, Robert Giannoni, assistant mayor of Menton, sums up the main obstacles as threefold: first, the lack of knowledge of the neighbour's language; bilingualism, until the recent past common on both sides of the frontier, is in rapid decline. Second is the differences in laws and regulations between the countries. The third and major difficulty is the persistence of mental barriers which are perverse effects of the national educational policies. All three encourage negative thinking and over-cautious behaviour when innovative projects are proposed (Giannoni 1998).[13]

As on the Franco-Spanish frontier, there is still an expectation on the part of affected groups that the frontier should serve as a protection, especially against the alleged cavalier behaviour of Italian firms. These firms are very active in the Alpes Maritimes, and certain sectors of the economy of the *département*, such as the property market, have in the past suffered a sharp depression when exchange rate fluctuations have temporarily diminished the Italian presence. There is no evidence yet of a merging of patterns of behaviour and of practices on this frontier, although interpersonal relations amongst elite groups are good.

The Pyrenees frontier

The Pyrenees frontier (Map 4.3), sometimes regarded as the first modern frontier, was agreed by France and Spain in the 1659 Treaty of the Pyrenees. The Pyrenees provide the archetypal 'natural' land frontier, although the medieval and early modern Pyrenees kingdoms (of which Andorra is the only survivor) took little account of the crest-line frontier. The drawing of clear distinctions between the populations separated by the frontier, through the establishment of national identities, was a long historical process (Bourret 1995, Sahlins 1989). The frontier was clearly demarcated only in the mid nineteenth century, by the Treaties of Bayonne of 1866 and 1868. As on all long-established frontiers, there are many agreements on local matters, from the siting of frontier posts and management of water supplies to access to pastures (Casadevante Romani 1985). From the victory of Franco in 1939 until the mid-1950s, the frontier was strongly policed, and it did not lose its militarised, tightly controlled, character until the death of Franco in 1975.

Despite the stable location for over three centuries of the French–Spanish frontier, 'the borderlands themselves are in a constant state of flux. ... Thus, how, as opposed to where, north meets south is subject to constant negotiation' (Douglass 1998). Since 1975, political violence in the Spanish Basque provinces and its implications for France have preoccupied both governments. Although this problem diminished in the 1990s, the Pyrenees continue to pose other problems of law enforcement, particularly in drug trafficking and illegal immigration. Traffic flows[14] and the improvement of communications have created conflict between economic development and environmental protection. The interface between two different economies has produced complications for which officially negotiated solutions are only a partial remedy.

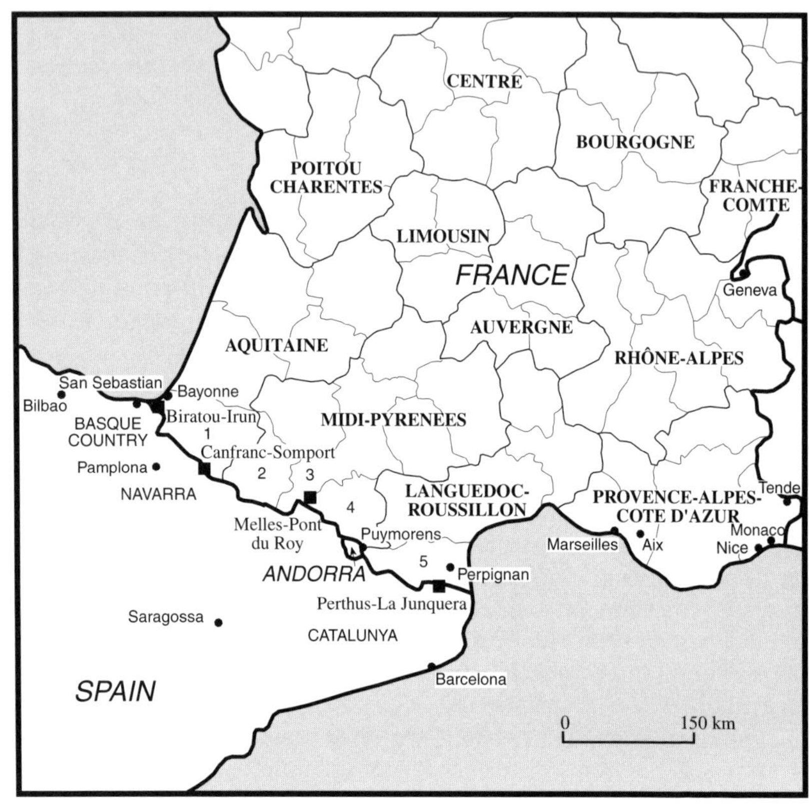

Départements

1   Pyrénées Atlantiques
2   Hautes-Pyrénées
3   Haute Garonne
4   Ariège
5   Pyrénées Orientales

■ Joint police stations

Map 4.3   France: the Pyrenean frontier

The Basques

Transfrontier implications of Basque terrorism cover a wide range of political, police and judicial co-operation, as well as cultural and social issues. During the Franco period, there was widespread sympathy in France, especially on the left, for militant Basque nationalism. The restoration of democracy and the speedy response, allowed under the new Spanish Constitution of 1978, to demands for Basque autonomy did not immediately result in a change of French attitudes. The main reason was a conviction that a highly repressive mentality persisted in the legal, police and administrative authorities. Beliefs prevailed that Basque nationalists were ill-treated by Spanish police and that judicial procedures were unfair to them. Members and supporters of ETA used French territory as a refuge from the Spanish police and it was difficult for the Spanish authorities to extradite them, even when they were charged with violent offences.

The French government was unwilling to expel Basque nationalists except through the normal extradition procedures, often impossible in the case of political offenders. Mistrust between the two countries was exacerbated by the locus of conflict in the Spanish Basque country – very close to France around San Sebastián and Bilbao (Raento 1997a) – and the fact that the most successful ETA commando group was composed of French nationals. The atmosphere began to change after 1982, with Socialist governments in power in both countries, but it was not until 1986 that France agreed to expel Basque militants from France, and an effective system of police co-operation was put in place. This co-operation was very quickly put at risk by evidence that elements of the Spanish police and Ministry of the Interior were involved in the assassination of Basque militants on French soil through the GAL, now known to have been sponsored by the Spanish Ministry of the Interior.

Militant Basque nationalists envisaged a setting up of a Basque state, changing the location of the international frontier. The Madrid and Paris governments regarded this as out of the question, and it has not been taken seriously by more than a minority of the Basque population. The militant Basque organisations have not made headway against the resolve of the governments and the large majority of the population of the Basque provinces. The Basque problem is nonetheless difficult to manage because repressive measures can increase the sympathy for Basque nationalists inside and outside the Basque provinces. Moderate non-violent nationalists can be induced to side with the militants, although this has been progressively less frequent in recent years, especially after highly unpopular assassinations of PP politicians.

Members of central governments sometimes have difficulty in identifying the motives underlying ambitions for greater autonomy in Spain and for a Basque *département* in France and are uncertain of the consequences of making concessions. Suspicions arise that moderate nationalists are 'objective' allies of violent militants. There is also an infiltration of moderate Basque nationalism into the aspiration for improved transfrontier co-operation (Borja et al. 1998). The political/ policing problem posed by militant Basque nationalism provides an uneasy background to transfrontier co-operation. Nonetheless, co-operation between the urban areas of the Basque littoral has not been seriously disrupted. Well-established forms of transfrontier co-operation concern the promotion of the Basque language and culture, the Basque Academy, the Society for Basque Studies, the Confederation of Ikastolas (Basque language schools), the periodical *Egunkaria* (founded 1991) which is distributed on both sides of the frontier, and EITB, the Basque radio and television station (founded in 1983).

Co-operation in the absence of violence

A parallel issue of a 'greater Catalunya', without the political violence, arose in the eastern Pyrenees when the incoming (1993) Mayor of Perpignan, Jean-Paul Alduy, promoted, with considerable success, the slogan 'Perpignan la Catalane'. He emphasised the importance of the 1987 convention signed between Perpignan and the Generalitat de Catalunya; he signed an agreement with Barcelona in 1994, established a consortium with Catalan towns (Figueres, Girona, Calella, Vic, Granollers, Tarragona, Lleida) and a 'delegation' of the city of Perpignan in Barcelona to promote closer links. The town also offered a prestigious building, the Hôtel Pams, as the headquarters of the Euroregion.

Alduy insists that the Catalan identity of Perpignan enhanced the profile of the town and promoted economic and urban development. Nonetheless, his transfrontier enthusiasm aroused opposition in the Conseil Général of the Pyrénées Orientales – mainly based on a hostility to the dominance of Perpignan on the part of outlying districts – and from the Prefect, Christian Bonnet (transferred to Corsica in 1998 and disgraced in 1999 for alleged illegal acts). The Prefect consistently refused to approve any INTERREG project in which the town of Perpignan was involved and failed to support the town in any of its major initiatives to play its role as the seat of the Euroregion. French centralists suspected that Perpignan, despite the denials, would be drawn into the orbit of Barcelona to the possible detriment of French interests.

Conflict between economic and environmental concerns

Most of the political actors along the Pyrenees frontier are not preoccupied with culture and ethnicity but with environmental protection and economic development. These are electorally sensitive issues and sometimes trigger off demonstrations. Among the issues in the 1990s are whether the transport infrastructure should be improved at the cost of environmental damage, how community support for economically fragile zones relates to EU policies, whether the Pyrenees should be managed in the interests of the, often very small, local populations in the mountains, valleys and small towns at the entrance to the valleys, or the large regional centres – Toulouse, Bordeaux, Bilbao, Pamplona, Saragossa and Barcelona – or indeed in the wider interests of France, Spain and the EU. The conflicts between the various levels of government and economic interest are a crucial element in policy debates.

Transport links are a case of Braudel's generalisation that the Pyrenees gateways have never been equally used in both directions at the same time (Braudel 1973). In the Pyrenean valleys improved roads have been built, or are planned, to provide a basis for better access to northern European markets, but with little direct benefit to French frontier regions and with considerable potential environmental damage. In 1997, the two motorways carried most of the traffic – at the eastern, Le Perthus, and at the western, Hendaye, crossings. The total for all other crossings was about 5 per cent of the traffic carried by these motorways. This led to proposals for a tunnel in the central Pyrenees, in addition to the Somport (opening in 2000) and the Puymorens tunnels. But the development of transport links is widely perceived as leading to noise, pollution and nuisance in the formerly secluded Pyrenean valleys. Opposition came from environmentalist groups and some local authorities. The association of some 30 French and Spanish ecological groups, 'Initiatives Pyrénées', has campaigned for comprehensive and stable management of the mountains, which would displace the priority of north–south transport links by giving priority to an east–west management of the environment.

Environmental and development issues are the main concerns of transfrontier co-operation along the Pyrenees. A tissue of social, economic and political contacts, north–south and east–west, have developed along the Pyrenees which did not exist in 1980 (Cuatrecasas interview). These involve all levels of government, from central government to municipalities, chambers of commerce, chambers of trades, chambers of agriculture, educational and cultural institutions, semi-public firms, private associations and private sector firms. One transfrontier association covers the whole frontier – the Working Committee for the Pyrenees.[15] It has produced glossy publications, ambitious declarations at the end of meetings of heads of regional governments, an Action Charter (Communauté de Travail des Pyrénées 1994), reports identifying problems and some ambitious schemes for transfrontier co-operative projects but, in effect, it has exercised little direct influence over policy decisions. The European structural, agricultural and social funds, co-ordinated by the regional Prefect of Midi-Pyrénées, came to be another important source of money to support projects in the massif (Préfet de Région 1995).

A change in the configuration of transfrontier co-operation occurred in the early 1990s. Two Euroregions (involving Aquitaine, Midi-Pyrénées, Euskadi and Navarre; Midi-Pyrénées, Languedoc-Roussillon and Catalunya) were established in 1991, triggered by the completion of the internal market and the announcement of the INTERREG programme (Gomez-Matarán 1998, Morata 1995). The first objective of the two Euroregions on the Pyrenees frontier was to develop co-operative policies; the second was to 'rebalance Europe', away from the north to the benefit of southern regions. Three types of actions were envisaged: first, interregional co-operative projects financed by the regions' own funds; second, projects initiated by the three regions in the framework of EC policies, co-ordinated by the central governments, but allowing the regions to have relations with the EC at the highest level; third, convergent and co-ordinated actions by the French and Spanish central governments – concerning which the regions acted as lobbies putting pressure on central governments (Euregió: Eurorégion 1993).

Several local initiatives brought together the cities within the Euroregion, and associated the *département* of Ariège and Catalan local authorities, and Bayonne, San Sebastián and smaller towns on the Basque littoral represent a more local tier of co-operation. The Transpireneus association links Ariège and six Spanish local authorities; on the French side, CAP DELTA (a semi-public development agency), and on the Spanish side, CFI (Consorci de Formacio i d'Iniciatives de Bergueda) were established in order to facilitate and manage projects; the Centre de Ressources Franco-Espagnol at Foix, and Transpyr, a consortium of communes financed by INTERREG for a transfrontier tourist zone (Pays d'Ariège n.d.) were set up. The chambers of commerce were active in providing via COPEF, the Association of French and Spanish Chambers of Commerce, studies of transfrontier exchanges (COPEF n.d.). These local initiatives did not usually produce immediate practical results, because of lack of resources, but they are symptomatic of a desire to break down barriers.

Ambitious Bayonne–San Sebastián co-operation, Eurocity, launched in July 1993, was aimed to take advantage of the new situation (the dismantling of frontier controls, the INTERREG programme and the establishment of the Euroregion of the western Pyrenees). The objective of the transfrontier alliance was to achieve a new 'territorial balance' – to create a medium-sized conurbation with a strong European profile, with the capacity to promote an ambitious development scheme (Solano interview). Eurocity has as its core an office (*observatoire*) in Bayonne for gathering and communicating information, formulating plans and for taking a strategic view of transfrontier activities (Bayonne–San Sebastián 1997). Seven transfrontier technical committees assist the office in reviewing current arrangements and policies, with a view to co-ordinating or harmonising them. The 1997 work programme included a range of objectives, some directly related to the work of the office such as the creation of a web page, communication within the area, promoting the project externally (specifically with the European Commission), creating a data base, organising seminars, promoting and co-ordinating projects for transfrontier co-operation through technical committees.

The different competences of regional governments (Dussourd interview) and the vastly different resources at their disposal (the budget of the Basque Autonomous Community was, in 1995, approximately ten times that of the Aquitaine region) are obstacles frequently mentioned by Spanish Basque policy makers. Contact with the Regional Prefects, necessary for the INTERREG programme and other transfrontier business, is unwelcome to the Basque Autonomous government because this necessarily brings into play the Spanish central authorities (Muñoa interview). On the French side, the dominant view is that if both sides are committed to the implementation of practical co-operative schemes, different structures and different financial arrangements will not stand in their way. However, there are certain constants in the Basque government's position, despite reservations about the quality of co-operation – for example, support for a Basque cultural identity in the Pyrénées Atlantiques is an enduring commitment (Letamendia 1997).

Some French reticences are based on the actual or potential economic impact, especially in the immediate frontier zone, of Spanish policies and practices. Some French interests react negatively to the increase in Spanish investment in the French Basque country, the numbers of Spanish tourists in the Pyrénées Atlantiques, and Spanish purchases of property. The Chamber of Commerce in Bayonne reported in 1997 that over 40 firms in the town had Spanish capital in them. The greater entrepreneurial dynamism on the Spanish side of the frontier provoked sporadic fears of domination of areas of French territory close to the frontier. There are few locally based French firms which invest on the other side of the frontier.[16] Despite initial French pessimism at the time of Spanish entry to the EC about the comparative advantage of Spanish goods, the balance of trade has been in France's favour since 1990, and French investment in Spain has grown at a rapid rate, outdistancing Spanish investment in France (Darré 1997). Benefits have been mutual – most industries in the Spanish autonomies adjacent to France have benefited from entry into the EC and from French investment.[17] The longer-term prospects cannot, of course, be predicted with any certainty, and one commentator has sketched six widely different possible scenarios for the Basque provinces (Borja 1997).

Points of conflict

However, a multiplicity of problems are associated with the interface between two very different political and economic cultures. The labour market is not integrated, although there are some south–north frontier workers at the western end of the Pyrenees. The frontier workers (with the exception of a very small number of Spanish professionals who have bought houses in France) are predominantly in the building and public works sector and, to a lesser extent, in transport. They tend to be male and older than average for these sectors, suggesting that the French labour market has become less dynamic and less attractive to a younger generation of Spaniards (Gandiaga 1998). The areas of transfrontier contracting and the transfrontier retail trade are much more sensitive; they have been the subject of Chamber of Commerce enquiries (Chambre de Commerce et d'Industrie de Perpignan 1997).

Spanish tax rates on firms and for VAT, as well as social security charges, are lower than in France – in some sectors such as hotels and restaurants the divergence is even greater than average. Spanish contractors, particularly in the building industry, enjoy very considerable comparative advantage. Moreover, although the Spanish are subject to

French legislation when operating in France, there are complaints that it is not the case in areas such as payment of taxes, building permissions, health and safety standards, hours of work permitted, and posting their name outside premises on which they are carrying out building work. Retail businesses in Spain publicise their cheaper prices in France, and this especially affects furniture and jewellery sales (prices are routinely 30 per cent cheaper). The purchase of motor vehicles in Spain is much cheaper and, although this is not publicised, it is well known and distorts the local car market. Proposals for a frontier 'free zone' have been made but rejected as impractical. A long-term solution cannot be achieved without harmonisation of tax burdens.

Some problems, however, cannot easily be made the subject of negotiation, either at the local or national levels, because they involve differences in attitudes, values and institutional organisation. The majority of firms in Pyrénées Orientales are forced into bankruptcy not by private creditors, but by tax demands; this virtually never happens in Catalunya which, according to French competitors, gives Spanish firms a competitive advantage. A highly competitive banking system on the Spanish side, which results in a great variety of forms of credit to small and medium-sized firms, contrasts with the allegedly more centralised and rigid French banking system. The working practices within firms are much more flexible, by tradition and by law, on the Spanish side. There are also complaints of hidden Spanish protectionism because of complex administrative requirements which Spanish firms either ignore or are sufficiently familiar with to find their way through them (Delcasso, Royer and Salgues interviews; CCI de Perpignan et des Pyrénées Orientales 1997). This is one reason why, with the exception of some transportation firms, there has been so little delocalisation to take advantage of the more favourable circumstances on the Spanish side of the frontier. However, the anxieties expressed about Spanish economic activity are mainly the views of economic interests exposed to Spanish competitors and do not give an accurate assessment of the balance of economic strength.

Policing the frontiers

The policing of French frontiers is a sensitive political issue because of anxieties and fears in the French electorate about immigration and crime. According to opinion polls, strong anti-immigrant sentiment is expressed by up to a third of the French electorate, although this may be declining. A sometimes exaggerated association is made between immigrants and criminality, particularly with political violence and drug trafficking.[18] Fear of crime is exploited by right-wing groups and is a matter of concern for policy makers at the national and European levels. The European Commission sponsored a study on the issues (Palidda 1996). Closer transfrontier co-operation between police forces has helped to diminish the suspicion that other jurisdictions are lax in controlling both clandestine immigrants and drugs.

The external frontier

The EU external frontier, in the French case, is the coastline, seaports, airports and the land frontier with Switzerland. The French coastline, relatively well policed, is less vulnerable than that of other EU member states such as Britain, Spain, Italy and Greece. Most of the coastline is without serious continuing problems, although tobacco and drugs smuggling cases in which small craft are involved regularly come to light. Light aircraft pose similar intermittent problems. For this reason, the French Ministry of the Interior has insisted that light aircraft crossing internal EU frontiers should land at designated international airports. Major seaports are regarded by the ministry as more difficult to control than airports, for three reasons: first, illegal immigrants, because of health and sanitary regulations, cannot be immediately expelled to be returned to the countries from which they came or to their countries of origin; second, the physical layout of ports means that there are usually more easy accessible than airports; third, the volume of container traffic and the imperfect technology of scanning, which cannot infallibly reveal illegal contents of containers, are problems shared with all member states.

Calais (the largest port for passengers) and Marseilles (the premier port for goods and for passengers passing the external frontier) present difficult policing problems. Almost all the drugs seized by French Customs in the Channel ports are destined for the United Kingdom. Smuggling beer and wine across the Channel costs the British Exchequer about £1bn a year. Cross-Channel smuggling is an example of different tax regimes providing clear opportunities for criminal profits, because British excise duties make them significantly more expensive in the UK than in France. Illegal immigration produces hostile reporting in the British press, critical of the efforts of the French police to stop cross-Channel movement of clandestine immigrants. Despite the British abolition of exit controls on passengers, these are maintained by the French, and the Prefect of the Pas de Calais in 1999 adopted vigorous methods to round up persons suspected of wishing to gain illegal entry to Britain. In 1998, faced by an increase in illegal immigration into Britain via the Channel ports, the British Home Office expressed concern that the French did not use sniffer dogs to detect people (although they used them to detect drugs).

The Channel frontier has the oldest developed form in Europe of transfrontier co-operation on a direct police-to-police basis. This began in the late 1960s between Kent Constabulary and French, Belgian and Dutch police forces as a result of an increase in illegal immigration. A Cross-Channel Intelligence Conference was established in 1968. It went through four phases (Sheptycki 1998): the setting up of a transfrontier police network from 1969 to 1970; the period from 1971 to 1986, when the liaison officers of the various police forces played a vital role in the exchange of information, and strategic as well as tactical intelligence was exchanged, multi-jurisdictional enquiries lasting long periods were launched and Interpol played a relatively minor role in the background; 1986–91 was a transitional phase, when the arrangements for policing the Channel Tunnel were put in place; 1991 to the present begins a new phase in police communications, marked by new communications technologies, with a consequent devaluation of the importance of the CCIC. If the UK remains outside the Schengen system, this will cause increasing difficulties for practical cross-Channel police co-operation.

A Channel Tunnel Policing Unit was set up in 1989, and the Channel Tunnel Policing Protocol was signed in 1991. The Protocol allowed the setting up of juxtaposed controls with a DICCILEC (Central Directorate for the Repression of Illegal Immigration and Clandestine Employment) presence at Folkestone and the Kent Constabulary presence at Fréthun, resulting in a daily movement of police officers through the Tunnel. Powers of arrest are authorised so that anyone who arrives at the English entry of the Tunnel can be arrested and transferred to France if the person is shown as wanted on the French criminal intelligence computer, without any formal extradition procedure. Normal criminal and public order offences remain the responsibility of the British police. The most contentious issue to arise concerned the presence of armed French police on British soil. Both sides held strong views on the matter, but a compromise was eventually arrived at, allowing the French to retain their personal weapons subject to stringent controls.

Given adequate resources available for the task, French airports are relatively easy to control. As in other EU member states, part of the responsibility for identity checks have been privatised, with the implementation of carriers' liability legislation; the airlines now have a financial interest in scrupulously checking the documentation of passengers. As a result, only a small proportion of illegal immigrants apprehended attempt to enter through airports – 13 per cent (5809 individuals) of those refused entry in 1997 were stopped at the airports, a decline of 5 per cent from the previous year. Although cabotage by non-French airlines to provincial airports will bring increased volumes of non-EU traffic to these airports, this traffic is overwhelmingly to the Paris airports, with the partial exception of North African traffic arriving at Nice and Aix-Marseille. The scale of passenger traffic means that drug carriers frequently get through. Seizures in recent years suggest that major traffickers prefer to move large consignments by road and sea rather than the relatively small amounts which can be carried on flights by 'mules'. They are also deterred because the obligations of the Schengen agreements and the high visibility of the Paris airports ensure that airports are strongly policed.

The Swiss frontier

The Franco-Swiss frontier causes relatively few policing problems. But it has a common characteristic shared with all of Switzerland's neighbours. The entire length of the Swiss land frontier is an EU external frontier, and the neighbouring states of Switzerland are all members of Schengen. The Schengen countries refuse to treat multilaterally with Switzerland. Instead, despite the stated wish of the Swiss confederal government, all frontier agreements are bilateral. This contrasts with the treatment given to the non-EU Scandinavian countries who adopt Schengen norms and have consultative status within the system. Swiss border controls are generally recognised as competent and Schengen technical inspection teams have, on occasion, met with Swiss border police. Swiss passengers are often processed in the same channels as EU citizens in the airports of EU member states because Swiss airports handle such a large number of EU citizens.

The anomalous position of Switzerland arises from general political considerations. The Swiss rejected by referendum membership of the European Economic Area and therefore implicitly any prospect of EU membership. The EU member states therefore wish to prevent Switzerland getting informal access to EU decision-making processes. A number of issues have irritated Switzerland's neighbours, such as the Swiss attitude towards transit traffic, and the arrival of large numbers of would-be immigrants at the Swiss–German frontier because Switzerland has no legislation for detaining undocumented immigrants and its readmission treaty with Italy is not yet ratified. Lack of a multi-lateral agreement between Switzerland and Schengen causes neighbouring countries some difficulties, but it causes more to Switzerland. Those directly involved in managing Swiss frontier controls would welcome an association agreement on Schengen, but there seems little immediate prospect of this happening.

Land frontiers with EU member states

A quest for 'control in depth' of the land frontiers, after the signing of the 1985 Schengen agreement, commenced as a search for a method of apprehending illegal immigrants and of reassuring sections of public opinion. The internal land frontier zones are the location in which most illegal immigrants (84 per cent in 1997) are apprehended.[19] On the Franco-Italian frontier there was an increase of 35 per cent in 1997 (15 525 individuals), but on the only external land frontier a decrease of 6 per cent was reported. At the border crossing at Strasbourg/Pont de l'Europe, 2770 Kurds were arrested by the German Bundesgrenzschutz in 1997. These arrests are now taken as evidence of the effectiveness of police co-operation, although they illustrate the porous nature of the external frontier. However, France was ceasing in the late 1990s to be predominantly a destination country for illegal immigrants and becoming a transit country.

France refused in 1996 to implement the Schengen agreement on the Belgian and Luxembourg frontier, arguing that unless the Netherlands changed its drugs policies, 'drug tourism' and trafficking across this frontier were inevitable. An underlying motive was to show that the French state could continue to control its frontiers, when necessary. The maintenance of controls remains a persistent source of difficulty between France and Belgium. When the Belgian government announced that, from 20 April 1998, cannabis use would no longer be prosecuted, that position was deliberately between the continued repression of soft drugs by the police and the criminal law in France, and the tolerated retail sale of cannabis in the Netherlands.

The intensity of patrolling frontier zones on the German, Italian and Spanish frontiers is usually based on risk analysis of the likelihood of illegal immigrantss and drugs being found. Risk analysis uses statistical data, some of which can be misleading,[20] intelligence reports on particular cases and the judgements of experienced police officials. Knowledge of local situations is essential for balanced risk assessment. There is sometimes a clash of appreciation of risks between central and local agencies. There was, for example, a difference of view between the Saarland and Bonn over the maintenance of a regular police presence after 1993 on the Saarbrücken–Metz motorway, with the *Land* in favour and the Federal government opposed (Basset interview).

On the Pyrenees frontier, drug smugglers usually take advantage of the cover of heavy goods traffic, especially at the eastern (Le Perthus), and also at the western (Hendaye), extremities of the mountain range. Joint police stations are now established at these crossing points and there are four high-level meetings a year between the French frontier police, the Spanish Guardia Civil and Customs to co-ordinate operations. Small-scale smugglers often use the less-frequented crossings such as Le Somport, and a particular watch is often mounted on certain kinds of tourist traffic. Mobile patrols, based on risk assessment, operate on both sides of the frontier. This may also be supplemented by undercover teams.

Customs services establish formal systems of communication; usually there is one centre of communication for each sector of the frontier. This is illustrated by a recent agreement at the ministerial level for the *Oberfinanzdirektionen* of Freiburg, Karlsruhe and Saarbrücken and the interregional directorate of Metz and the regional directorates of Strasbourg and Mulhouse (*Accord* 12 March 1997). Contracting parties nominate official contacts in the frontier zone for a direct exchange of information; for the rest, information exchange was to take place through national offices – the Direction Nationale du Renseignement et des Enquêtes Douanières and the Zollkriminalamt.

Impact on police organisation

Abolition of frontier controls, the internationalisation of crime, and government action to modernise the police services have combined to produce new practices and attitudes within law enforcement agencies. The difficult territorial division and overlapping responsibilities of the National Police and the Gendarmerie, and the competition between them in their criminal investigation role, resulted in tense relationships. In policing the frontiers, these relations are now based on a ministerial circular of 1996 establishing complementarity between them.

Both the National Police and the Gendarmerie tended to disdain Customs as a 'civilian' administration, even though Customs had extensive powers of search and seizure. The introduction by Customs, in the early 1990s, of the technique of 'controlled delivery' in drugs investigations (contained in the 1988 Vienna Convention but not, at that time, legal in French law) was disrupted by a police operation against it. Customs retaliated by requesting criminal investigation police powers

to put them on an equal footing with the Gendarmerie and the police –
a power which they eventually acquired in 1999. Customs also had,
since 1982, the legal authority to check the identities of persons at the
frontier. The long-standing feuds between law enforcement agencies in
France have not disappeared, but in matters where transfrontier co-
operation is involved they have significantly diminished.

The abolishing of frontier controls resulted in the radical (although
temporary) reorganisation of one agency. In October 1994, PAF (the
Airport and Frontier Police) was transformed into DICCILEC. PAF was
orientated towards the geographical frontier, whereas DICCILEC aimed
to cover the whole territory. This involved both regular contact with
other law enforcement agencies and continuous transfrontier co-operation with neighbouring countries. This coverage was not achieved, and
even Paris lacked a dedicated office. Co-operation with other police services, the Gendarmerie and the Labour Inspectorate, became essential to
fulfil its role. However, the reorganisation proved too ambitious – it over-
stretched the resources of DICCILEC and caused overlapping responsibilities with other police services – and PAF was reinvented in 1999.

Another innovation was the establishment of the joint police stations
on the British, Spanish, German and Italian frontiers – commonly
known as BCNJ (*bureaux à contrôles nationaux juxtaposés*).[21] Two of them
long pre-dated the implementation of the Schengen system – at
Ventimiglia on the Franco-Italian frontier, and the two on exits to the
Channel tunnel. The others were set up with the abolishing of frontier
controls in immediate prospect and may initiate a general European
pattern. Joint police stations allowed regular and speedy communication of information between the police agencies of the states involved
and the exchange, on a confidential basis, of sensitive intelligence.

The increased pace of reform of law enforcement services and
improved co-ordination between them are partly attributable to open
frontiers.[22] The abolishing of frontier controls provided new arguments
for the modernisers within the law enforcement establishment. The relative backwardness of French police technologies, training and organisation, against other comparable countries, had been noted in the early
1980s (Belorgey 1991). The preparation for Schengen and new systems
for tracking goods in a borderless Europe[23] gave it an urgency and focus.
The introduction of new IT technologies, scanning technologies, and
sophisticated equipment for detecting forged documents, was stimulated by pressure arising from the abolition of frontier controls.

An increased emphasis on research and training was encouraged by
Europeanisation. The programmes of the Institut des Hautes Etudes de

la Sécurité Intérieure in the fields of immigration, fraud, traffic in illegal goods, customs and police co-operation were linked to the prospect of a 'borderless' Europe. The international role and contacts of police and Customs have increased very rapidly, particularly through liaison officers posted to other countries and to international agencies. A range of international activities are now routine – acceptance by the police services of *stagiaires* from other countries, international training courses, missions to European and extra-European countries as expert advisers on matters such as security of ports and airports, security of air and maritime traffic, security equipment, and methods of detection of forged or false documents, implications of national and international legislation and other matters.

The cultural frontier

The term 'culture' in France is usually closely linked with the French language, with territory and with a 'patrimony' or national heritage. A threat to the French nation is often conceived to be associated with the idea of globalisation – domination of English as the international language, homogenisation of tastes (particularly popular tastes), cultural production dominated by the global market place. These are considered responsible for the spread of cosmopolitan values, the undermining of elite culture and the diminishing power of the state to preserve cultural identity. The threat allegedly also posed from within – by the local languages so disapproved of by Jacobins and centralisers since the Revolution – has been taken much less seriously in recent years, although the speaking of a local language defines certain local communities. But the general question, whether control of territory still makes it possible to maintain cultural characteristics, is a persistent anxiety. The cultural frontier is a virtual frontier whose location and character depend on the notion of culture adopted.

Three approaches in France to this question can be identified. The first is that cultural frontiers, under the twin pressures of technological change and shifts in distribution of political and economic power, evolve in ways independent of any attempts to control or shape them. The second is support for an active but flexible promotion of French culture, abandoning defensive attitudes (a fixed frontier line), and adopting cultural products from abroad. English should, according to this view, be accepted as the leading international language, and French promoted, where possible, as the second international language. The promotion of French cultural products outside France should be done in a co-operative dialogue with other cultures. The third is cultural closure (a defensive frontier), which includes resistance to the cultural encroachment of the 'Anglo-Saxons', negotiation of 'cultural exception clauses' to all international trade agreements to allow protectionist measures, use control of territory to defend, through the educational system and other public institutions, the purity of the French language, and enhance the prestige of the cultural patrimony. The boundaries between these approaches are not rigid – for example, someone who is broadly in line with the second approach may favour cultural exception clauses in international agreements.

The first position is a minority view in France, but the second is discreetly adopted by some of the country's leading educational and research establishments, as well as underpinning France's cultural diplomacy. The necessity of publishing scientific papers in English (the Institut Pasteur decided to publish its scientific journal in English in 1996), the recognition of English as the international language in communications, commerce and finance must, according to this point of view, be accepted. French will remain an important international language, and one with considerable prestige, provided that the language is intelligently promoted. The idea of a standard French, defined by the Academy as the only language officially approved should, in this view, be abandoned in favour of a diversity of language use, including local non-French languages and styles of French used by immigrant groups.

The third approach is dominated by resistance to the English-speaking world. An enduring and complex theme is the mixture of fascination, attraction and repulsion characterising the French relationship with the English-speaking world since American independence. Anxiety about America as a cultural threat – incipient in Alexis de Tocqueville's classic, *Democracy in America* (1835), which treated the United States, in certain respects, as an unattractive model for a democratic future – reached extreme levels in Georges Duhamel, *America the Menace* (1931). After the end of the Second World War, when American political, military and economic hegemony became a reality, French resistance to American domination took a variety of forms – including neutralism, de Gaulle's withdrawal from the military structure of NATO, the promotion of specifically French policies in European and international affairs, and the partially successful attempt to resist American direct investment in France in the 1960s.

During this period, the influence of the USA, and even the English language itself, was regarded by some French milieux as a cultural threat. As Richard Kuisel shows, this was largely an elite reaction (Kuisel 1993), although on the left there has been popular support. It took many different forms, such as the resistance to Coca Cola in

France in the late 1940s, the criticisms of American consumerism and the import of Hollywood films in the 1950s, and the description of Disneyland at Marne la Vallée as a 'cultural Chernobyl' and 'a giant step toward world homogenisation'. Although broad sections of the French population may have been converted to the consumer goods and lifestyles which in the 1950s were regarded as the epitome of Americanisation, there remains strong elite resistance to manifestations of American cultural domination.

A number of practical measures were based on this third approach. The 1997 Toubon law restricted foreign-language use in public documents and in the description of goods (the attempt to impose the same standards to other sectors such as advertising was declared contrary to freedom of speech by the Constitutional Council), as well as the administrative resistance to the adoption of foreign (English) words in France by finding French substitutes, the legal requirement that French popular songs constitute at least half the output broadcast by French radio stations, and the negotiation of 'cultural exception' in the Uruguay round of GATT, allowing protection of cultural products, particularly French films. The issue of 'cultural exception' re-emerged in 1998 during the failed negotiations on the Multilateral Investment Agreement and the failed Seattle World Trade Conference in 1999. The French Minister of Culture, Catherine Trautman, in 1998, described the principle of free trade in cultural goods as shocking because cultural production was not a matter for the market to determine – states must be in a position to protect creative activity.

The apparently inexorable decline of French as a language of diplomacy and culture is considered by some elite groups, and the neo-Gaullist right, as reducing the international influence of France. One measure favoured by supporters of both the second and third positions is to organise the countries where French is widely spoken into a grouping along the lines of the British Commonwealth (Barrat 1997). The idea of 'la Francophonie' emerged in the period of decolonisation. According to Xavier Deniau, Francophonie has four meanings: a linguistic meaning – 'those who speak French'; a geographical meaning, covering those areas where French is used as a mother tongue, as the normal language of communication, or as an official language; a 'mystical and spiritual sense' of belonging to the same community; and a cluster of institutions and associations (Deniau 1995). The French government's approach to the biennial summit meetings of heads of state and government of Francophonie, begun in 1986, tends to be pragmatic, regarding it as a useful tool for spreading French influence.

Local languages

Local languages are no longer regarded, by the neo-Gaullist President, Jacques Chirac, and the Socialist Prime Minister, Lionel Jospin, as a threat to national unity and Republican values. In July 1998, the government announced that it was prepared to sign the European Charter of Minority Languages and implement many of its provisions. The argument that local languages were part of the Republican patrimony and of the cultural heritage of France seemed to mark the end of Republican hostility to them. But an important legal obstacle to signature and ratification of the Charter was the revised (1992) Article 2 of the Constitution, which states that 'the language of the Republic is French'. In 1999, the Constitutional Council declared several important articles contrary to the Constitution. President Chirac was not prepared to countenance a revision of the Constitution. He was supported by some members of the government majority as well as the right-wing opposition, revealing that reservations about local languages, as a factor dividing the nation, had not entirely disappeared.

One of the arguments used in favour of local languages is that they blur the clearly defined language frontiers created by the nation states. This is true only to a very limited degree and, whether or not local languages serve this purpose, they are all in serious long-term decline. In French Flanders, Flemish has disappeared; the Mosellan and Alsatian Alemanic dialects in Alsace and Lorraine are mainly spoken by the older generation in rural or semi-rural communes, although there is a revival of interest in them amongst the younger generation. In the former Piedmontese territory, ceded to France in 1860, and in Haute-Savoie and Alpes Maritimes, Italian is no longer spoken as a mother tongue, except by immigrants.

Catalan and Basque are spoken by very small numbers of people at the eastern and western ends of the Pyrenees.[24] In terms of the learning the languages of neighbours, the teaching of Dutch/Flemish scarcely exists; German has rapidly declined even in the secondary schools of the eastern Academies (the decline may now have been arrested in Alsace), despite the provisions to encourage each others' languages in the 1963 Franco-German Treaty of Friendship; only Spanish has maintained a strong position in the educational system. Regional languages are taught to approximately 2 per cent of the school population (*Le Monde*, 3 July 1998) and of these only Catalan, Basque and Alemanic assist transfrontier comprehension.

Broadcasting may help to preserve some minority-language use. The ending of Spanish (1977) and French (1980) state broadcasting led to a flourishing of Basque and Catalan stations, although most of the new private stations were ephemeral. French state broadcasting set up a network of local stations, and Radio France Pays Basque, founded in 1984, introduced transfrontier programming (Boure 1996). It broadcasts both in Basque and Spanish. Radio France Roussillon broadcasts short programmes in Catalan and also gives a prominent place to events in Catalunya. There is an exchange of news stories between the FR 3 regional television and Catalan and Basque stations. In 1992, the Basque channel ETB 1 created a seven-minute news broadcast from Bayonne, and both ETB 1 and 2 (Spanish) give time to transfrontier news. Proposals for a unified transfrontier television service have, however, foundered for lack of political and financial support. Local newspapers have also given prominence to news and activities of localities across the frontier and occasionally publish items in the local language.

The boundaries of community are often felt to be the boundaries of the language group. Occasionally this is contested. In the Saar-Lor-Lux transfrontier region (Saarland, Rhineland-Palatinate, Lorraine, Luxembourg, Belgium) some informants in interviews emphasised that, despite the lack of a common language, mutual comprehension exists in this transfrontier region which could be characterised as a kind of biculturalism. This was not a unanimous view – others simply denied that such a bicultural space existed and asserted that all traces of a cultural community, which had existed historically, had been effaced by national educational systems. There is, however, no longer any political drive to put up cultural walls between France and the neighbouring EU member states. A posture of increasing cultural openness has accompanied a policy of promoting practical co-operation in the frontier regions. This has become particularly clear since the election of the Socialist-led government in 1997.[25]

Conclusion – the local, the European and the global

The frontiers of France show a variety of local experience and a complexity of attitudes regarding frontiers; the policing of frontiers is a mixture of pragmatism in deployment of resources and a response to European policy changes; the use of the control of territory to conserve language and culture is a sometimes nebulous, but persistent concern. But in all these areas, the frontier is no longer the clear line of division between one sovereign state and another. It is a perimeter open to constant negotiation and adjustment.

The debate over globalisation has sensitised public opinion to the decline of frontiers as a means of protection. The French debate has been characterised by a higher level of anxiety than in the other European countries. There are two main explanations. The first is that full exposure to the global market means the dismantling of the special features of French capitalism. This transformation has disturbed powerful interests and runs counter to widespread beliefs that major French industries should be French controlled, often considered as a condition of national independence. The close relationships between banks, government and industry is no longer possible in a world of shareholder sovereignty and global capital markets. French dirigisme – a dominant public sector, a regulated labour market, a high degree of social protection, and 'capitalism without capitalists' – has been eroding since the 1960s, but remnants remain strong, particularly in terms of both elite and popular attitudes.

The second reason is that globalisation is felt as a cultural threat at three levels. First, the technological revolution, associated with computerisation and the Internet, is regarded as the death knell of the book and of the educational values, especially the literary values, which characterise France. Second, the new technology breaks down frontiers in an anarchic and uncontrollable way. The French state is incapable of regulating this domain, which implies a downgrading of the role of the state. Third, the globalisation process seems to encourage the inexorable progress of English as the lingua franca of communication, which further undermines French culture. In all three domains, control of frontiers – which in the past implied the ability to control activities on the national territory – is of limited use.

The issues are complicated further because some of the frontiers to be controlled are now external EU frontiers. For some economic and social purposes the EU is a single territory. The French government has to persuade – sometimes sceptical – European partners of the necessity for, for example, trade rules which allow for the protection of cultural products. The implications of the Single Market on the Europeanisation of the national territory are dramatised by specific incidents and crises.

During the French lorry drivers' strikes of 1996 and 1997 when, for considerable periods of time, all major international crossing points were blocked, the EU Commissioner for Transport, Neil Kinnock, protested to the French government that the behaviour of the strikers was an infringement of the Single Market. The British, German, Dutch and Spanish governments denounced the failure of the French government to uphold the law and the principle of free movement. In December 1997, after the strike was over, the European Court of Justice, in a landmark judgement, declared the French government in breach of the rules of the Single Market by failing to control demonstrators. The reactions of neighbouring states, the European Commission, the European Court of Justice and lorry drivers from other EU member states clearly showed that interruption of traffic was no longer a French domestic matter. This Europeanisation of the territory of France is difficult to reconcile with the Republican tradition of popular sovereignty and of the nation. Ambivalence to the openness of frontiers will, therefore, continue to imbue French attitudes.

5
The External Frontier of the European Union

External frontiers and the European state

The location and the character of the external frontier of the European Union profoundly affect the institutions of the EU, the security of its members and the nature of an emerging European identity. The way the external frontier is managed and how policies for this frontier are developed shows the degree of integration which the EU has achieved. Whether it is an 'open' or a 'closed' frontier, and whether the frontiers established represent a 'sieve' or a 'fortress' Europe or neither (Bigo 1998: 153–5) has profound implications for the nature of the EU as a political community. Shifting the common external frontier by taking in new members produces pressing demands for internal institutional reform; whether effective decision-making will still be possible or whether the EU will be paralysed as the number of member states increases, remains unresolved.

Despite some state-like features, the EU external frontier is not the same as a state frontier because the EU is a curious, mixed regime with various levels of governance. Waever and Kelstrup (1993: 68) define the current 'complex nature of European transformation' as taking 'the form of an illogical mix of three processes':

- standard inter-governmental co-operation, especially in the fields of security
- elements of a superstate, with a number of state-like traits without approaching the character of a nation-state or a sovereign territorial state
- many 'sub-state' and 'around-state' structures, especially German *Länder* and other regions, business and similar networks.

Waever and Kelstrup (1993: 68) see this as representing 'the tendency towards dissolution of the modern state system' – in a move towards dissemination of power in a multi-level, multi-layered system of governance, 'which undermines the exclusive, sovereign, territorial state'. Thus, there are overlapping frontiers, different in kind and quality. The EU external frontier and the frontiers of the member states remain, for the time being, the most important.

The external frontier is an economic frontier even though doubts remain about the degree to which the EU is a genuinely unified economic territory. Lack of tax harmonisation means that Europe, from one point of view, is a segmented market and far from being a unified economic territory. The most radical means of spatial differentiation within the EU is the creation of special fiscal regimes. An example of this was the promulgation, with the agreement of the EU, of a law in December 1996 making Corsica a 'free zone'. In practice this meant the removal of tax on profits below a certain threshold, no professional tax for five years, decrease of social security charges for employers on low-paid employees. The intention, although not the result, was to revive the economy of the island to remove the bases of political violence.

In internal and external security, the EU remains geographically divided. All EU members are members of Europol but not of Schengen; all participate in developing a common foreign and security policy for the EU but not all are members of the WEU and NATO. Internal and external security are often assessed in different ways across the EU. There is no longer any immediate perceived danger of massive military attack and the governments of EU member states, except Britain and France, see very little security advantage in military intervention in conflicts in other parts of the world. This has made it difficult to establish a new security doctrine, or even an agreed concept of security, which finds widespread support. When the term 'insecurity' is used in EU member states, excepting of Greece where the military threat posed by Turkey is keenly felt, it generally refers to concerns about crime and the spillover effects of social and political disorder in neighbouring states. It also refers to the effects of armed conflict in the wider neighbourhood of the EU – in Algeria, Bosnia and the Kurd regions of Turkey and Iraq.

The lack of a security identity is mirrored by the uncertainty about a European identity *tout court*. Frontiers defined the limits of the (nation-) state, but Europe is not a nation. Can it ever be a nation? A widespread view is expressed by Anthony Smith (1992: 58, 62, 75), for whom Europe lacks a set of 'shared memories or a sense of continuity', 'a pre-modern past – a "prehistory" which can provide ... emotional sustenance and historical depth'. To achieve a common identity, the boundary defining 'us' and 'them' has to be constructed around 'shared experiences, memories and myths, in relation to those of other collective identities'. Awareness of a common external frontier, dividing 'Europeans' from 'non-Europeans', may promote such a sense of solidarity across the EU territory. This is more likely to be based on identification with institutions, rather than a cultural–historical construction of a European identity. As Jürgen Habermas (1992: 12) argued: 'Our task is less to reassure ourselves of our common origins in the European Middle ages than to develop a new political self-confidence commensurate with the role of Europe in the world of the twenty-first century.' What he calls 'a European constitutional patriotism' 'would have to grow out of different interpretations of the same universalist rights and constitutional principles which are marked by the context of different national histories'. This formula has implications for the frontiers because it allows EU enlargement, without asking whether a state, such as Turkey, is culturally European. But it involves a weaker and more cerebral construction of identity in which the emotions are less involved than in national identity. It implies an external frontier policy based on rational calculations of cost/benefit rather than on the cultural and identity issues, involved in nation state frontiers.

Categories of external frontiers

There are two broad classes of external frontiers of the EU: first, those with the rich non-EU countries like Norway and Switzerland or with microstates like Andorra or Monaco, and those with relatively poor Central and, second, Eastern European and Mediterranean countries. External borderlands of the EU 'range from the most advanced regions in the core (EU borders with Switzerland) and northern periphery (outer borders with Norway) to the most poorly developed regions in the east' (AEBR 1997: A2/10). A more refined typology gives four different categories of external frontiers:

- with highly developed EFTA/EEA countries and rich microstates
- with Central and Eastern European countries on the threshold of becoming members of the EU, including the Baltic states, Cyprus and Malta
- with other Central and Eastern European countries like Albania, Macedonia, Croatia, Yugoslavia, Turkey, Moldova and Russia, which have no immediate perspective of membership

- with African and Middle Eastern countries around the Mediterranean.

The first category of frontiers can be considered 'as if' frontiers. The countries themselves and the EU tend to treat these common borders 'as if' they were internal frontiers. Bilateral agreements attempt to bring co-operation and control mechanisms in line with standards of the Schengen countries.[1] EU funding for frontier region co-operation on the EU side of the frontier is matched by national funding on the other side because INTERREG funds can only be used on EU territory. Financing of joint programmes at the external frontier is done in co-operation with other EU programmes such as TACIS, PHARE and ECOS/OUVERTURE.[2]

All EU member states, except landlocked Luxembourg and Austria, have sea frontiers. Sea frontiers are very diverse but, except for fisheries where there is a common regime for the territorial waters of the EU states, both seas and seaports form part of the external frontier. Some areas of the sea have pollution and coastal protection problems which can only be solved by cross-border co-operation. Other areas for co-operation include improvements of sea infrastructure (transport, tourism and safety/emergency measures). Still perceived as natural barriers, 'maritime borders are often characterised by common historic and cultural links and trading traditions' (AEBR 1997: A2/12). Under the INTERREG programmes, maritime borders were included as 'exceptional', and programmes for external maritime frontiers supported initiatives for the Baltic, the North Sea, Greece and Cyprus, and Spain and Morocco.

Microstates, overseas territories and autonomous regions

These entities illustrate the uncertain and fragmented character of the external frontier. These entities have varied and anomalous relationships with member states and the EU. The status of Europe's microstates, overseas territories and autonomous regions, and their relation to the framework of the European treaties, is, to say the least, complex. They thus form a penumbra of territories, a vague frontier zone, which could become highly problematic.

Anomalous relationships fall into four categories:

- independent countries (microstates) within the European Community's boundaries
- French overseas *départements*
- European or nearby regions of member states which enjoy autonomous or semi-autonomous status

- overseas countries and territories referred to in Part Four of the Treaty of Rome and listed in Annex I to the Council Decision of 25 July 1991, which retain ties of varying intensity with a member state

Notions of sovereignty are scarcely relevant for microstates. Their very existence has depended on the goodwill of, and negotiated arrangements with, their larger neighbours (Nairn 1998, 2000).

Although Andorra, Monaco, Liechtenstein, San Marino and the Vatican City are often regarded as charming historical relics, they have a role and an influence out of proportion to their size and population. As independent financial jurisdictions (and suspected of being used by transnational criminal organisations), these microstates have a flourishing international banking and financial services sector, mainly because they are tax havens. Their governments mainly deal with the central governments of neighbouring states and have little contact with their immediate hinterland in the neighbouring countries. Transfrontier co-operation at the local regional level between these microstates and their EU neighbours is rare, although Andorra is a member of the Working Committee of the Pyrenees (see Chapter 4).

Each microstate has a special relationship with the EU and the member states. In April 1993, Andorra (with a population of 54 500, the majority foreigners) adopted, by a 75 per cent majority in a referendum, a new democratic constitution and reacquired full sovereignty from its 'co-princes', the head of the French state and the bishop of Urgel. Two months later the country was admitted as a full member of UNO. Andorra has not signed the EEC Treaty and is fiscally independent. A trade agreement with the EC in 1990, which established a customs union between the EC and Andorra for a range of products, but excluding agricultural products, although agricultural products which originate in Andorra are exempt from import duties when imported into the Community. Imports from third countries into Andorra are not to be treated more favourably than imports from the Community:

> Until 1993, the statelet had Home Rule, and got the best of both worlds from France and Spain. Now it has Independence, it gets the best of all worlds from Community Europe as a whole, and is even admitted to the Council of Europe. Not bad for a despicable relic of feudal times (Nairn 2000: 102).

Monaco and San Marino are also not members of the European Community and are considered by the EC as foreign countries.

Monaco has, however, been part of the customs territory of the Community since 1984, and EC rules of free circulation of goods apply. Monaco has no agreements with the EC on taxes on investment income, tax on casinos, and residence of individuals. The Republic of San Marino, though independent, is closely linked with Italy through a co-operation treaty which, when Italy joined the EC, meant that San Marino was included in the Community's customs territory. The EC and San Marino signed in 1991 an agreement which resolved judicial and economic problems concerning external trade, customs, transport and social security; it includes a customs union, a variety of co-operative relations, and mutual non-discrimination against workers.[3] The Vatican City is even more detached from the EU than San Marino. Although located in the capital city of a member state, it is not a party to the treaties and is treated by the EU as a foreign country. No special agreements exist between the Community and the Vatican City.

Liechtenstein, situated between Austria and Switzerland, has traditionally been politically close to Austria, but economically closely connected with Switzerland. When Austria joined the EU while Switzerland rejected joining the European Economic Area, Liechtenstein was relatively unaffected, demonstrating the resilience and adaptability of microstates. There is no income tax in Liechtenstein (tax revenue is raised from the foreign-owned Liechtenstein-based companies) but the provision of public services is of high quality, demonstrating the privileged position of the microstates.

The main difficulties posed by the microstates is they are tax havens and bankers for illicit profits. On both counts the European Commission and some member states, particularly France, would like a regime which severely limited these activities. Since influential banks and firms have branches in them, and some have headquarters in the microstates, many powerful interests would be disturbed by any radical change in the status quo. The main deterrent to decisive action against the microstates, and against the Channel Islands and the Isle of Man, is that funds would simply move to non-European tax havens.

French overseas *départements*

The French overseas *départements* (Réunion, Guadeloupe, Guyane and Martinique) form an integral part of the EC, since Article 227 of the Treaty of Rome provides that the Treaty shall apply to the French Republic in its entirety. Since 1960, all provisions of the EEC Treaty and secondary law applied to these overseas departments. A programme called POSEIDOM (Programme d'Options Spécifique à l'Éloignement et à l'Insularité des Départements français d'Outre Mer) was adopted by the EC in 1989, which set up a framework for the Community's contribution to the economic and social development of the islands. POSEIDOM promotes co-operation and regional commercial agreements between the territories and their neighbours. The programme is the legal model on the basis of which all other 'ultra-peripheral' programmes are drafted. Along similar lines, POSEICAN, applying to the Canary Islands, and POSEIMA, applying to the Azores and Madeira, were adopted in June 1991.

The main problem, in the 1990s, concerning the French overseas *départements* was the deteriorating economic, social and political climate in them, particularly in the West Indies. This resulted in out-migration but, since numbers were relatively small, this was not experienced by the EU as a difficulty. At the moment, their political relationship with France is regarded as purely a French matter, but all economic assistance to them has, in principle, to be within EU guidelines.

Special relationships with a member state

Ceuta and Melilla, cities on the Mediterranean coast of Morocco, are autonomous regions of Spain. Under the Spanish Accession Act and the derogations set out within it, Ceuta and Melilla are excluded from the Community's customs territory and from application of the common commercial, fisheries and agricultural policies. These territories are particularly sensitive from the point of view of clandestine immigration, and the Spanish authorities have taken stringent measures to prevent African migrants entering the territories. The Spanish authorities are confident that very few clandestine immigrants get through (Diaz-Pintado and Prieto Montero interviews).

The Canary Islands are an autonomous region of Spain. In 1991, following a request from Spain, the European Council decided that the islands should be gradually incorporated into the customs territory of the Community, accompanied by suitable measures to compensate them for their insular character and remoteness. The Azores and Madeira, situated in the Atlantic Ocean, are autonomous regions of Portugal. By virtue of the 1985 Portuguese Act of Accession, the islands belong politically and economically to the Community. A Joint Declaration on their economic and social development, annexed to the Act of Accession, calls on the Community to devote special attention to the development policies of the islands.

The Channel Islands and the Isle of Man are not part of the UK, but are Crown dependencies. The UK is responsible for the foreign relations and external defence of the islands and has ultimate responsibility for their good government. In domestic affairs, however, the islands govern themselves, although laws passed by their legislatures must receive Royal Assent. The islands' relationship with the Community is governed by Articles 25–27 and Protocol 3 of the UK's Act of Accession, which states that the islands are included in the EC customs territory. Goods imported into the islands from outside the Community are subject to the same Common Customs Tariff and agricultural levies as goods imported into the EC. Apart from ensuring the proper functioning of free trade, the islands are excluded from the provisions of the EEC Treaty. Although Treaty provisions relating to free movement of workers and the right of establishment do not apply to the islanders, nationals of all EC countries must receive identical treatment within the territories, while islanders enjoy the same rights in the UK as UK citizens. The islands' virtual exclusion from Community responsibilities enables them to retain the proceeds from import duties and agricultural levies on imports from third countries.

The Faroe Islands, with a population of 45 000, annexed to Denmark from 1814, have had an autonomy statute since 1948. Since 1970, Faroe has been an independent member of the Nordic Council (Davies 1996: 63). The Faroe Islands are in a similar position to the other non-EU Scandinavian countries, having free trade in goods and free movement of persons, but no rights of residence in the non-Scandinavian EU countries.

The Gibraltar dispute is mainly about sovereignty over the territory which is claimed by Spain. It is also a dispute about where the external frontier lies, with the Spanish government regarding the external frontier between Spain and Gibraltar, and the UK government regarding Gibraltar as part of EU territory (Morris and Haigh 1991, Gold 1994, O'Reilly 1999). The British and Spanish governments agreed under the Brussels Agreement of 1984 to grant EC rights for Spaniards in Gibraltar and Gibraltarians in Spain in advance of Spain's entry in the Community. This established free movement of persons, vehicles and goods between Gibraltar and the EC. Yet the 30 000 inhabitants of Gibraltar remain the only European citizens excluded from voting rights in the European parliamentary elections, as London failed to secure that right when the UK joined the EC – now any move towards it is blocked by Spain.

One justification for the Spanish position is the clearly anomalous relationship of Gibraltar to the EU. When the UK joined the European Community in 1973, Gibraltar was included under Article 227 of the

Treaty of Rome relating to European territories for whose external relations a member state is responsible. At Gibraltar's request, however, certain exceptions were negotiated, which exclude it from the Common Customs Tariff, the CAP and the need to apply VAT. Community Directives, where of local practical application, are given legal force in Gibraltar by means of locally enacted ordinances.

A further difficulty was created by the 1995 implementation of the Schengen system. Spain's inclusion in the Schengen system made the Gibraltar–Spain border an external Schengen frontier, which is used by Spain against the UK and Gibraltar. Between 1996 and 1999, Spain has used border controls repeatedly as a means of putting pressure on Gibraltar, by punctilious checking of cars and documentation, limiting crossings to as few as 12 cars in an hour. Part of the Spanish case for doing this is allegations of criminal activity in Gibraltar. The Spanish government allege that Gibraltar is a centre of money laundering and is used, directly and indirectly, for tobacco and drug smuggling.

The conflict over Gibraltar is a stalemate and although relations between the parties are unlikely to degenerate into violence in the near future, it is a serious conflict. The parties are obdurate but there is an asymmetry in the seriousness with which the dispute is regarded. Felipe González said, in an interview in the *Financial Times* (9 May 1991), that Gibraltar is 'a stone in the shoe' of Spain but only a minor irritant to Britain. Britain cannot legally grant the colony independence because this is contrary to the clause of the 1713 Treaty of Utrecht, giving Spain the right of reversion. The UK accepted the principle of self-determination (the status of the territory cannot be changed without the consent of the inhabitants), which the Spanish reject, in the Preamble to the 1969 Order in Council promulgating the Gibraltar Constitution. The Spanish government, backed by an overwhelming majority of the Spanish population, regards Gibraltar as an integral part of Spain with a population too small to enjoy the right to self-determination. The Gibraltarians feel most threatened by the conflict and remain virtually unanimous in their rejection of the Spanish claim. Although Spain is prepared to grant internal autonomy to Gibraltar, neither it nor the British government has shown any sign of changing their position.

Overseas countries and territories

Part Four of the Treaty of Rome deals with the association of overseas countries and territories. Member states agree to associate with the Community the non-European countries and territories which have special relations with a particular member state. An updated list of the countries and territories is published in Annex I to the Council Decision of 25 July 1991.

The overseas countries and territories are:

- country having special relations with the Kingdom of Denmark: Greenland[4]
- overseas territories of the French Republic: New Caledonia and Dependencies, French Polynesia, French Southern and Antarctic Territories, Wallis and Futuna Islands
- territorial 'collectivities' of the French Republic: Mayotte, Saint Pierre and Miquelon
- non-European countries of the Kingdom of the Netherlands: Aruba, the Netherlands Antilles (Bonaire, Curacao, Saba, Saint Eustatius, Saint Martin)
- overseas countries and territories of the United Kingdom: Anguilla, Cayman Islands, Falkland Islands, South Georgia and the Sandwich Islands, Montserrat, Pitcairn, Saint Helena and Dependencies, British Antarctic Territory, British Indian Ocean Territory, Turks and Caicos Islands, British Virgin Islands

The association of these territories and the EEC was intended to promote their economic and social development and to establish close economic relations between them and the Community. Occasionally trade issues disturb relationships with these territories as when the World Trade Organisation ruled in 1999 against EC preferential treatment of bananas from the Antilles, which discriminated against Central American bananas. But there are many possible problems with these territories concerning tax havens, drug trafficking, criminal influence over their governments, and territorial disputes. The EU has connections with, and takes some responsibility for, widely scattered territories at very different stages of economic and social development. As the EU develops more state-like characteristics, involvement in thorny and obscure disputes is probable.

Scandinavian external frontiers

The Norwegian and Icelandic decisions to stay outside the EU did not create trade and economic problems since both have open access to the EU market through EFTA and EEA agreements. However, the implementation of the Schengen system in March 1995 created a difficult situation for Scandinavia because of the existence of the Nordic free movement area, the only great achievement of the Nordic Union and a symbol of Scandinavian identity. The options for the countries concerned were, first, the maintenance of the Scandinavian free movement area, the exclusion of Denmark from Schengen, with the imposition of external frontier controls on the German–Danish frontier. Second, the Scandinavian passport and labour mobility agreements could be revoked and the external frontier could be drawn along the Norwegian–Swedish frontier. Third, an association agreement between Schengen and the non-EU Scandinavian states – Norway and Iceland – could be negotiated. Creating external border controls against Denmark would have contradicted the core principles of the EU; the drawing of the Schengen frontier between Sweden and Norway would have been impractical and caused offence as an affront to Nordic solidarity. The third option was therefore chosen.

The Nordic free movement area is based on conventions agreed in 1954 and 1957. There are three differences between its modus operandi and the Schengen system: random controls at the internal Scandinavian frontiers are allowed; external frontier checks are regulated by a five-paragraph guideline, rather than the 250 pages of the Schengen manual; and exchange of information between frontier police is decentralised, contrasting with the centralised Schengen Information System in Strasbourg. Formal negotiations between the Scandinavian countries resulted in the granting of observer status of Schengen to Norway and Iceland in May 1996. Neither country saw difficulties in applying the Schengen standards at their frontiers and accepting the Schengen *acquis* as long as no supranational elements were introduced and as long as goods were not involved (Eikas interview). Since Norway is the only country ever to reject, in 1972, full EC membership (Kuhnle 1992: 19), a potential problem was the integration of Schengen into the Treaty of European Union, which implied the opting in by Norway to part of the EU. This formal difficulty was overcome by the negotiation of the association agreement.

All parties adopted a pragmatic approach and the problems were of a manageable nature. The clandestine immigration issue was relatively minor – very few non-Scandinavians cross the principal frontier involved (the Swedish–Norwegian) because the main transport links with third countries do not pass this frontier. There is a very low incidence of cross-border crime – no Swedish criminals in the 1990s have been engaged in cross-border crime, although an Oslo group has been raiding Swedish country cottages. Smuggling, especially liquor by Norwegian nationals and drugs by foreigners, is common but most illegal goods come in by sea and not across the land border. There is good informal co-operation between Swedish and Norwegian police in the frontier regions, and hot pursuit has been tolerated in practice, without formal agreement. There has been only one important incident involving frontier policing in the 1990s. On the Trondheim highway into Sweden, Norwegian police entered Swedish territory to arrest Swedish bikers (and inappropriate police behaviour was video-taped). There are usually no problems over mutual assistance in criminal matters because the criminal law and criminal law procedures are very similar, although the organisation of the police and prosecution services are very different (Ahnfelt and Ulrich interviews).

The Baltic

The disintegration of the USSR in 1991 created a radically new situation in the Baltic. The immediate military threat of the USSR disappeared, but social and economic conditions in Russia were potentially destabilising for the region. The environmental threat of the decaying Russian nuclear northern fleet was serious. New and vulnerable Baltic states re-emerged. The different forms of neutrality of Sweden and Finland seemed to lose some relevance. Poland unequivocally 'joined' the West and aspired to membership of both NATO and the EC. A new co-operative framework to stabilise the region was felt as an urgent necessity by the smaller powers. The big powers, Germany and Russia, could only play a passive role. A German view, not officially expressed, was that a positive German approach would be considered threatening by the smaller countries, as prefiguring a drive to achieve a hegemonic position in the region. The initiative was therefore left to the Scandinavian countries.

One such initiative came in the 1999 Finnish EU presidency when Finland promoted the idea of an EU 'Northern Dimension',[5] focusing on trade with Russia and establishing regional co-operation between the countries bordering the Baltic Sea. The intention was to create a complement and a counterbalance to the Euro-Med Partnership. The Finnish government argued that there was a 'Baltic opportunity' – a huge field for investment and trade. Russia's north has one-third of the world's gas resources, is oil-rich and the location of one-fifth of the world's forests.

The Arctic frontier is a particular source of concern for the Norwegians, although the opening of this frontier with Russia created the possibility of re-establishing traditional trading relationships. Norway is neither a major power nor a country with a Baltic coastline.

But it has a general interest in Baltic stability and, more specifically, in stabilising relations with Russia. Foreign Minister Stoltenberg's 1997 statement that 'Norway is a power at the mouth of the Baltic Sea' indicated that Norway wished to participate in all initiatives concerning the Baltic. Sweden has vital interests in the Baltic region, and with greater resources than either Finland and Norway, became the unofficial leader of Baltic Sea co-operation.

The 1992 Copenhagen summit of foreign ministers initiated the Baltic Sea Region Council of States (Joenniemi 1997: 67–8). The practical problem confronting the countries concerned was the difficulty of identifying concrete measures which were not better done through bilateral co-operation – such as technical assistance to the former communist states, educational exchanges, scientific co-operation. Some areas indicated for multilateral co-operation were unwelcome to some of the partners. Pollution of the Baltic was high on the Scandinavian agenda but low on the Russian since most of the pollution came from the Russian coast on the Gulf of Finland. Pollution was nonetheless made a priority for multilateral action by the Baltic Sea Conference. The other priority was organised crime; a conference on organised crime and a task force were organised.

In the area of organised crime, Sweden assumed the leading role, with the Swedish Prime Minister given the responsibility for co-ordinating an action programme. A task force, composed of the personal representatives of the heads of government, was established. The Swedish representative, Per Nuder, described the Baltic, in a term more often used for the Mediterranean, as Europe's Rio Grande because of the difference in income levels and social development between Russia and the Scandinavian countries. The opening of frontiers and increased personal mobility created a threat of organised crime in areas such as drug trafficking, fraud, prostitution and racketeering, damaging to individual citizens and to the progress of integration in the region and to the enlargement of the EU. The task force produced, in 1997, a series of practical measures concerning information exchange between police, customs, tax, and other agencies which held data useful in investigating organised crime; increased exchanges of police liaison officers; improved judicial co-operation; and an educational effort supported by a programme of exchanges. There was also to be close co-operation between the FBI offices in Moscow, Warsaw and Copenhagen (Nuder interview).

The Swedish government's main concern was the general security of the Baltic area. The initiative on organised crime was a useful step towards contact between security and intelligence services as a stage to reaching a common understanding of security issues, perceptions of which varied very considerably in the riparian states. However, there is a cautious approach – one official expressed the view that some of the EU partners had tried to assign too big a security role to Sweden and that Baltic security issues should not be regionalised (Kettis interview). Nonetheless, the Baltic region remains an area of potential instability with small, vulnerable states, a neighbouring great power, Russia, going through a period of disorder, the large Russian arsenal of weapons, and vastly different levels of economic development.

The Swiss frontiers

Switzerland provokes irritation in neighbouring states for a variety of reasons – amongst others, banking secrecy laws, determination to keep EU heavy goods vehicles from transiting Switzerland, and voluntary isolation from European institutions. Frontiers are relatively far down the agenda of issues between Switzerland and its neighbours, even though the present frontier regime is flawed.

The main issue concerning frontier control is that Switzerland has been used as a transit country for undocumented migrants. The absence, until 1999, of a readmission agreement with Italy meant that very large numbers of undocumented immigrants reached the German frontier having crossed Italy and Switzerland. When clandestine immi-grants are apprehended in the country, according to Swiss law, they cannot be held in custody and therefore tend to disappear. The Swiss–German frontier, in the later 1990s, has the highest numbers of people returned in accordance with a readmission agreement, and not the Polish–German frontier as commonly supposed. Another sensitive area is that a systematic individual check on all persons (a requirement of Schengen for the external frontier of member states) is impossible because of the volume of traffic. Switzerland is prepared to accept light and flexible controls.[6] But the EU's eastern neighbours notice what occurs at the Swiss frontier with the EU, and suggest that the same regime be applied to them.

There are about 700 000 border crossings each day at Swiss frontiers. The exact number is not known because at busy frontiers statistics are rough estimates. The less frequented crossings are monitored more closely to see whether a change in the pattern of traffic occurs which warrants a change in the system of control. Overall, between 6 and 10 per cent of individuals are checked. The responsibility for policing the frontier is a mixed one. In principle, policing the frontier is in the hands of the cantonal police. The Gardes Frontières, a confederal force of about 1900 officials (about one official per kilometre of frontier), are customs officers. However, they have full police powers in the frontier zone (a vague concept but usually regarded as about 10 km). In practice, therefore, the responsibility is shared and, in the less populated cantons, the Gardes Frontières are the dominant partner.

Topographically, the characteristics of Swiss frontiers are very diverse, with high mountain ranges the norm, and densely populated areas like Basel or Geneva the exception. The physical difficulties in Swiss frontier surveillance are obvious (Caluori 1994: 33) but there is very little evidence of significant illegal frontier crossing in difficult terrain, even though the financial interest in encouraging tourism means that some frontiers are deliberately unpoliced. Local agreements have been made to remove frontier controls in some places such as the footpath around Mont Blanc and certain ski runs. There is no evidence that undocumented immigrants or criminals exploit these exceptions.

In the past, there had been a Swiss tendency to downplay the importance of frontier controls. In 1947, the Conseil Fédéral resolved to abolish completely frontier controls, subject to certain conditions (which were never met). This illustrates a Swiss perspective – controls on foreigners are exercised, not at the frontier, but in the interior of the territory. This is no longer the case because of a change in the political atmosphere about immigration and, from the 1980s, about frontier controls. Frontier controls have been politicised by ultranationalists. Christoph Blocher, leader of the Swiss People's Party which made considerable gains in the 1999 elections, calls for stricter frontier controls and a tightening of asylum law.

Greater co-operation in criminal and immigration matters has been a priority of Swiss policy since the Confederal government attempted, from the late 1980s, to draw closer to the EC (Rossi, Strahm and Théraulaz interviews). The impact, previously regarded as a matter of purely internal concern, of frontier controls on neighbouring states is also taken more seriously. The Confederal authorities and the frontier police would welcome an association agreement with Schengen, but this does not seem possible because the Schengen countries are opposed to it, and Switzerland is not prepared to join Schengen by dismantling frontier controls, a move which would almost certainly be rejected by a referendum. Since the late 1980s, informal contacts between Switzerland and Schengen have taken place and a Swiss working group is examining ways of becoming closer to the Schengen system. Practical police co-operation takes place with the police in the neighbouring countries on the basis of bilateral agreements (trilateral in the case of Basel).

There is virtually no cross-border crime from Switzerland into the neighbouring countries. Most crime in the other direction is petty, with some exceptions – Italian criminals enter Tessin to rob banks, and drugs come into Switzerland from Milan. Drugs present a difficult policing problem, in Switzerland and elsewhere, because as soon as controls are tightened in one place, the traffickers quickly switch to another. Where there is a large city at the frontier there are often people crossing to steal car radios, and shoplift – presenting problems of identification, extradition and prosecution. Two out of three people arrested in Basel are foreigners, although some are resident foreigners (Auf der Maur interview).

Frontier controls at the Swiss frontier, therefore, present only low-key problems for the neighbouring countries. This allows the EU countries at the main ports of entry to treat Swiss citizens as if they are EU citizens. Since there is a free trade agreement between the EU and Switzerland, and the Swiss cantons have become, in the 1990s, very active promoters of transfrontier co-operation at the local and regional levels (see Chapter 3), Swiss territory can be seen, in important respects, as slowly merging with the EU territory. Opinion surveys, referenda results and elections show a majority of Swiss opinion usually rejects joining the EU, but the prospect of aligning Swiss with EU policies, without being able to influence the content of them, could effect a long-term change in attitudes.

The Mediterranean frontier

The Mediterranean 'blue frontier' is the most problematic of the external maritime frontiers of the EU. Intractable political conflicts, resulting in both wars and terrorist action, complicate political relationships between the EU and its neighbours. Trafficking and landing of illegal goods and persons occur on all sea frontiers of the EU, but the Mediterranean presents the most difficult problems. Greece, Italy and Spain have long coastal and island frontiers, in close proximity to unstable and relatively poor neighbouring countries. Migratory pressure and cross-border crime present serious policing problems. The gulf between the northern and southern shores of the Mediterranean is wide and getting wider. The disparities are sometimes referred to as the three Ds – demography, development and democracy – which present formidable barriers to close co-operation between the EU and the southern shore countries.

Intractable disputes

All the numerous disputes in the region affect, to a degree, the EU and its member states. If a common EU foreign and security policy, and a independent military capability, become a reality, the EU will have to exercise an influence in these disputes which at least equals that of the USA. This is still a distant prospect. The EU lacks a coherent strategy for its frontiers and its immediate neighbourhood. From the western (the western Sahara problem) to the eastern end of the Mediterranean (the Israeli–Palestinian–Arab conflict), most of the disputes are beyond the power of the EU, or its members, to influence let alone resolve. But there are important disputes which directly affect the EU and its member states. In addition to the Spanish–UK dispute over Gibraltar, the Greek–Turkish disputes involve a member state and, from the end of 1999, a candidate member.

The origins of these disputes go back to the foundation of the Greek state and the collapse of the Ottoman empire, and cannot be described here. Two disputes are of crucial importance and must be resolved before Turkish EU entry – the Aegean and Cyprus. Disputes about the Aegean frontier with Turkey led to the brink of armed conflict between NATO partners Greece and Turkey in 1996 and 1997. The conflict originates in the Treaty of Lausanne (1923), concerning islands, some of them close to the Turkish coastline, which came from Italian into Greek possession after the Second World War. Turkey never accepted all the implications of this situation. Conflicts over airspace, over the seabed and over territorial waters, particularly the proposal to extend Greek territorial waters from 6 to 12 miles, have led to repeated naval incidents (M. Anderson 1996: 158–60).

Under pressure to come to an agreement on Cyprus, proximity talks started at the UN in New York in December 1999. The Turkish part of the island, backed by Turkey, insists that negotiations must be held on the basis of two Cypriot states. The Turkish Republic of North Cyprus, established after the Turkish invasion of 1974, is internationally unrecognised. The justification for a separate Turkish Cyprus is, according to its leader, Rauf Denktash: 'There is no Cypriot nation. There are two parts of two nations: Greek Cypriots call themselves Greeks; and we are from Turkey, settled here 400 years ago. No intermarriage. Religions different. Languages different' (Burke-Kennedy 1999).

At the dividing 'green line' two imperial concepts clash: *enosis* (union with Greece), and *taksim* (separation or partition), aiming at the preservation of the Turkish presence on the island (Banos 1998: 141). The green line, a buffer zone separating Greek and Turkish Cyprus, is policed by the UN; and the British, more and more irrelevantly, control two sovereign bases. Both Turkey and Greece regard the green line as a military frontier and maintain forces in a state of readiness, which makes it a unique frontier between NATO partners (Hitchens 1990: 120). If Turkish Cypriots enter the southern part of the island or Greek Cypriots enter the north they are immediately deported (Burke-Kennedy 1999). There is therefore no possibility of contact between the two populations – an intolerable situation if Turkey draws closer to the EU.

The 1999 earthquakes, in both Greece and Turkey, brought these traditional enemies closer together in mutual assistance, and have even initiated an apparent change of the Greek policy of blocking Turkey's EU membership aspirations. The resolution of territorial disputes seems, for the first time since the First World War, a possibility in the medium term. If and when Turkey becomes a member, the EU will have a common frontier with the conflict-riven regions of the Middle East and the Caucasus.[7] Having a coherent frontier policy will then be not only desirable but an urgent necessity.

Europe's Rio Grande

It has become a commonplace to describe the EU's Mediterranean as Europe's Rio Grande.[8] In Russell King's words, 'the Mediterranean represents a sharp, even brutal divide between "developed" Europe and the less developed regions of North Africa and the Middle East' (King 1998: 109), a divide in economic, demographic, geopolitical, cultural and migratory terms. Roberto Aliboni writes: 'The Mediterranean is not ... a "centre", naturally destined to breed solidarity, but rather a "frontier" separating worlds that are culturally, economically and politically very far apart – the Judæo-Christian and the Islamic; the developed and the underdeveloped; the democratic and the authoritarian' (Aliboni 1991: 1). The contemporary Mediterranean is far removed from the Roman *mare nostrum*, the centre of the civilised world, even if it remains a region with 'a self-consciously glorious past' (King 1998: 111).

It is seen as one of the sites of the 'clash of civilisations' predicted by Samuel Huntington. Huntington argues that ideological conflict ended with the collapse of the USSR, but that it will be replaced by conflict between religious/cultural groupings (Huntington 1996). The overt hostility of Islamic 'fundamentalists' to the rich 'North' and the Islamophobia of sections of opinion in Europe give a superficial credibility to this argument. Despite some blurrings of the cultural frontier (e.g. Israel and Morocco taking part in the Eurovision Song Contest, and in European sports competitions), Middle Eastern and North African states are regarded as non-European (Vrbetic 1995: 5). This was made explicit in the rejection of Morocco's application to join the EC in 1987. But it is an oversimplification to regard the cultural/religious frontier between the northern and southern shores of the Mediterranean as an inevitable cause of conflict. There have been long periods of coexistence and interpenetration; relations between the northern and southern shores are of a complexity and variety which cannot be encompassed in Huntington's scenario (Holmes 1998: 39).

The economic data illustrate the depth of the divide between North and South. Between the 1980s and 1990s, the divide was getting deeper. GNP figures for the Mediterranean countries (in the *World Bank Atlas*) show rapid increases for the main countries on the northern shore: France from $667 700 to 1 355 039 between 1980 and 1994, Italy from 368 860 to 1 101 258, Spain from 199 780 to 525 334. For the North African countries the comparable figures are Algeria from $36 410 to 46 115, Egypt 23 140 to 40 950, Morocco from 23 788 to 30 330 and Tunisia from 8340 to 15 873. The GNP per capita show an even more dramatic widening gap, with France increasing from $11 730 to 23 470 by comparison with Egypt from 580 to 710, Tunisia from 1310 to 1800, Algeria from 860 to 1150 and Morocco from 860 to 1150. Israel is the great exception in the non-European Mediterranean and the islands of Cyprus and Malta are partial exceptions. GDP per capita in France is about 13 times higher than in Tunisia, in Spain about 12 times higher than in Morocco, and in Italy about 11 times higher than in Algeria. 'Clearly', Tovias writes, 'the Mediterranean is a border zone between the industrialised and the Third World' (Tovias 1997: 122).

The widening gap is accentuated by economic and demographic transformation of the Mediterranean states of the EU and by the demographic explosion in North Africa. This is a relatively new development and a success story of European integration. Only 30 years ago, southern Europe was relatively poor. Franco's Spain and Salazar's Portugal, the Italian Mezzogiorno and Greece under the dictatorship of the colonels were peripheral countries marked by high degrees of poverty, emigration and political violence (Rufin 1991). Accession to the EC was followed by a radical improvement in the economic performance of these countries, even if the Italian Mezzogiorno and Greece remain relatively poor by EU standards. Italy and Spain have made progress in catching up with France.

Spain and Italy have also changed from countries of high birth rates to countries whose birth rate is at or below the normal rate of replacement. They, even more than the north European countries, are condemned to an ageing population. The demographic explosion in North Africa is in sharp contrast and could, unless drastic action is taken to contain it, make the poverty gap much worse. The current population of Egypt alone is estimated to be in the region of 60 million, yet is expected to increase to around 100 million within the next 30 years. According to the United Nations Environmental Programme projections, by the early twenty-first century more than 65 per cent of coastal Mediterranean people will dwell on its non-European shore compared with 1950, when two-thirds lived on the European shore.[9] In the 1990s, those on the southern shore have only approximately 10 per cent of the wealth (Fox 1997).

This dynamic demographic growth on the southern shore compounds the other disparities – economic prosperity, the lack of freedom and democracy, and the repressive nature of the regimes on the southern shore. The cancelling of the 1991 elections in Algeria, followed by eight years of violence and repression (followed by a very fragile peace) seem the quasi-inevitable outcome of economic and demographic circumstances. The populations on the southern shore are overwhelmingly young, and no employment prospects exist for most young people. This increases both the probability of political violence, and the propensity to migrate to the EU countries. As the intra-EU frontiers between northern and southern countries, and indeed the dividing lines between south and north within these countries, became less marked economically, socially and politically, the Mediterranean frontier increased in salience.

A neglected frontier?

A common complaint, most frequently expressed in the first half of the 1990s, was that the Mediterranean frontier was neglected by the EU because of its preoccupation with Central and Eastern Europe (Pisani 1992, Dinan 1994: 459). However, in recent years, 're-inventing' (Balta 1992) the Mediterranean frontier has been increasingly on the agenda of the EU (Sultana 1999: 181). The Italian EU presidency in 1990 initiated this by redirecting some attention to the southern frontier but progress has been punctuated by political difficulties, such as the alleged Libyan involvement in the placing of bombs on French and American aircraft and withdrawal of aid packages because of concern for human rights.[10]

The countries on the southern shore of the Mediterranean have not been and are not regarded as potential EU members (although the 1999 acceptance of the candidature of Turkey as a candidate broke an important taboo widely assumed to exist against candidacies of Muslim countries). Among current candidate members, Malta[11] and Cyprus, although they are not southern shore countries, have important links with them. As Marengo (1998: 99) notes, 'attention is being drawn to the EU's southern boundary not for the purpose of reaching out for new members, but of refocusing the EU's attention on its existing southern members and their problems'.

The two pressing preoccupations of the EU countries bordering the Mediterranean are negative ones – security against political violence spilling over from North Africa, and stemming the flow of immigrants. Emphasis on these issues has led to the characterisation of the southern shore states as a non-military menace (Khader 1994). There is a general awareness that the solution to problems of migration and violence is economic development but this is regarded as a long-term objective and no consensus exists about how it can be achieved.

Two important conferences in the early 1990s attempted to address co-operation in the Mediterranean basin on a multilateral basis. The first, an initiative launched by Spain and Italy in 1990, the Conference on Security and Co-operation in the Mediterranean, aimed to place security issues in the context of trade, development and political relationships. The conference lacked a concrete outcome, but it opened up the possibility of a more practical project. The second, the Barcelona Conference of November 1995, in which 15 EU members and 12 non-EU Mediterranean states (Albania, Libya and Yugoslavia were absentees), launched the Euromed partnership. This attempted to establish a comprehensive framework of co-operation in the Mediterranean region, aiming at the progressive establishment of a Euro-Mediterranean free trade zone by 2010. In addition to trade, the agenda included aid, cultural co-operation and the control of immigration.

The Barcelona Euromed partnership increased the EU's financial commitment towards the Mediterranean, bringing it up to about two-thirds of the level of aid to East Central European states, totalling 4.7 billion ECU for the 12 non-EU member states in the Mediterranean for the period 1996–99 (9.1 billion ECU from 1991 to 1999). These are large sums, but the Mediterranean countries contain nearly twice the population of Eastern Europe and there are enormous differences in projected demographic growth rates. Hence the real EU support is three to four times higher in Eastern Europe than the Mediterranean (King 1998: 121).

Many of the proposed priority areas of Euro-Mediterranean co-operation involve flexibility in the frontier regime between the EU and the southern shore states. Amongst these are: a substantial enlargement of tariff quotas for fruit, vegetables and other agricultural produce from the Mediterranean countries; rules of origin should be made as simple as possible so that not only large exporters profit; working towards a Euro-Mediterranean Economic Area in the field of industrial goods (Tovias 1997: 128–9). Whether these are achieved depends on a favourable combination of circumstances and the emergence of a strong consensus on aims, both in the EU and the southern shore countries. All the latter, even Libya in the later 1990s, would welcome additional aid from the EU and some, such as Israel and Morocco, with long-standing association agreements, aspire to a close relationship with, or membership of, the Union (Vasconcelos 1996). But the policies of these two states, and the other southern shore states, is to gain a comparative advantage over their neighbours. Intense competition rather than co-operation is the normal relationship between the non-EU Mediterranean states. Promoting the idea of the Mediterranean Sea as a common patrimony of all the riparian states, preserving the quality of water in the sea, the coastlines and the historic sites on the coasts is the one joint venture which has made progress. Several local and multilateral agreements in this domain have been achieved and further progress is likely.[12]

The indicators of trade, investment and aid give little room for optimism, despite the clear interest of the EU in having a zone of peace and stability in the Mediterranean basin (Hilpold 1996: 230–1). 'Despite the clear strategic need to preserve and improve relations' (Guizzi 1997: 50), the internal problems of the southern countries are too great to be solved by EU initiatives. The EU countries remain cautious about aid because of the potential instability of the North African countries and the uses to which the aid might be put (such as the corrupt siphoning off of funds, or applied to increase the repressive apparatus of the state). Trade is of relatively small volumes and expanding these would cause political difficulties within the EU. The Mediterranean, in figures for 1990, depended on the European Community for nearly 50 per cent of its total trade; yet, conversely, the

Mediterranean countries only accounted for 4 per cent of total EC trade (Aliboni 1991: 19). Tovias argues that immigration can only be stemmed by 'importing more agricultural and labour-intensive goods from Mediterranean non-EU-member countries' (Tovias 1997: 130). A more flexible immigration regime taking account of both the development needs of the southern shore countries and labour market of the northern is also an essential component. Provided that they do not result in further conflicts, these measures would create greater mutual confidence across Europe's Rio Grande (Fabre 1997).

Immigration

Sources and destinations of immigrants, as well as their socio-economic characteristics, from the Mediterranean region to the EU countries vary considerably. Migration from the Maghreb countries and Francophone Africa is mainly aimed at France, with Belgium a second important destination. It is estimated that there are already more than 2 million emigrants from North Africa in the EU – 70 per cent of them in France. Most of them are legal immigrants, although the extreme right National Front allege that there are 1.5 million illegal immigrants living in France. This is a wildly exaggerated figure. In 1988–89, during a partial amnesty in France, 143 000 illegal immigrants (*sans papiers*) applied for regularisation. Official and unofficial estimates generally agree that perhaps the same number again did not apply for regularisation. The migratory potential of North Africa is difficult to quantify but, if only every fifth of the currently unemployed young men between 20 and 30 years of age decided to emigrate, this would result in another million immigrants.

Albanians are the single most important group of immigrants reaching Greece but various East European nationalities, often trying to use Greece as a staging post to the rest of the EU, are also present. Influxes of illegal immigrants from Albania and from Eastern Europe have resulted in increased crime problems in a country which previously had very low crime figures and no record of organised crime. The result has been a growing rejection of foreigners, particularly Albanians. In 1998, Greece attempted to reduce the social problems created by illegal immigration by regularising the status of the immigrants and bringing them within the social security system (Nikolopoulos 1998: 108–10).

Italy was placed in severe difficulties by the influx of Albanians in 1996, dropping towards the end of 1997. But Italy remained an important destination for clandestine immigrants from Turkey, Sri Lanka, Bangladesh, Rwanda and, especially in the autumn of 1997, Kurds from Iraq. In late 1997 and early 1998, the arrival of Kurds revived controversies over immigration. A ship, the *Ararat*, was wrecked on the Cantabrian coast in December 1997 with 835 clandestine immigrants. Another boat, abandoned by its crew, was found in the Otranto Straits with 326 immigrants on board. Up to 3000 illegal migrants a month were arrested on Lampedusa and Sicily in 1998 and 1999. Even after the end of the intervention in Kosovo by NATO, the stream of Albanian/Kosovar refugees showed no signs of abating. According to official figures, 120 died in the attempt to cross the Adriatic between April and November 1999, but the true figure could, according to the Italian Ministry of the Interior, be four times higher. A new generation of human traffickers, often young and reckless, smuggle not only refugees, but also prostitutes, drugs, weapons and cigarettes.

Spain is also a route for illegal immigrants, and for cannabis and heroin imports into northern Europe. In the second half of the 1990s, the flow of illegal immigrants into southern Spain appeared to increase at the same time as in Italy. In the last six months of 1996 the Spanish authorities stopped 24 vessels with 315 illegal immigrants; during the first nine months of 1997, 129 vessels with 1374 illegal immigrants (figures supplied by the Oficina Policial Central de Asilio, Fronteras e Immigración). The Ceuta and Melilla exclaves present local problems (the EU helped to fund a security fence around them), and there are tight controls on persons entering mainland Spain from these territories and on ferries from Morocco generally. A number of immigrants, mainly from sub-Saharan Africa, make their way in small boats across the straits of Gibraltar – many clandestine immigrants on this crossing die in the attempt (about 60 bodies a year are found, with many others probably never discovered).

In 1997 the Spanish Ministry of the Interior estimated over 100 000 undocumented immigrants in Spain, from all over the world (Prieto interview). Their origins vary over time, and Eastern Europe is sometimes a more important region of origin than Africa. Illegal immigrants are regularly picked up on the Franco-Spanish border, and drugs moving north are also seized at this frontier. Spain has not, however, attracted suspicions suffered by Italy, partly because there are no Spanish equivalents of Italian Mafia organisations and partly because, as a result of preparations for the Seville Universal Exhibition and the Barcelona Olympics, Spain's border controls were relatively efficient (Fernández interview).[13]

Portugal has a geographical peculiarity in that access by land to other EU member states is only possible through Spain. Its external frontier (airports, seaports and coastline) are relatively easy to police. The peculiarity of Portugal is that it wishes to be regarded as a Mediterranean country (in the same way as Norway wishes to be regarded as a Baltic power) although it has no coastline on that sea. There are a growing number of immigrants in the country, mainly from former Portuguese possessions, but also some East Europeans. Some illegal immigrants are a policing problem – such as prostitutes from San Domingo. These problems are not on a scale which are likely to cause its Schengen partners serious concern, but the Portuguese authorities consider them serious enough to warrant close attention to how they have been confronted elsewhere (Burke 1998).

The arrival of refugees and undocumented immigrants in southern Europe causes tension between EU members because it is often assumed that the majority of these are trying to reach northern Europe. For example, 4000 undocumented Kurdish immigrants were apprehended in France alone in 1997 – to French complaints of inadequate control by the Italian authorities and allegations that Turkish gangs organised this influx via Italy (*Le Monde* 31 March 1997, 10 January 1998). Despite press outrage, the estimates of numbers of undocumented immigrants in the southern member states remained very much smaller than those in northern Europe for the first half of the 1990s.

A corrective to the view that illegal immigration is always a problem of movement from south to north are the readmission figures for France and Spain. In 1996 France asked Spain to readmit 1810 undocumented entrants (Spain accepted 1710) and Spain asked France to readmit 982 (892 accepted). However, the proportion accepted by Spain fell by a half in the first nine months of 1997, with France asking for 1076 readmissions (1061 accepted) and Spain asking for 426 (411 accepted). France does not criticise Spain in the way that Italy has, until 1998, been criticised by both the French press and by the government because it is accepted that there is a problem of undocumented individuals moving from France to Spain.

Policing

Effective co-operation on immigration and law enforcement requires a convergence of interests among like-minded states. The states of the northern and southern shores of the Mediterranean have remarkably different political systems and foreign policy interests. If the Euromed programme launched at Barcelona results in 'a Euro-Mediterranean economic space' by 2010, then a convergence might occur, but a darker, more pessimistic scenario of a continuing deep divide between northern and southern shores seems more probable. Difficult problems of policing the Mediterranean frontier are likely to remain. They may be grouped under four headings – problems of co-operating between the north and the south, problems of co-operation and understanding among EU member countries, material difficulties and human rights considerations.

Until 1999, EU governments, backed by public opinion, were determined to resist migratory pressure from the south by all practical means. The co-operation they can get from the southern states is limited, for two main reasons. First, although the southern shore countries have, in general, a positive view of the EU because it offers a promise of improved north–south relations, bilateral relations with the member states are complicated and sometimes conflictual. Second, the southern shore countries do not have the technical capacity to co-operate in controlling out-migration even if they had the political will to do so. There is little evidence that they have such a will.[14] Moreover, by asking them to do so, the northern shore countries are in conflict with one of the most cherished principles of liberalism – the right to leave one's country.

The EU, as a collective entity, is present in policing immigration across the Mediterranean through the Schengen system. In the southern shore countries, the system is often stigmatised, along with readmission agreements and other bases of summary expulsion of third-country nationals (which give particular offence in Black Africa), as part of fortress Europe. It is this clear desire to exclude persons from the southern shore of the Mediterranean, and the non-white world generally, rather than the Schengen system itself, which is at the root of resentments. There is very little direct contact between the southern shore countries and the Schengen system. In 1993, the Moroccans were invited to the Schengen technical inspection of the Spanish frontier controls; the Moroccan Ministry of the Interior was interested in the system but not disposed to co-operate in joint management of the sea frontier unless significant financial aid was provided (it was not forthcoming).

Mutual legal assistance between the northern and southern shore countries, which affect co-operation both over illegal immigration and criminal law enforcement issues, is not straightforward. The juridical systems and legal practices on the southern shore, despite strong French influence, are very different from those in the north, and can contribute to misunderstandings. Though they exist, bilateral agreements on mutual legal assistance are either not as fully developed as they are between, for example, European and North American countries, or are underutilised. The expulsion of clandestine immigrants to North Africa is hindered by legal and practical difficulties. Southern shore countries are reluctant to readmit any but their own nationals; determining where the immigrants who arrive in Lampedusa and Sicily have commenced their sea crossing, is difficult; and identifying the nationality of immigrants who have destroyed all their papers is sometimes impossible.

An obstacle to efficient mutual legal assistance is that crimes and offences are perceived in different ways. For example, Algeria has been prone since the early 1990s to politico-religious violence bordering on civil war. Co-operating with EU states to prevent Algerian nationals illegally entering the EU is not a priority for the Algerian authorities, and they will only do so if they are offered something in return. A relatively peaceful country like Morocco, with a long tradition of tolerating cannabis, will only co-operate with its northern neighbours to suppress trade in the drug in return for economic assistance – even then, because of traditional Moroccan attitudes, it is difficult for the Moroccan government to co-operate effectively. When Libya was treated as a pariah state, Libyan co-operation in law enforcement and illegal migration was bound to be highly selective.[15]

Compared to the difficulties which divide EU and non-EU countries bordering the Mediterranean, the differences between the four southern members of the EU – Greece, Italy, Spain and Portugal – are relatively limited but significant. Until the implementation of Schengen in 1995, the Schengen system was driven by Germany and France, both very restrictionist on immigration matters. According to this view, the southern EU member states were carried along by their determined and powerful northern neighbours. Although the southern countries were required to change their laws and practices to accommodate Schengen requirements, there is little evidence that they did this unwillingly, because they were beginning to feel the effects of migratory pressures.

In order to satisfy Schengen norms, Greece tightened up its legislation on the entry and residence of foreigners and put in place a system of surveillance in depth of its frontiers. This consisted of two zones – a 20 km zone patrolled by 46 mobile police units; then a band of 50 km patrolled by 25 mobile units. Each unit consists of about 25 police officers. Controls of foreigners are also carried out anywhere on the national territory. The number of officers involved in frontier posts, the land and sea frontiers, and immigration control was increased by about 2000, making a total of 12 000 in 1997.

The Italian case is the leading illustration of how suspicions between EU partners can complicate the policing of the external frontier. France and Germany would, in the early stages of negotiating and developing the Schengen system, have liked to have excluded Italy on grounds of lack of appropriate legislation and police standards, and failure to control the most notorious criminal conspiracy in Europe – the Sicilian Mafia. In Germany, as recently as 1997, the Minister of the Interior, Manfred Kanther, made alarmist statements to the effect that 'hordes' of Kurds were about to arrive on German territory, and the Minister of the Interior of Lower Saxony requested the suspension of the Schengen agreements. In January 1998, the Austrian Minister of the Interior, Karl Schloegl, accused Italy of 'getting rid of the problem [of illegal immigration] on to others' and threatened to close the frontier (*Le Monde* 3 January 1998).

Visits by German journalists, MEPs and MPs gave reassurance about the seriousness of the Italian approach to frontier controls and helped to further understanding of the difficulties faced. Applying minimum force to prevent desperate people landing and treating refugees humanely when they arrived in a country were recognised as part of all EU member states' international obligations (Scivoletto interview). Human rights considerations became even more pressing when the EU was compelled to take stands in Bosnia and Kosovo on human rights grounds. Doubts remained about the security of information held by the Italian police and about the technical quality of Italian frontier controls. Italy, however, passed the Schengen technical inspection in February 1997 and was admitted to full membership of the system in October 1997. Schengen became fully operational for Italy on 1 April 1998.

Greek frontier controls are also a target for severe criticisms from France, particularly in the French Senate (République Française – Sénat 1997). Greece has not yet fully joined the system, apart from Athens airport.[16] Greece, like the UK and Ireland, has no land border with another EU member state, and none of Greece's immediate neighbours are candidates for early EU membership. Greece has the most difficult sea frontier to police, with over 400 islands (many more if uninhabited islets, rocks and reefs are counted) as well as a mountainous northern frontier, difficult to police, not least due to lack of surveillance technology and sufficient manpower (Nikolopoulos 1998: 108, Angouras 1998). Standards of Greek frontier controls do not yet meet the technical requirements of the Schengen system. By contrast, Spain and Portugal, despite criticisms of some inadequacies within the law enforcement establishments, escape the public censure which has been directed both against Greece and Italy by their northern partners.

French parliamentary, official and press criticism of the other states has been driven by the political sensitivity within France on immigration, and the electoral threat of the anti-immigrant National Front. France has, since the 1970s, been in favour of strict control of immigration and, of all the countries of the southern façade, has been the one in which a belief has been the strongest that frontier controls can effectively exclude immigrants. A complete cessation of further immigration from the south has been regarded as a proper aim of policy. In 1993, the Interior Minister Charles Pasqua said that zero immigration was the objective. But even Pasqua admitted in 1998 that frontier controls were not effective against people determined to enter the country. Also, France continued to receive legally about 100 000 immigrants a year for reasons of family regroupment, asylum, study and skill shortages. The main preoccupation of France has been to prevent the import of violence from Algeria during the long crisis in that country which commenced in 1991. To this end it reinforced frontier controls from 1995 with the introduction of an anti-terrorist programme named Vigipirate, which strengthened frontier controls and remained in effect after the implementation of Schengen.[17] Whether French immigration controls are more effective than those of its southern EU partners is impossible to establish, but there is some evidence that France had, by the end of the 1990s, become a country of transit rather than of destination of clandestine immigrants.

There are, therefore, tensions between Schengen member states. Nonetheless, the system provides an incentive to EU countries (and indirectly their neighbours) to think in overall terms about the best interests of the EU in immigration policy and how to tackle transfrontier crime. A beginning has been made. The 1999 Tampere Declaration of the EU heads of state and government showed that there is a willingness to consider future immigration needs on the basis of economic and demographic data. Tight immigration control may no longer be in the economic interests of the EU states because of the unsatisfied demand for labour in certain sectors and the ageing of the EU population.

Conclusion

The external frontier still is a hybrid: for one set of functions (legal, tax, finance regulation, social and health systems, etc.) member states' frontiers are fundamental, for another agreed set of functions (movement of people, customs) it is the European or at least Schengen external frontier which predominates. But this review of the northern, Swiss, Mediterranean and the anomalous territories' frontiers shows how varied in character, difficult to manage and control, this frontier is. Although, in principle, common technical standards are applied to the whole length of the external frontier, in practice they vary. Moreover, they affect different populations differently. The most important respect in which they differ is the movement of persons.

In terms of relations with neighbours, the frontier is not a clear line but a complex system of relationships. In this sense, the frontier is more like that of an old imperial frontier or *limes*. Michel Foucher writes about the Mediterranean:

> To the extent that a comparison is possible, the interaction between the EU and its southern flank, from Morocco to Turkey, is similar to a '*limes*-style' strategy, where the border is closed to migrations and citizenship but open to trade, ideas, and languages, in an asymmetrical relationship which remains a permanent source of tension (Foucher 1998: 236).

The complexity and haziness of the external frontier and, as will be discussed in Chapter 6, the fact that the frontier is relocated from time to time, make it very difficult to have a mental map of it. It is therefore virtually impossible that the frontier will play a role in creating and shaping a *single* European identity (Koivumaa 1998), analogous to the process of the formation of national identities. It is the moving character of this frontier (with EU enlargement) which poses the most difficult problem of governance for the EU.

6
The Case of the Eastern Frontier of the European Union

The eastern frontier is mobile, a characteristic which distinguishes it from the other EU frontiers.[1] The October 1990 unification of Germany resulted in a new EU border with Poland. The accession of Finland and Austria in 1995 established an EU external border with Russia and Hungary. Association agreements in the 1990s with all Central and Eastern European states between the EU and the former USSR were the first step towards further enlargement, which will, in the new millennium, move the external frontier further east. Schengen frontier controls have already been exported to the first tier of applicant states, requiring of them a policing role on behalf of the EU at their own eastern frontiers.

The 1990s have thus seen the transformation of a rigid boundary line between east and west – the Iron Curtain – into a more diffuse frontier zone, which includes 'a certain de-localisation ... of European frontier controls' (M. Anderson 2000a: 23). By contrast with Turner's conception of the American frontier (also a moving zone), expansion of the EU is the enlargement of a union of states; it is not the spread of a people or a 'civilisation' across a continent. The EU expansion may diffuse certain norms, values and practices, but it leaves many others in place.

This chapter charts the recent developments at the present eastern frontier of the EU since the changes of 1989–91. It then assesses the risks and opportunities concerning this frontier: the main themes are security, migration, cross-border crime and cross-border co-operation.

Enlargement: setting the scene

Much high-flown rhetoric surrounded the 1989 destruction of the Berlin Wall and the 1991 disintegration of the USSR. These pivotal events provided the opportunity of overcoming the Cold War division of Europe and, of building, in Gorbachev's words, a 'common European house'. For the former satellites of the Soviet Union, and some of the republics of the former USSR, 'now that the blocs had been dissolved without resort to violence, it became possible for them to contemplate "a return to Europe"' (Croft et al. 1999: 6). What this meant was the adoption of certain principles – liberal constitutions, free elections, rule of law and market economies.

Almost a decade elapsed before the EU opened accession negotiations with five former Eastern bloc countries (the Czech Republic, Estonia, Hungary, Poland), plus Slovenia and Cyprus (Map 6.1). The Polish Foreign Minister Bronislaw Geremek declared that this marked the true end of the Second World War. The entry date for new members, initially thought before the end of the millennium, was postponed; at the time of writing, the first new entries are expected around 2004. NATO membership proceeded more quickly, with Poland, the Czech Republic and Hungary joining on 1 April 1999, but further expansion of membership is now stalled.

Two main reasons account for the slow progress: first, changes happening contemporaneously in the West and in the East were not in harmony, and, second, fears were provoked by the prospect of open frontiers and by vague security concerns. At the end of the 1980s and at the beginning of the 1990s, Western Europe was in a dynamic phase of integration, following the 1986 Single European Act, the completion of the Single Market through the 1992 programme, the 1985 Schengen Agreement and the 1990 Schengen Implementation Conventions. Contemporaneously with these changes, the East Central European countries were struggling with the transformation to a market economy, establishment of democratic institutions, and rebuilding of their legal and bureaucratic systems.

The EU was alleged, by friends of East Central Europe, to be preoccupied with internal affairs, such as the common currency (Ash 1999). However, the resources made available by the EU were substantial. Between 1995 and 1999, EU subsidies for Central and Eastern European states amounted to 6.7 billion ECU, with most of it going to the three countries favoured for early entry: Poland, the Czech Republic and Hungary. 'Hungary, with a per capita income four times that of Macedonia, got 12 times as much aid' (P. Anderson 1999). The Mediterranean countries argued that concentration on East Central Europe prevented funds being directed to much poorer countries in the south. The economic aid policy of the EU may also have been aimed

Map 6.1   EU enlargement

less at the preparation of the East Central European countries for membership than at the creation of a 'buffer zone' – 'new areas of social, economic and cultural interaction between East and West' (C. Wallace et al. 1997: 1).

EU strategy

The issues of 'deepening versus widening' of the EU were sometimes presented as an either/or alternative. In the event, the member states of the EU decided to follow a 'both at the same time' strategy – both to press on with further integration, while assisting the applicant countries to prepare for accession. From 1991, association agreements were negotiated with all potential candidate states. Between 1994 and 1996, all eastern neighbours of the EU formally applied for EU membership. The 1993 Copenhagen summit fixed the criteria for accession,[2] and decided that negotiations should start with all candidate countries simultaneously. Given the different economic, demographic and political characteristics of the applicant states, this meant further slowing the accession process.

Of the six countries under consideration for rapid admission to the EU, Poland is the largest in terms of population (with 38.6 million, it is almost twice as big as the other five combined); but in terms of gross domestic product per head, according to European Commission figures, it reached only 31 per cent of the EU average. The two smallest applicants, Cyprus (0.7 million inhabitants) and Slovenia (2 million) had, in 1997, the highest GDP per head with 59 per cent of the EU average, followed by the Czech Republic (10.3 million) with 55 per cent, Hungary (10.2 million) 37 per cent and Estonia (1.5 million) 23 per cent.

The five other candidates for delayed membership – Bulgaria, Lithuania, Latvia, Romania and Slovakia – all had GDP per head of less than a quarter of the EU average. Slovakia was an exception with 41 per cent, but for political and human rights reasons was excluded from early consideration for entry to the EU. Although the eastern borderlands of the EU (mostly German) also suffered from their peripheral frontier status (Neuss et al. 1998: 160), there is, nonetheless, a very steep gradient in economic terms and sharp differences in demography between the EU, its immediate neighbours and the outer circle of applicant states (Langer 1996, Krämer 1997: 68–88). In terms of trade, there has been a coming together with the EU: by the mid 1990s, 60 per cent of the Central and Eastern European applicant states' export trade went to the EU, a radical change from the pre-1989 trade flows (Tebbe 1998: 67–88).

The possibility of political instability, huge differentials in wage levels,[3] security risks coming from the east, and illegal trafficking of persons (including prostitutes) and goods (especially drugs) created apprehensions which slowed down the accession process. Priority was given to practical 'compensatory measures' to control the risks. The eastern neighbours of the EU experienced these compensatory measures as limiting access to the EU, and as imposing policies on them. The incorporation of Schengen into the Treaty on European Union (TEU) requires the acceptance of the Schengen *acquis* by all states acceding to the EU (without the possibility of opt-outs along the lines of those negotiated by the UK, Ireland or Denmark). Negative reactions among the applicant members, to the effect that the Schengen *acquis* was an imposed regime, were inevitable.

Strictly policed frontiers impeded attempts at establishing institutionalised cross-border co-operation along the EU eastern frontier. The aim to create interdependent border regions on the model of the borderlands along the internal frontiers of the EU required freedom of movement. Long waiting times spent in queues at frontier checkpoints were unhelpful; even though there were ways to cut the queue, relaxed social contact between people not involved in official meetings was inhibited. In addition, Central and Eastern European representatives remarked on the obvious contradiction between heavy investments in border control facilities when, according to declared policies of the EU, the frontiers would shortly become internal ones without any controls.

In general, the difficulties of transition to EU membership caused the 'profound disillusionment which has gripped Central Europe progressively these past 10 years' (Lloyd 1999). In Central and Eastern European applicant states, the initial overwhelming support for accession to the EU has been in decline (Bretherton 1999: 200). Figures in Hungary show a substantial erosion of popular backing for EU membership (Bort 1996: 102–3, Czaban 1999: 288). Czech opinion was always the most negative about the cost of EU membership and the immigration which could result from the abandonment of frontier controls (Newton and Walsh 1999: 240–2). From February to October 1999, Polish support had, according to one polling institute, fallen from 64 per cent to (for the first time) below 50 per cent.

Polish farmers feared that Polish agriculture would not be viable, and coal miners were anxious about the future of their jobs, should Poland join the EU (Francis 1999: 313). Popular fears that Germans might 'return' to buy up land and house property complicated accession negotiations concerning the freedoms of movement, settlement and establishment. The reforms in health, education and pensions necessary to meet EU criteria were also unpopular. Economic reforms have also encountered difficulties. While the privatisation of small and medium-sized enterprises progressed, big state concerns, particularly in Poland and in the Czech Republic, have not been privatised.[4] Further restructuring of the economy is likely to have, at least initially, a negative effect on employment.

Questions of cultural autonomy have also been raised in the applicant states. Frontiers in an enlarged EU would, it is feared, no longer protect their cultures against the intrusion of Western (i.e. Americanised) culture and cultural products. Anxieties about cultural homogenisation are, in the EU, predominantly voiced by French elites (see Chapter 3), and in the east in Hungary which, due to its unique language and relatively autonomous economic policy, preserved a protected cultural enclave for its art and folklore behind the Iron Curtain (Szász 1997).

Geopolitical change

The Iron Curtain was a highly policed frontier but variations in different sectors of that frontier were obscured by a simplistic ideological presentation of the line of division by both sides. Willy Brandt's 'Ostpolitik' and the détente of the 1970s, culminating in the Final Act of Helsinki in 1975, led to the acceptance of the post-war frontiers[5] and some relaxing of border regimes.[6] The Final Act guaranteed the inviolability of those frontiers. Notwithstanding this, 15 years later some 20 000 km of new international frontiers would be created in Central and Eastern Europe (Grimm 1995: 11–12) and one, the 'inner German frontier', would be abolished.[7]

The destruction of the Iron Curtain left some legacies and revived historical memories. There was a risk that territorial claims might resurface, as many state borders were imposed by the victors of the Second World War. The most sensitive frontier, the Oder–Neisse line, was confirmed as the eastern frontier of Germany, after several months' hesitation by Chancellor Kohl. Minority issues remained, such as the 180 000 Polish living in the Ukraine, in the area of Lvov (Lemberg) annexed by Stalin (Nowak 1994: 94). Romania's frontiers were complicated. While Romania could make claims on Moldova, neighbouring states could also make claims on Romanian territory; it has declared a readiness 'to contemplate peaceful, negotiated border changes' (Dunay 1995: 54). EU candidate members have been under pressure to abandon any claim to frontier change and this was made part of the

Copenhagen criteria for accession to the EU. Post-Cold War Hungary, after initial hesitation, signed and ratified two treaties dealing with borders and territory, with Ukraine in December 1991, and with Slovakia in 1995 (Dunay 1995: 55).

The aftermath of the collapse of communism revived disputes on the northern frontier of Greece. One was a relatively minor dispute with Albania, involving the Hellenic population (the existence of which was disputed by Albania) north of the Greek border. Another dispute isolated Greece within the EU. While most of the EU countries recognised Macedonia as an independent state in 1993, Greece refused to accept the name of Macedonia and the national symbols of FYROM (Former Yugoslav Republic of Macedonia – the designation which Greece finally accepted). As Bulgaria was also willing to recognise the new Macedonia, this put strain on Greek–Bulgarian relations. Towards the north-east, Greece has differences with Ankara over the Turkish minority in Thrace, one part of the Greek–Turkish territorial tension which also involves the Aegean and the partition of Cyprus (Anderson 1996: 181–4, Angouras 1998).

Mental maps, or images, of the regions of Europe were radically revised as a result of the decline and fall of communism. One example was the revival of the discourse on *Mitteleuropa*. During the 1980s, intellectuals like Milan Kundera, György Konrád or Günter Grass argued that the fate of this imaginary zone, *Mitteleuropa*, was to be caught between two superpowers (Kundera 1984, Konrád 1985). A role of the 'intermediary' was forced on the peoples of this zone to avoid the catastrophe of war in the heart of Europe. In this period, 'no country or region in central and eastern Europe thought of itself as being at the centre. All looked somewhere else for a model of how really to be advanced and modern ...' (Hobsbawm 1997: 3). The end of the Cold War made the concept of *Mitteleuropa* – 'the classic example of political programmes disguised as geography' (Hobsbawm 1997: 219) – in the sense given to it by Friedrich Naumann[8] very unattractive.

The former Czech Ambassador in Bonn, Jiři Gruša, has remarked how much he prefers the American term 'Central-East Europe' to the German term *Mitteleuropa* (Grusa 1996: 27–8). *Mitteleuropa*, in his view, is by definition a *Zwischen-Europa*, the limits of which are set by the powers surrounding it to the east and west. Eric Hobsbawm notes that 'the present government in Prague does not even wish to be called 'central-European' for fear of being contaminated by contact with the east. It insists that it belongs exclusively to the West' (Hobsbawm

1997: 3). Tendencies in Poland have been similar: Polish politicians claimed that post-Cold War Poland was part of Western Europe, putting any notion of 'middle' even further to the east. This debate is not merely about semantics – it represents the difference between self-defining and being defined by others.

Security

The possibility of violent aggression against, and military defence of, the eastern frontier, as symbolised by the confrontations over the building of the Berlin Wall in 1961, and the deployment of SS20 and Pershing missiles in the 1970s and 1980s, faded after the 1985 arrival of Gorbachev in power in the USSR. From 1989, the official security agenda for the EU countries changed, at first slowly, from planning for the possibility of massive military attack to peacekeeping, humanitarian and crisis-management tasks, specified in the Amsterdam Treaty and the 1999 Tampere Declaration. All countries, except Russia which vociferously opposed it, accepted the idea of NATO enlargement. In the words of the Estonian Foreign Minister, Toomas Hendrik Ilves:

> The consensus in the 11 applicant countries is clear. From Tallin to Ljubljana, it is accepted that NATO enlargement is a fitting conclusion to the Cold War, an integrative, unifying step in European affairs and a key-move toward guaranteeing Euro-Atlantic stability (Ilves 1997).

The objective (but not the achievement) of enlargement was to prevent confusing security boundaries in Central and Eastern Europe, thus avoiding grey zones which could imperil future stability.

Uncertainty remains about the location and the quality of the new military security frontier, and about what is to be defended against whom. The motives for opening negotiations with Estonia and Lithuania about NATO membership remained unclear. The status of Slovakia, Bulgaria and Romania has not yet been decided. One possibility is a new dividing line, further to the east than the old Iron Curtain and clearly dividing east from west. An alternative is a buffer between the EU and Russia, consisting perhaps of ex-Soviet Republics – Belarus, Ukraine, Moldova – or a wider 'grey zone'. The underlying issue is whether there will be just one frontier, or non-coinciding economic, political and security frontiers (Grabbe and Hughes 1998). Eric Hobsbawm's sombre prediction may prevail, that 'the people of central and eastern Europe will go on living in countries disappointed in their past, probably largely disappointed with their present, and uncertain about their future' (Hobsbawm 1997: 4–5).

Following the frustrating experience of Bosnia and Kosovo in the second half of the 1990s, another uncertainty emerged. The need was felt, and expressed by the 1998 Anglo-French Saint Malo declaration, for the establishment of a stronger EU security and foreign policy identity. Decisions were taken to integrate the Western European Union (WEU) into the EU and to create a European rapid reaction corps by 2003. The former NATO Secretary-General Javier Solana was appointed EU foreign and security policy chief, and combined this post with the position of Secretary-General of the WEU. The objective of the EU security and foreign policy identity remained nebulous.

There was no clarification of what to do about disorder on the eastern frontier, which took a variety of forms, commencing with wars in former Yugoslavia and in Chechnya. In addition, military materials became available on the international black market. Criminal activities and 'soft security' threats were perceived as endangering the stability of Western European societies (Algieri 1996: 204). Immigration was regarded as part of these threats (Weiner 1995: 2). Threats to cultures and ways of life became an integral part of the security field (Huysmans 1995: 61). As the military threat receded, these other threats seemed to replace it and the previously clear categories of internal and external security merged. Soft security threats were also perceived to come from the southern shore of the Mediterranean, but the eastern march remained the most important preoccupation of most of the EU countries.

Cross-border crime

From the early 1990s, crime from the east came to be represented as a major security threat. A typical newspaper report on EUROPOL suggested:

> a grim post-Cold War pattern of crime ..., with gangsters from the former Soviet bloc having a stranglehold in the West on prostitution, racketeering and the trade in stolen cars. Drugs are also pouring in from the east, with Poland now the third largest producer of amphetamines (Smart 1995).

It became a theme of the populist right, illustrated by the following outburst by the Austrian Freedom Party leader, Jörg Haider:

> We've got the Poles who concentrate on car theft. We've got the former Yugoslavs who are burglary experts. We've got the Turks

who are superbly organised in the heroin trade. And we've got the Russians who are experts in blackmail and mugging (Staunton 1999).

Crime problems were not simply a figment of the fevered imaginings of the xenophobic right and of a certain security discourse. Even EU governments geographically far removed from the eastern frontier were concerned by criminal incidents. When the Irish President, Mary McAleese, and the Irish head of government, Bertie Ahern, paid state visits to the Czech Republic and to Hungary in 1999, they brought up the issues of 'illegal drug trafficking, money-laundering and other cross-border criminal activity' (Brennock 1999, Sheridan 1999).

The increased level of crime in Eastern Europe and the former Soviet Union is symptomatic of the difficult transformation of these countries. Post-communist states were attempting, in Claus Offe's term, a 'triple transition': the simultaneous transformation of their political systems, economic systems, and boundaries and identities (Offe 1996, Ágh 1998: 49–83). In addition, the legacy of communism, where corruption and avoiding the state were part of the political culture, had created 'an environment of institutionalised illegality' (Galeotti 1995: 1). Economic decline under communism encouraged a flourishing extra-legal economy, even before the transition to market economies provided new opportunities for criminals. Eastern criminal activity did not remain an internal problem of the post-communist countries. Co-operation was established between organised criminals in post-communist states and established criminal structures in the West (Galeotti 1995: 6).

But the size of the threat of organised cross-border crime is 'a matter of judgement rather than fact' (Holmes forthcoming, Raith 1995: 8). The campaign against organised crime appears to serve as a surrogate for the Cold War enemy: 'The defeat of communism has created a "threat vacuum" that has given rise to a search for new enemies' (Esposito 1994: 19). Law enforcement agencies 'have an obvious institutional interest in painting the picture blacker than the reality' (Cullen 1997: 5). The discourse on organised and cross-border crime has undoubtedly been used by them 'to endorse the "modernization" and "professionalization" of the German police force and to legitimize the extension of its arsenal of legal investigative tools to include, for example, electronic surveillance' (von Lampe 1995: 2).[9]

A survey of crime statistics (which must be treated with caution) in Central and East European states appears to show that 'crime rates in the post-communist states have remained still considerably below those of many leading Western states' (Holmes forthcoming). But alarmist reports contribute to the image of the eastern frontier and the threat it represents. Certain categories of crime have been much publicised. Street prostitution visibly increased on the German–Polish, German–Czech, Austro-Czech and Austro-Slovak borders. In 1999 Peter Schatzer of the International Organisation for Migration (IOM) said that kidnapping and smuggling of women have become lucrative activities: 175 000 women and girls are estimated to be smuggled annually from Eastern Europe and the former Soviet Union into Western Europe.

Prague is reported by Interpol to be a centre for money laundering for the Chechnya mafia, operating in conjunction with dubious Liechtenstein-based firms. The financial centres of Geneva, Zurich, Zug and Lugano in Switzerland are used by eastern criminals, according to a report by the Federal Police Office in Berne, for money laundering. Bratislava, only 60 km from Vienna, is alleged to be both a centre for the 'car-smuggling mafia', and organised drug-trafficking, profiting from the substantial price difference between the two cities (Berger 1997). Large drug depots exist in the Slovak Republic, set up by ethnic Albanian and Turkish trafficking gangs, according to reports by the German *Bundeskriminalamt* (BKA). Poland has become a major drug manufacturing country for laboratory-based drugs, particularly for amphetamines.

Illegal trade – stolen goods, drugs, cigarettes, alcohol – has dramatically increased since 1989. In Poland, 3000 stolen cars were seized in 1995, representing a value of $37 million. The record year concerning cars stolen in Germany and illegally smuggled over the border to Poland was 1993 (144 000 cars). The number has declined to an estimated 90 000 in 1999 (Urban 1999). There is evidence of illegal trade in arms and weaponry, and the possible smuggling of nuclear substances, across the former Iron Curtain was deemed possible; customs officers at the German border have found quantities of up to 1000 rounds of ammunition, anti-tank weapons, and hand grenades, often in small cars (Bauer and Kauper interviews).[10]

A common crime is passport and document forgery. In 1995, 1319 false passports were confiscated at the Polish–German border, 400 false visas and 500 other forged travel documents. In 1997, German border police confiscated 1700 false passports at the Polish border. The intractable problem is genuine documents – stolen passports, passports corruptly issued under false names and passports sold to potential illegal migrants. These are hard to identify, even when checked against the Schengen data base. Human trafficking syndicates, operating from Russia, Georgia, Armenia and Asian countries, use the infrastructure of Red Army barracks, former Intourist agencies and the latest navigation technology to facilitate clandestine migration (Raith 1995: 19, Severin 1997). The tightening of the German asylum laws in 1993 made refugees turn to human smuggling organisations. The latter charge a modest £70, for a tip about where to cross the frontier, to £15 000 per individual, for a complete package, including false identity papers, and travel from place of origin to final destination (Schwennicke 1997, Loose 1998). Tightening border controls, according to Peter Schatzer (IOM), increases the price exacted by the traffickers and increases their propensity to violence (Blechschmidt 1999).

According to the German Ministry of the Interior, German border guards intervened in 1780 cases of human trafficking in the first half of 1999 – an increase of 50 per cent against the previous year. Two-thirds of these were concentrated on the borders with Austria and the Czech Republic. During the same period of time, German border authorities arrested 18 754 illegal migrants (which is an increase of 8 per cent against the same period of the previous year, and smuggling gangs have been brought to trial (Pfeiffer 1999). Between January and September 1998, more than 650 *Schleuser* (human traffickers) were arrested at the Czech–German border (Mrkvica interview). On the Polish–German border, the activities of traffickers frequently result in casualties. Many would-be migrants drown in the Oder and Neisse rivers, led by their smugglers to remote river banks and places with dangerous currents, because these are the least policed sectors of the border (Kaltenborn 1997, Lesch 1998).

Human trafficking and drug smuggling are often done by the same gangs; passport forgery and human smuggling are clearly connected. But there has been a tendency to link all kinds of cross-border crime to issues of migration, even in official policy documents. In a 1998 strategy paper about the Geneva Convention, drafted by the Austrian presidency of the EU but withdrawn after strong criticism, the refugee problem was grouped with 'illegal migration', and migration policy was explicitly linked with policies against organised crime (Prantl 1998). As Achim Hildebrandt of the German Project Group on Visa Harmonisation in the Ministry of the Interior stated, 'the migrant is not the criminal; he or she is the victim of crime'.[11]

Refugees and immigrants

In 1999 Amnesty International pointed out that the EU received 16.5 per cent of the world's 16.5 million refugees and displaced persons in 1998. Even when crises arise in Europe, the EU is not faced with massive influxes. For example of the 880 000 persons displaced from Kosovo, only some 100 000 applied for asylum outside the region, and most of them returned after NATO military action succeeded.[12] In 1998, fewer than 30 000 persons were granted asylum in EU member states. Dennis McNamara, director of the international protection division of the United Nations Commission for Refugees, said that 'the number of refugees in the whole of Europe was about the same as the number in one camp in Tanzania' (Coulter 1998).

In 1992, Germany received around 80 per cent of all asylum seekers of all EU member states. After the tightening of asylum laws in 1993, Germany experienced a rapid fall in numbers as shown in Table 6.1. In addition, about 2.5 million ethnic German *Aussiedler* have arrived since 1987 from the former Soviet Union.[13] Yet, the data for 1997 indicate that more foreigners left the country than entered it – 615 000 new arrivals were outnumbered by 637 000 who left.

Nonetheless, mass migration of refugees and economic migrants from the east is widely seen as threatening 'social cohesion, international solidarity, and peace' (Widgren 1990: 749). Even legal labour migration from new members in an enlarged EU, or facilitated by changes in nationality laws, has caused moral panics, particularly among conservative politicians in Germany. The Christian Democrats have therefore demanded that freedom of movement should only be introduced for new EU members, at the earliest, in 2015. The Bavarian government encouraged these fears by stating that they expected another 2 million ethnic Germans from the former Soviet Union to exercise their right to come to Germany (*Süddeutsche Zeitung* 9 January 1999), a figure which seems grossly exaggerated. Even the Social Democratic Chancellor

Table 6.1

Year	No. of asylum seekers
1989	121 318
1991	256 112
1992	438 191
1994	127 210
1995	127 937
1996	116 367
1997	104 353
1998	98 644
1999	95 113

Source: German Federal Ministry of the Interior.

Schröder declared, shortly after his election in 1998, that 'the limit of Germany's tolerance of immigration has been surpassed'.

The debate about the changes of citizenship laws proposed by the new German SPD–Green coalition government at the beginning of 1999, and especially the possibility of dual citizenship, produced highly speculative figures of a massive influx of relatives of foreigners with dual citizenship, in particular from Turkey. Politicians of the Bavarian CSU forecast up to 600 000 additional immigrants. Yet, as Klaus Barwig shows, this was a 'horror scenario' without any foundation. He calculated that, had the reform succeeded, the number of relatives benefiting from it would be closer to 4000.

Fear of labour migration in an enlarged EU is not just a theme of the German right. In the Austrian borderlands, there is a reluctance to welcome Hungary into the EU:

> Many Austrians actively oppose it, especially those living in border regions such as Burgenland, in the belief that free labour migration will endanger their jobs and an increased flow of refugees put pressure on already stretched Austrian capacity to receive the 500 000 or so people they have absorbed in recent years (Gillespie 1999a).

The EU commissioner in charge of enlargement, Günter Verheugen who, as an MP, represented a German constituency bordering on the Czech Republic, said that he was conscious of caution, even scepticism, of Germans living near the border about the opening of this frontier (Bergdoll and Oldag 1999). These anxieties are not diminished by the historical fact that the widely predicted 'wave' of labour migration, when Spain and Portugal joined the EU in the early 1980s, did not materialise.

Anxieties about waves of immigrants are a cyclical phenomenon which started in the early 1990s, partly encouraged by the declining USSR, which warned the EC Commission in 1991 of the possibility of 7 million migrants, in order to get aid from the West. Alarmist reports then declined, only to revive again in the last years of the decade. In August 1998, unidentified secret services were warning of 2.5 to 3 million potential migrants in Russia, Belarus and the Ukraine (Scherer 1998). However, a recent survey, published in January 1999 and conducted in all the major sender countries in Eastern Europe by the European Observatory for Migrations, contradicted these prognostications, suggesting that though the propensity to emigrate is high, potential immigrants want to go to the US, Canada, Australia and New Zealand rather than to the EU.

Nevertheless, populist statements of politicians and media coverage of illegal migration have effects which endanger the authority of the state, such as, in 1998, 'civic guards' on the German side of the German–Polish border who patrol the border zone looking for clandestine immigrants. But clandestine migration is not a figment of the imagination – it constitutes a genuine problem. On the German–Czech border, 43 000 undocumented immigrants were detected in 1993; the figure then declined to 19 000 in 1995, rising again to 32 000 in 1997 (out of 210 million legal crossings in 1997).[14]

Despite the popular appeal of anti-immigrant sentiment, in 1999 a more positive approach to immigrants was proposed in France by former neo-Gaullist Prime Minister Alain Juppé and by well-informed German circles. Herwig Birg, the Director of the Institute of Demographic Research and Social Policy at the University of Bielefeld, has argued that Germany 'has no longer any choice whether or not it wants to be an immigration country'. Due to low birth rates, the population of West Germany would fall between 1990 and 2050 from 64 to 39 million, and that of East Germany from 16 to 9 million – if there was not permanent immigration. The situation in other EU countries is similar. The reproduction rate of 2.1 children per family is needed for a stable population, in the UK it is 1.7, and in Spain only 1.15. Thus, the issue of immigration is not just an issue of human rights. There are compelling economic and demographic reasons for a regulated, yet open and positive policy on immigration (Leonard 1999).

Environmental hazards

The EU's eastern frontier is an environmental frontier because it marks the limits of relatively strict controls on pollution. Although the candidate members are adopting the EU's environmental norms, important problems remain unresolved for economic reasons. Further east problems are much worse. The Finnish President Marrti Ahtisaari said (*Financial Times* 25 November 1997) that the threat from Russian pollution was his greatest security problem and added: 'I would be much happier if I could clean up the Baltic and swim in the sea than join NATO.' He complained that 70–80 per cent of Baltic Sea pollution was created by St Petersburg and that there was an urgent need to clean up the Russian military and civil nuclear facilities.

In the north, environmental problems are particularly pressing in the borderlands between the environmentally conscious Nordic countries and Russia. The Kola peninsula has been used as a nuclear dump by the Soviet Union and become the most nuclear-contaminated area of the world: 'Rusting nuclear submarines, dilapidated nuclear power stations and enormous toxin emissions by antediluvian industrial plant pose a threat to northern Europe well beyond Russia's borders' (Gamillscheg 1999). The 1996 arrest on espionage charges of the Russian former officer, Alexander Nikitin, for his collaboration with the Norwegian ecological organisation, Belluna, on the risks of nuclear pollution in the Sea of Murmansk, suggested that very limited co-operation would be forthcoming from Russia.[15] The Barents Council, formed in 1993, has repeatedly voiced its concern about the increasing threat of nuclear pollution on the Kola peninsula, both as a health threat in itself and a potential disaster for the fish industry (Blake et al. 1997, Stokke and Tunander 1994).

Poor security standards in eastern nuclear power stations resulted in the notorious 1986 Chernobyl accident, whose damaging effects were felt as far away as the UK. But below-standard security standards in nuclear installations can be found across East Central Europe (Auffermann 1992: 43). Throughout the 1990s, the Central and Eastern European states have made efforts to raise environmental awareness and standards. Poland initiated a National Environmental Policy in 1991. The Czech environment ministry announced in April 1998 that it would cost $15 billion to achieve EU standards in the environmental sector (Francis 1999: 178–9). Environmentally sensitive governments, and non-governmental organisations, within the EU remain highly critical of the actions of East Central European governments.

When the Slovak nuclear power plant at Mochovce, 100 km from the Austrian border, was connected to the grid in June 1998, the Austrian Chancellor Viktor Klima spoke of 'an extremely irresponsible and unfriendly act' (*Süddeutsche Zeitung* 9 June 1998). The Austrians were even more annoyed that promises were not honoured to shut down the obsolescent plant at Bohunice (near Bratislava), described as one of the most dangerous nuclear power stations in the world. Nonetheless, the Austrian government declared before the 1999 Helsinki summit that it would not veto accession negotiations, despite the continuing operation of Soviet-built nuclear reactors in most of the countries concerned, and reports of radioactive ash being dumped on open tips.

The level of air pollution in the newly democratised states[16] has posed a threat to health, has contributed to the contamination of forests,[17] soil and underground water in neighbouring countries. Border rivers have been badly polluted by untreated sewage and emissions from the chemical industry. The almost landlocked and shallow

Baltic Sea also suffered from the heavily industrialised, oil-shale mining regions in north-east Estonia and the aluminium industry of Saldus in Latvia. Cleaning the rivers and the Baltic requires large financial resources and can only be achieved by close East–West co-operation (Hilz 1998: 132–5).

River pollution usually raises more local concerns but major rivers can cause international tensions. Austria, Slovakia and Hungary have had a long-lasting dispute about the use of the Danube for energy generation – both as a reservoir of water power and as provider of potential sites for nuclear power stations (Wösendorfer 1997). One of the main problems has been the Gabcikovo–Nagymaros hydroelectric project on the Danube which has caused serious conflict between Slovakia and Hungary, as Hungary cancelled its part in the partnership project, while Slovakia finished the Gabcikovo dam in 1992, allegedly violating the boundary agreement between the two countries of 1947 (Gerner 1997: 156).

Strategies

All EU member governments support the principle of EU eastern enlargement, but they are aware that the interests of some of their citizens could be adversely affected. Also, member states with different foreign policy and economic interests developed somewhat different strategies with regard to the countries on the eastern frontier. Italy developed a Central European Initiative based on its close relationship with the western Republics of the former Yugoslavia and Hungary, which eventually extended as far as Poland (Newton and Walsh 1999: 236–7). Britain was consistently an enthusiast for eastern expansion of the EC/EU in order, so its partners suspected, to slow the pace of integration and turn the EU into a loose association of states (Mannin 1999b: 35). The Nordic countries focused on the development of a Baltic partnership, involving Russia as a partner (Platzöder and Verlaan 1997).

Finland went the furthest in engaging Russia as a partner on practical projects. The 1999 Finnish EU presidency proposed improved cross-border links, assisted by EU finance, between Finland and Russia, enhancing Finland's role as the 'gateway to Russia'. These include a gas pipeline from Russia via Finland, a motorway linking Helsinki, St Petersburg and Moscow, as well as upgrading roads from Moscow to Berlin and Paris. Important upgrading of the main rail link between Russia and Finland was also proposed.

Germany and France gave priority to eastern enlargement as the proper response to the new post-communist situation, whilst insisting that further moves towards integration, such as the introduction of the common currency and setting up the European Central Bank, should take place at the same time. Germany, in particular, urged that the applicant states, as soon as possible, be given responsibilities in migration and crime control. This transformed the eastern frontier into an extended zone of influence, with neighbours sharing the burden of controlling access to the EU. France and Italy tried to balance the preoccupation of the EU with its eastern frontier by emphasising the importance of their southern perimeter, and launched the Euromed partnership (see Chapter 4). Most of these strategies were designed to increase openness of frontiers for trade and communication but not for migrants.

Resources for border crossings

Opening of frontiers required increased investment on roads, railways, checkpoints and law enforcement personnel. At the eastern borders of Germany there is a higher concentration of border police than at any other border of Europe – 6500 border guards and a further 1500 unskilled semi-official 'auxiliaries'. Surveillance technique is state of the art, and highly expensive. One infrared nightvision instrument costs about £70 000 and, in 1997, 100 of these were in use (Rippert 1998: 98). Following German unification, the manpower of the *Bundesgrenzschutz* (BGS) was nearly doubled between 1989 and 1997, from 24 982 to 40 100 border guards; the budget of the BGS rose in the same period from £0.43 bn to £0.96 bn.[18]

When the eastern frontier was opened for the movement of persons, the border posts and crossing-points could not cope with the traffic (Grimm 1995: 10). Increased trade and a rapid increase in border crossings brought with them long waiting times and queues.[19] Transport links – roads and rail – had to be modernised, border crossings upgraded and new ones built.[20] Parallel moves were made by the EU's eastern neighbours. In Poland in 1991, border police replaced the army, with a fundamental change of attitude towards border control. In the Euregio Neiße, a German–Polish Commission was formed, with INTERREG II support, to develop plans for a common border crossing near Görlitz, a bridge-crossing near Podrosche-Przewoz. Another priority was the development of public transport across the frontier (AEBR/LACE 1993: 8).

At the German–Czech frontier traffic increased explosively. While in 1989 3.5 million vehicles crossed this border, the figure had reached

77 million by 1995. Due to restrictive planning laws, it took the German side almost a decade to complete upgrading its border posts (Bauer and Kauper interviews). Immediately after the opening of the border, the Czech Republic started a programme of renovating and enlarging border crossings along the 810 km-long frontier with Germany, including a motorway and 38 minor cross-border roads, providing alternatives for pedestrians and cars (*Kleiner Grenzverkehr*). Some have been restricted to 'pedestrians only' crossings (Mrkvica and Schwarz interviews).

The net effect of improvement of transport links and strengthened controls at crossing points is hard to establish. Even hardliners – like the former German Minister of the Interior, Manfred Kanther – admit that there are limits to the effectiveness of frontier controls. But the evaluation of investment in law enforcement at the EU eastern border crossings faces similar problems to value for money assessments as all forms of policing. The greater the manpower and technology deployed, the more crimes and offences discovered. The impact on the 'true' rate is not a matter of objective analysis of statistics but of judgement.

Export of Schengen

The European Commission's Task Force on Enlargement screens the legal provisions and practical measures taken by the six candidate countries. Although this process involves justice and home affairs as a whole, particular emphasis has been laid on matters relating to the Schengen *acquis*. These include asylum procedures, external border management, immigration controls, repression of organised crime, drug trafficking and terrorism, and police, customs and judicial co-operation. The extent to which EU countries are willing to relax controls on their present eastern external border depends on the willingness of the candidate countries to impose Schengen norms at their eastern borders. Pressure from the EU can take a direct and insistent form. EU Commissioner Hans von Broek, for example, told the Polish government that the country's chances of joining the EU depended a great deal on how well it could police its borders (*Die Welt* 17 February 1998). The candidate states are thus co-opted into the EU for this purpose.

Since 1991, readmission treaties have been signed between Schengen states and the first-tier candidate countries, and between the latter and almost all states in the east and south-east: Bulgaria, Ukraine, Moldova, Belarus and Russia. All applicant states have been designated as 'safe havens', so that asylum seekers approaching the EU from their territories are being sent back immediately. The states closer to the countries of origin of the migrants are being turned into frontier guards, although this does not always work. Difficulties arise in establishing with certainty whether clandestine immigrants travelled, for example, to Germany from Poland, or from another country, because they destroy identity papers and travel documentation. Despite difficulties, the strengthening of Poland's eastern frontier is seen – particularly in Germany – as the attempt to erect an obstacle to illegal migration and illegal trade from east to west.[21]

The export of Schengen standards to the eastern neighbours of the EU has caused unease among the candidate states. This is partly because they did not participate in the negotiation of the Schengen accords, nor the development of the Schengen system, nor its incorporation into the structures of the EU (Gasperlin 1997). But the main reason is that, seen from East Central Europe, the Schengen frontier threatened to become a new Iron Curtain, a rigorously controlled frontier which separated those within the system from those without. Although the Iron Curtain analogy is an exaggeration, the imposition of tight controls has important symbolic, psychological and practical effects. This new line of separation initially affected countries negotiating for membership of the EU.

Hungary and Slovenia were the two most offended because prior to the full implementation of Schengen the Austrian–Hungarian and the Slovene–Italian borders had been relatively open and, at least for the states directly concerned, relatively problem free.[22] In 1997, a trial run of the application of Schengen norms to border controls on these borders caused local indignation and disruption (Richter-Malabotta 1998: 65–6). When the controls were instituted in 1998, modifications had been made for local traffic (Leo 1998) and, although not publicly admitted, some flexibility is allowed in the interpretation of Schengen rules. But there is a bitter sense of exclusion among the elites in countries further east, such as Romania and Bulgaria, often focused on the bureaucratic process of acquiring visas. Members of these elites claim that this impedes the preparation of these countries for future EU membership.

All candidate countries perceive some difficulties with applying Schengen norms in the short term. The Czech Republic, in January 1998, listed 12 countries – including the Ukraine, Russia and Belarus – for which it would introduce visa requirements, but had not acted upon it by the end of 1999 because of the serious administrative problems of issuing visas (Mrkvica interview). Poland introduced a new aliens law to conform with these norms at the beginning of 1998 (Hilz 1998: 137), which led to protests and blocking of several border crossings by Russia. In east Poland, more than 1000 local Polish traders rallied against the 'economic catastrophe' caused by tighter border controls. There was a 30 per cent fall in trading at Warsaw's economically important 'Russian bazaar', after the introduction of the new aliens' law and the new visa regime. The informal export trade is estimated to earn Poland £5.9 bn per annum (Traynor 1998).

The Estonian–Russian border remains militarised with barbed wire and watchtowers, reminiscent of the Iron Curtain. These fortifications were put in place unilaterally by the Russians, partly because Estonia claimed a strip of territory which had been annexed by Russia (a claim dropped at EU insistence). Tension on this border, based on the exclusion of Russophones from Estonian citizenship, is increased by the fact that the Russian border region of Pskov returned, in the 1990s, an ultranationalist governor of Zhirinovsky's LDPR party as regional governor; this party calls for the restoration of the Soviet borders. The Estonian government tolerates a tightly controlled frontier with Russia, it does not want a closed border regime with the other Baltic states – Latvia and Lithuania.

The main problem for the first tier of candidate countries is lack of effective co-operation with their neighbours to the east, without which it is impossible to have efficient control of the border. Even at the Slovak–Austrian border post of Bratislava/Berg, during the Meciar administration, only the commander on the Slovak side spoke German, none of the Austrians Slovak. Communication was poor and, as a rule, conducted through interpreters. Co-operation between Austria and Slovakia was virtually at a standstill because of tense bilateral relations between the two governments for political, environmental and human rights reasons. Poland faces much greater difficulties with Belarus and Ukraine. When Ukrainian frontier guards temporarily ceased to receive their salaries in 1997, they were alleged to recoup the money by assisting illegal migrants to cross the frontier. Poland nevertheless attempts a delicate balancing act – stabilising relations and trying to control the border (since 1991, more than 80 000 undocumented immigrants have been arrested at the Ukrainian border alone), and avoiding total closure towards the east (Gerner 1997: 153).

Minority problems (600 000 Hungarians live in Slovakia, 2.7 million in Romania[23]) are seen as potentially exacerbated by new dividing Schengen frontiers (Czaban 1999: 289–90). A Polish minority of perhaps 120 000 is in Ukraine, in and around Lvov. The most potentially dangerous minority problems are the Russian-speaking minorities in Estonia and Latvia. Cutting these off from Russia by a Schengen frontier could incite Russian reprisals. A hardened frontier, in these cases, may cause serious political conflicts, and possibly further migratory pressure. Other general problems of introducing tight controls on persons and inspection of all vehicles is that they impose costs, disrupt local markets, inhibit close transfrontier social relations and represent a symbolic exclusion.

Police co-operation

Early in the 1990s France, Germany and the UK all had bilateral programmes of assistance in police matters and all complained about insufficient information about what each other were doing. Some of the early programmes of assistance, such as the UK's 'know how' programme, have been phased out. EU police forces have subsequently developed practical bilateral co-operation across the eastern frontier and have been keeping each other informed; the practice of posting police liaison officers to the East Central European countries has become standard practice.[24] Initiatives involving neighbouring countries are particularly important.

In 1994, a tripartite co-operation of border guards was initiated between Finland, Russia and Estonia, subsequently extended to Sweden, which is envisaged to encompass the entire Baltic region (Veijalainen 1998: 102). Co-operation between border police at the German–Polish and the German–Czech borders has made progress, with permanent exchange of notes, common training and daily communication. After every shift in the border control points, there is an exchange of information between the Polish and the German side. This co-operation was put on a more secure legal basis in April 1995, when the Treaty of Co-operation between police and border police in the German–Polish borderlands was signed by the two governments. At the Austro-Slovak, Austro-Hungarian and Italian–Slovene frontiers, the quality of co-operation is less good, but systematic cross-border contacts are now established.

The EU itself has, until recently, had a low profile because of its lack of legal competence in policing matters, and the recent establishment, on an intergovernmental basis, of a semi-operational role for EUROPOL.[25] The efforts at police co-operation are now concentrated on education and training, police equipment, encouraging involvement of private sector actors in law enforcement, and co-ordination of police operations in investigating serious crime. In 1996, the European

Commission started to sponsor seminars and a placement scheme for EU border police (Molle 1996). In October 1999, the European Commission announced the launch of a 4.5 million euro programme to help Central and Eastern European countries to combat drug trafficking, money laundering, car theft and other crimes. This programme involves collaboration with the Association of European Police Colleges (AEPC) in Budapest in the 'Curriculum' project – to improve police training standards in the applicant countries – which commenced in March 1999 and is to assist candidate states in their preparation for accession.[26]

Seminars on detecting fraudulent documents, drugs and stolen works of art and corruption are being held under various auspices, including Interpol and national police training institutions and specialist law enforcement agencies. An example is the College for Police Training in Rothenburg, Saxony, holding multinational seminars on topics like car smuggling or transnational fraud (Hilz 1998: 141). In 1995, the International Law Enforcement Academy (ILEA) was founded in Budapest, offering eight-week courses for law enforcement agents from Hungary and other East Central European states, concentrating on combating terrorism, drug-related crime and economic crime. Most of the candidate members are also lacking in police equipment, especially in scanning devices, detection of fraudulent documents and drug detection procedures. Further east the situation is worse, with sometimes a chronic lack of police vehicles. These technical deficiencies are compounded by the vulnerability of all poorly paid police forces to corruption.

Further to the east co-operation is intermittent and marked by inefficiency, corruption and political interference. Poland's eastern neighbours do not co-operate. 'Chaos and corruption' was one reporter's verdict (*Süddeutsche Zeitung* 20 August 1998), summing up the situation at the frontiers between Poland and Kaliningrad (Russia) and between Lithuania, Belarus and the Ukraine. As with the virtual lack of co-operation on Greece's northern frontier with Albania, there is no technical solution to the problems. They can only be ameliorated by economic and social development in the countries concerned.

Despite the difficulties, some successes in operational co-operation are reported. International police co-ordination along the so-called 'Balkan route' has resulted in large-scale seizure of heroin in 1998: 8112 kg, an increase of 17.3 per cent over 1997. Along the route, 1736 alleged drug-traffickers were apprehended in 1998, compared with 1482 in 1997. Seizure of hard drugs was up 3 per cent from 1997 to 1998, Ecstasy pills

35 per cent, and the volume of intercepted hashish and marijuana doubled. It is impossible to establish whether the increases represented improvements in policing or reflected increased trafficking.

Co-operation between local and regional authorities

The establishment of co-operative structures across formerly closed frontiers is a profound change in the character and the perceptions of these frontiers. But this is difficult to achieve for political, social and constitutional reasons. The lack of party-political and institutional stability on the eastern side of the external frontier is compounded by a political culture in which democratic norms have not been internalised. A 'participant political culture', necessary for transfrontier co-operation, is only slowly emerging. Constitutional differences – and their manifestations in administrative and local government structures – play a similar, but even more divisive, role to that found in the EU. States on the western side of the frontier are federal (Austria or Germany) or decentralised, with strong regional structures (Finland or Italy), while the new democracies are trying to build a strong central state, thought necessary to rebuild their countries after communism. Faced with these difficulties, the experiments in transfrontier co-operation have been, of necessity, flexible. Polish communities and municipalities, for example, have the right to opt in or out of the agreements for transfrontier co-operation (Heffner 1998: 61).

Jutta Seidel of the State Chancellery of the Free State of Saxony, speaking about her experience in organising transfrontier co-operation between Saxony and Poland, and Saxony and the Czech Republic, emphasised the initial difficulties, mainly resulting from administrative centralisation in the Czech and Polish Republics. According to Frau Seidel, it took years to create trust and willingness in Warsaw and Prague to allow their western border regions a degree of autonomy to allow them to negotiate directly with their German counterparts (Seidel interview).

While the 'pooling' of sovereignty has been widely accepted in the West, newly regained independence has made sovereignty as an idea more precious for the eastern neighbours (Czachór 1998: 37–43). Close co-operation in the borderlands has been viewed in Prague and Warsaw as an erosion of territorial sovereignty and a threat to national and cultural identity.[27] In particular, it has been considered as a means of expanding German influence. Although there has been a subsequent modification of opinion, in June 1993, Václav Klaus called the Euroregions 'a German attempt at "creeping" reconquest of the

Sudetenland' (Gerner 1997: 157). This runs counter to an underlying motive in East Central Europe of wanting EU membership as a tool to dilute or contain German influence in Central Europe.

Euroregions have become a general feature of the eastern frontier (see Map 6.2) – set up from the Finno-Russian border to Austria, Slovakia and Hungary (Bort 1996). They now range from Kuhmo-Kostamuksha (1992) on the Finnish–Russian border (Tikkanen and Käkönen 1997), the Euroregion named Baltyk, involving Poland, Lithuania, Latvia, Kaliningrad, Bornholm (Denmark) and Sweden (1998),[28] and the German–Polish border region with the Euregios of Neisse–Nysa–Nisa, founded in Zittau in 1991,[29] Spree–Neisse–Bober (1993),[30] Pro Europa Viadrina (1993)[31] and Pomerania (1995),[32] the three Euregios on the German–Czech border – Elbe–Labe (1992), Erzgebirge (1992), Egrensis (Jurczek 1997, Heberlein 1996, Jerábek 1998: 90) – to Sumova/Bayerischer Wald/Mühlviertel in the borderlands of Germany, the Czech Republic and Austria (Jerábek 1998: 90), and the Businesspark Heiligenberg-Szentgotthárd at the Austro-Hungarian border. Further south, at the Slovene frontiers, cross-border co-operation was already well established through the *Arbeitsgemeinschaft Alpenländer* (see Chapter 3).

The project of transfrontier co-operation is spreading even further east, as the foundation of the first exclusively Eastern European Euroregion, the Carpathian Euroregion, in February 1993 indicates (Kurcz 1999: 63). Under the guidance (and financial aid) of the Institute of East–West Studies in New York, the foreign ministers of Hungary, Poland, Slovakia and Ukraine, representing around a dozen regions and a population of over 100 million people, signed the agreement on transfrontier co-operation. Since the break-up of the area in different nation states in the aftermath of the First World War, the number of road and rail links has shrunk. Transport and telecommunication are priority areas for co-operation (Illés 1996, Gerner 1997: 156–7). The Carpathian Euroregion is an example of macro-regional co-operation, such as the Baltic Sea co-operation or the ARGE Donauländer, which cover areas larger than some of the member states of the EU (Wösendorfer 1997). Also in the future eastern borderlands of an enlarged EU, Euroregions have been created between the Czech Republic and Poland (Euroregion Glacensis, 1996) at the Bug, in the Tatra, and around Niemen/Neman/Nemunas[33] (Neubauer 1997), as well as in the borders between Romania and Moldova (Euroregion Low, 1998).

The ostensible purposes of transfrontier regionalism in the eastern borderlands are threefold (Bort 1996: 99–100):

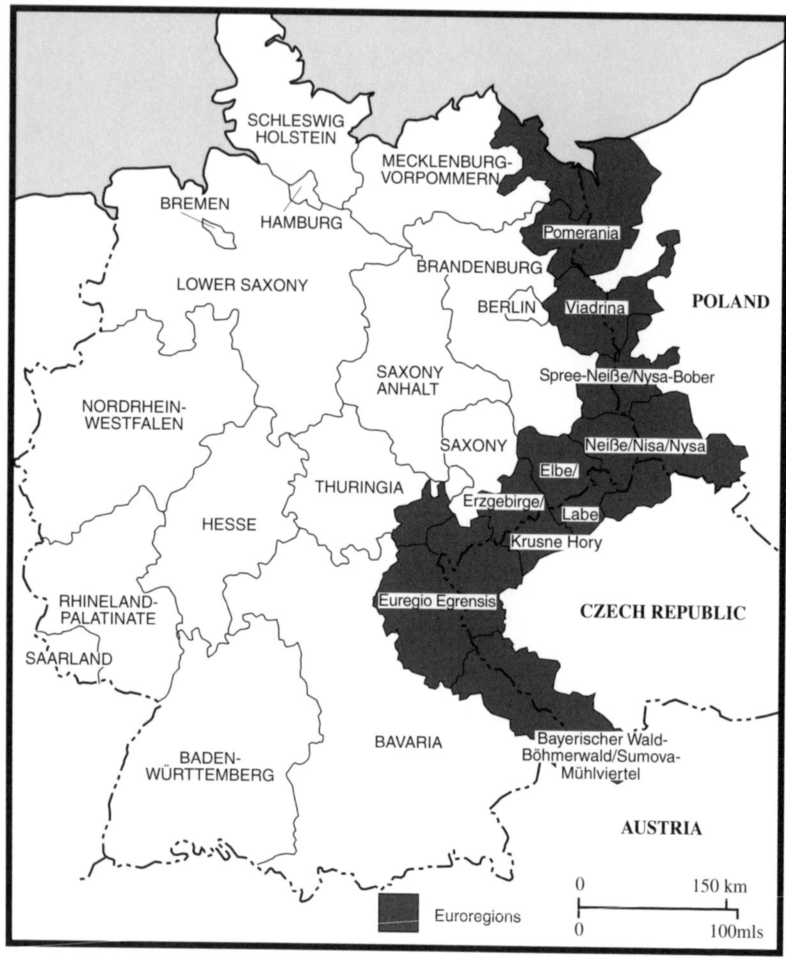

Map 6.2   Euroregions on the eastern frontier of the EU

- economic co-operation – investment in infrastructure, technology transfer, co-ordinated planning, optimising the use of resources and European funds, and making the border more permeable for trans-frontier workers
- the environment,[34] focusing on sustainable development and tourism[35]
- cultural exchange, based on common traditions, education and communication, forging, or reviving, a common regional identity[36]

Wherever possible, Euroregions are linked to common cultural and historical experience[37] but, primarily, they are pragmatic associations for economic development. They are funded by the EU's INTERREG and PHARE/CBC programmes. A key role in giving impetus to the Euroregions is often played by split or twin towns along the eastern frontier, from Frankfurt/Oder and Slubice through Guben/Gubin and Görlitz/Zgoralec on the German–Polish frontier (Horn 1997, Neuss et al. 1998, Jajesniak and Stoklosa 1999) to Gorizia and Nova Gorica (Strassoldo 1999) and Trieste and Koper (Richter-Malabotta 1998: 59–65) on the Italian–Slovene border (Skok 1998).

The published objectives of transfrontier regions are impressive and ambitious. An example is the Euroregion on the German–Polish frontier, Pro Europa Viadrina, initiated in 1993 by Frankfurt an der Oder, Eisenhüttenstadt, four German counties and two Polish community associations. Beneath general objectives of improvement in living standards and economic performance, and the promotion of European integration by creating an integrated transboundary region, 6 primary objectives and 27 individual objectives are listed. Neither the elaborate nature of the mechanisms for consultation nor the policy areas covered by formal agreements give an accurate picture of the success of co-operation. In general, the evidence about the Euroregions on the eastern frontier of Germany suggest a general lack of progress in fulfilling objectives (Lepesant 1996).[38]

Economic inequality is the single most important obstacle to the flourishing of transfrontier co-operation. Within the EU, especially along the German frontiers, there was a rough approximation of levels of economic development when authorities started collaborating across their borders. Although the eastern borderlands of the Federal Republic of Germany suffered – and continue to suffer[39] – from their peripheral location (Neuss et al. 1998: 160), the eastern frontier of the EU became, before 1989, a profound economic divide which left a legacy of extreme economic inequality. This legacy has four effects which hinder transfrontier co-operation. First, the amount of money the eastern partners can contribute to joint projects is minimal, unless there are grants from EU programmes or other western sources. Second, and partly as a consequence of the first, countries bordering the EU to the east have anxieties about economic and political subordination to the western partners. Third, complex financial procedures, involving the EU and central governments, lead to long delays, from application to actual payment of grants, and to disillusionment in the frontier regions (Kennard 1997: 56–7). Fourth, central governments and other regions in the Central and Eastern European countries sometimes object to the regions bordering on the EU being privileged by cross-border initiatives and subsidies, over regions in the interior in even greater need of economic development. By challenging state central-ism, these apparently privileged western frontier regions can cause per-ceptions of threats to the geographical integrity of the state itself (Dauderstädt 1996).

A second difficulty in the way of co-operation is that the present eastern frontier of the EU is a distinctive language barrier, which makes cross-border communication difficult. A survey in the Czech border-lands found 41 per cent of the respondents quoting the language barrier as the biggest obstacle obstructing improved cross-border co-operation (Jerábek 1998: 95–6).[40] Forced population movements during and after the Second World War meant that, on the Finno-Russian border, the Finnish-speaking Karelians were mostly resettled in Finland. Along parts of the Polish–German border incomers predomi-nate on both sides of the frontier: on the Polish side, eastern Poles were resettled from areas annexed by the USSR; and on the eastern front of the former GDR, Germans from Pomerania and East Prussia (which Germany lost to Poland and the Soviet Union after the war) found refuge. The Sudeten Germans were expelled by Czechoslovakia follow-ing the Beneš decrees (Brandes 1995: 61–3); large numbers of ethnic Germans were driven out of Hungary, Romania and Yugoslavia after the war. The political frontiers are therefore more clearly functioning as language frontiers than they were in 1939. Moreover, incentives to learn the neighbouring languages are asymmetrical; Poles and Czechs learn German (because there is an economic advantage), but very few Germans or Austrians learn Polish, Czech, Slovakian or Hungarian, let alone the Slavic languages of the Balkans.[41]

Nationalist sentiment is another factor which hinders transfrontier co-operation. Anti-Polish attitudes are evident in the borderlands of the former GDR. There are fears, especially among the older generation of Poles and Czechs, partly fuelled by memories of the war, partly by long years of anti-capitalist propaganda, of western expansion and domination. Surveys in the borderlands show that these xenophobic feelings may diminish through closer contact and interaction, but this is not inevitable (Heffner 1998: 65).[42]

More positively, transfrontier co-operation is now seen as a resilient development and survives periods of stress in high politics and diplomatic relations. For example, in the German–Czech borderlands co-operation continued despite disagreements between the countries on other matters. Difficult negotiations between Germany and the Czech Republic took place about the property of, and compensation for, the Sudeten Germans prior to the accord of January 1997 (Handl 1998, Kopstein 1998). Nonetheless, co-operation developed contemporaneously between the Technical University of Chemnitz and the West Bohemian University of Pilsen, which both recruit a large percentage of their students from the border regions. The universities are considered as 'two poles of cross-border co-operation' (Doukupil 1998: 87) in the German–Czech borderlands.[43] It prospered despite the unfavourable general political climate.

In the borderlands, any functional change of frontiers is felt immediately, and there is an awareness of the difficulties of transfrontier co-operation (Kräfke et al. 1997). Overall, cross-border co-operation along the eastern frontier is evaluated positively, as enhancing communications and collaboration, and contributing to stability (Machowicz 1997, Weissman 1997, Gasperlin 1997, Richter-Malabotta 1998, Leo 1998, Skok 1998, Roch 1999). For example, 56 per cent of respondents in a poll in the German–Czech borderlands, saw the role of the Elbe–Labe Euroregion as positive for the development of German–Czech relations; 54 per cent expect the intensity of co-operation to increase, because it was beneficial for mutual economic development (Jerabek 1998: 97–9). Despite some German impatience, commentators thought that remarkable progress had been achieved in a relatively short time (Jaedicke and Schwab 1999: 41, Grimm 1995: 13).

Cross-border co-operation is also seen as a major contribution towards solving, or at least easing, minority problems:

The integration of transportation and communication systems, common efforts for environment protection and cooperation in trade and education, etc., etc. facilitate the contacts among the members of the national minorities separated by the borders. It relieves the burden of being separated and belonging to different national states and, by promoting civic activities and associations on both sides of the border, it solves the conflicts of dual loyalty. These regional integrations ... accelerate local socio-economic development and make the national borders transparent for different kinds of minorities without changing the national borders and creating new frustrated minorities (Ágh 1998: 209).

Conclusion

The implementation of Schengen, the accession process of Central European states to the EU, and the establishment of Euroregions, create an ambiguous situation on the EU's eastern frontier. It is a frontier with elements of both openness and closure (Mannin 1999a: 25). Euroregions, in order to function effectively, require a high permeability of borders and attempt to make the border a bridge, a meeting point rather than a barrier. The accession process to the EU for the candidate countries also encourages greater openness of frontiers and will eventually involve the abolition of frontier controls, probably after a transition period.

Tight migration control has been justified, accompanied and supported by a security discourse, which emphasises closure. Identity checks, to exclude unwanted migrants and 'bogus' asylum seekers, have dominated consideration about, and practice on, the external frontier of the EU. Yet, migration control may well be in part ineffective and in part a myth (Bigo 1998), and over-concentration on it might obstruct more constructive solutions to immigration issues:

> The rigid border regime with eastern Europe, which the EU developed under the leadership of the FRG, is not contributing to the development of such political instruments that would control migration. To a great extent, it has blocked the search for such instruments (Funk 1994: 17).

The security discourse, linking terrorism, organised crime and illegal migration, was at its most pervasive in the mid 1990s. There was a wide tendency to link organised crime and immigration. Associations between these phenomena are often assumed, although there is no necessary connection between them (Bigo 1998, 1999). Misperceptions of threats lead to policies which, though appearing to counter genuine risks, may prove, in the long run, counter-productive.

The Tampere Declaration of EU heads of state and government in October 1999 marked a decisive step away from this way of conceiving the problem, towards one which envisaged regulated immigration, with renewed emphasis on individual rights and co-operation at the frontiers. The difficulty of this more positive approach is that the present EU eastern frontier, and the frontier after the next enlargement, separate societies with very different levels of economic and social development. The Copenhagen conditions for EU membership require applicant states to adopt many of the norms, laws and institutional arrangements current in the EU. Although the speed with which the Mediterranean EU members have been catching up with their northern partners is an encouraging precedent, a substantial risk remains that the present EU frontier will continue, for many decades, to mark an economic and social divide.

At present, the first tier of applicant states form a buffer zone between the EU and less developed societies, including Russia, to the east. Since the 1999 EU summit in Helsinki, Romania, Bulgaria, the Slovak Republic, Latvia, Lithuania and Turkey have been included in accession negotiations. Yet, even this next possible wave of enlargement will leave buffer states – Moldova, Belarus and Ukraine – between a future EU and Russia. Eastern Europe, or some parts of it, is likely for the foreseeable future to remain a large 'in-between' zone, a march or a *glacis*. But options remain open. The limits of the EU are not clearly defined in the east: the question of the final contours of Europe is yet to be decided (Schmidt-Häuer 1999). Where the eastern frontier of Europe ultimately resides, will not be determined by geography but is 'a matter of politics and ideology' (Wallace 1991: 8).

7
Conclusion

Norman Davies concludes his distinguished survey of European history with the words: '[Europe] has the chance to be less divided than for generations past. If fortune smiles, the physical and psychological barriers will be less brutal than at any time in living memory' (Davies 1996: 1136). The barriers which continue to divide Europeans are political and cultural frontiers, which in some cases are made more conflictual by economic inequalities. What are the main issues which European frontiers raise?

Two traditional questions about frontiers remain central in evaluating the frontiers of the EU and of the member states – where the frontiers are drawn and what purposes they serve. Location and function of frontiers are expressions of a political project. They are also, because they cannot easily be modified, limitations and constraints on what might be achieved by a state or a union of states. Frontiers partly influence, and partly reflect, a distribution of power and resources. They are instruments through which identities are created and defined. They have a basic role in meeting demand for security. For these reasons, an assessment of European frontiers is of fundamental practical, historical and theoretical importance.

I

In terms of their location, the frontiers of EU member states are conflict-free, with the troublesome exception of Gibraltar. After the unification of Germany, and the reaffirmation of the eastern frontier of Germany as the Oder–Neisse line, and the de facto, then the *de jure*, acceptance by the Republic of Ireland of Northern Ireland, no member state has a territorial dispute in Europe. Stability of frontiers was a basic principle of the 1975 Helsinki Final Act and is a condition of acceptance of new members by the EU. The Helsinki declaration of principle did not prevent the creation of new international frontiers following the collapse of communism and the disintegration of the USSR and Yugoslavia, because more important issues were thought to be at stake.

The EU's insistence on territorial stability for its members, in the absence of an unforeseeable political cataclysm, will almost certainly have more success than Helsinki. The latter was an agreement of a heterogeneous collection of states, with a profound 'Cold War' division between them. The eastern part of the continent was dominated, against the wishes of its population, by a communist autocracy. The EU integrates its members by consent in a trading bloc, an economic union and a system of law, capped by an aspiration to political unity. Whilst present conditions hold, no member state has an interest in pursuing territorial claims against another, and there is not the slightest chance that it would succeed.

The real tests of this territorial stability will come after the next and subsequent enlargements because the EU will absorb states with recent histories of territorial instability. This will bring the EU's external frontier into contact with states, all of which have current territorial disputes. Particular issues may be resolved easily by negotiation or remain a long-term focus of conflict. For example, the future is uncertain for Kaliningrad, the Russian exclave (formerly part of the German province of East Prussia, between Poland and Lithuania), and several solutions have been proposed for its future status. The factors involved are complex and the future unpredictable so that the status of Kaliningrad may either become a running sore like Gibraltar or may be resolved by peaceful change. Whether territorial stability can be secured in the whole 'shatter zone' between the Baltic and the Black Sea (and thence to the Adriatic) is uncertain.

II

The changing functions of the internal frontiers of the EU are bound up with the process of European integration and with globalisation. Internal frontiers are being divested of functions which formerly were attributed to them and which were thought basic expressions of state sovereignty. Nation states from the seventeenth to the nineteenth centuries established the Westphalian functions of frontiers – limits of legal jurisdiction, fiscal limits, lines of military protection and defence, customs borders, means of surveillance and control of the movement of persons, and the main socio-cultural boundary. All these functions had the effect of differentiating between inside and outside, between 'us' and 'them', and were powerful means of inclusion and exclusion.

The general purpose of frontiers of the sovereign state was to establish absolute physical control over a clearly defined area and to allow the exercise of exclusive legal, administrative and social control over its inhabitants. Many argue that we now live in an increasingly post-national, 'post-sovereign' (MacCormick 1999) Europe: '... it seems obvious that no state in Western Europe any longer is a sovereign state. None is in a position such that all the power exercised internally in it, whether politically or legally, derives from purely internal sources' (MacCormick 1993: 16). As the traditional attributes of sovereignty are eroded in Europe, frontiers are losing their hard-edged clarity (M. Anderson 1996: 189). States are going through a certain deterritorialisation in that defence of state interests is now pursued through European and global institutions rather than through unilateral action. State power is based less on control of territory and the military means of defending that territory and more on political and financial resources – the ability to mobilise influential networks.

The internal development of member states is also diminishing the centrality of the state frontier. Some sub-state boundaries and internal member state boundaries are becoming more similar in function to inter-state boundaries, as sub-state regions develop into actors in the system of European governance. Transfrontier co-operation is an illustration of how the frontiers of the state have ceased to be the exclusive frame of constitutional political activity. Multinational transfrontier co-operation, most significantly at the external frontier, is potentially 'reinventing' macro-regional bloc-building in Europe (the Baltic region, with the Euroregion 'Pomerania' at its heart; the Lake Constance region, straddling the EU frontier with Switzerland; the Arge Alpe-Adria; the Arge Donauländer; or the Euro-Med Partnership).

Profound changes in attitudes towards frontiers are occurring, in frontier regions, in populations at large and in elite thinking. These changes are associated with beliefs about sovereignty and identity. Sovereignty is a concept less used by governments (although it retains an important legal significance) and has become more a term used to oppose European integration. Rather than being static, identity is increasingly viewed as a process (McCrone 1998: 34) which implies constant change in the markers of identity. Cultural difference is a moving line of division whereas the older notion of national character was conceived as a quasi-permanent, indelible feature of nations.

The extent of the change should not be exaggerated. States remain important centres of power to the extent that it is difficult to envisage any process of deciding policy, on important matters, at the European level in their absence or against their opposition. Their frontiers, in some important senses, are intact. They have not simply been abolished, despite the rhetoric of the '1992 programme' and the abolition of frontier controls within Schengen. No European institution has (nor is likely to acquire) the authority to redraw state boundaries and no frontier functions can be withdrawn from them without their consent. A state without a territory is impractical in any foreseeable future, and states need territory for their most important political resource – the consent and the positive support of large populations. Support depends on a belief in political independence and self-government, and on identification with, and feelings of loyalty towards, a state.

All the evidence about culture and national identity in Europe suggests, in the absence of a revolutionary cataclysm, that change is slow. The cultural legacy of the nation state remains embedded in most of the frontiers of the member states of the EU, in terms of language use, forms and substance of education, and habitual ways of doing things. Exclusive loyalties to the nation and to the nation alone are, however, diminishing. Multiple identities are acquiring or reacquiring an important place across the EU. The hard shell of the old nation state is thus becoming less clear as a dividing line. As Edward Said writes:

> Gone are the binary oppositions dear to the nationalist and imperialist enterprise. Instead we begin to sense that old authority cannot simply be replaced by new authority, but that new alignments made across borders, types, nations, and essences are rapidly coming into view, and it is those new alignments that now provoke and challenge the fundamentally static notion of identity that has been the core of cultural thought during the era of imperialism (Said 1993: xxviii).

III

In terms of the location of the external frontier, the definition of its functions, the connections between security, economic and political boundaries, the EU is living with uncertainty. It will continue to do so for an indeterminate, but probably a long, period. Especially on the eastern frontier, policy makers will have to adopt 'a "fuzzy logic", less rational, less rigid, to allow for a complex historical transition to take place' (Foucher 1999: 169). Lack of consistency will also be necessary to preserve an openness of frontiers. As Didier Bigo writes, a free society

> is one with open frontiers and plural identities. This implies both that behaviour is adaptable and that there must be acceptance of illegality at the margins. Whether European politicians accept it or not, a free society now implies tolerance of international phenomena decoupled from territory, characterised by transnational networks and the penetration of national territories (Bigo 1998: 161).

The areas of uncertainty about the frontiers of the EU are even greater than those of the member states.

Recommending a lack of coherence and a rational model for the drawing of the external frontier is paradoxical. It seems that, almost for the first time, an important political frontier can be drawn as an outcome of a rational calculation of interests. Rational models of boundary drawing have been widely discussed in debates about the redrawing of regional and local government boundaries. One of the basic axioms derived from these debates is that boundaries should be drawn to include the population affected by a set of problems and therefore disposed to devoting the time and resources to addressing those problems. This justifies the existence of various levels of government in Europe (and has affected thinking about the organisation of spaces for transfrontier co-operation at the local and regional levels).

European integration provides an obvious example of how the frontiers of the state no longer coincide with the boundaries of problems and solutions have to be found within a new spatial framework. Crucial economic and environmental issues escape the capacity of an entity as large and rich as the EU, and therefore have to be treated at the global level through bodies such as the G7 or the World Trade Organisation (WTO). The difficulty with the EU frontiers (as with local government boundaries) is that there are different optimal areas for different policy areas, and there are no basic overriding interests. It is possible that the EU will become over-extended and face fragmentation by bringing in countries whose elites have different perceptions about what the important problems are and different levels of commitment to the wishes of the majority than the old core states of the EU. This has already been encountered with Britain and, in a different form, with Greece.

There are two other problems associated with the calculation of interest and the drawing of boundaries – the difference in the nature of short-term interests and long-term interests, and how to calculate the trade-off between different sorts of interest, in this case between security and economic interests. The boundaries of short-term and long-term communities of interests, and between economic and security interests, may not be the same or perceived to be the same. Neither long-term interests nor security interests can be precisely calculated – long-term interests depend on assumptions about preferences in a set of changed and unpredictable circumstances; even short-term security interests cannot, except in war, be calculated and are politically defined by the priority given to certain security objectives.

In broad terms, the movement of the EU frontier to the east will not result in economic benefits other than those already achieved through the existing trade agreements and aid from the EU, and may well involve costs both to the existing and new members. There are, however, considerable potential political and security gains in terms of stability. The enlargement towards the east will reduce insecurity and uneasy 'in-betweenness' for a number of, if not in the near future all, countries of Central and Eastern Europe and reduce anxieties in the core states about 'chaos on the doorstep'. However, fears that enlargement will make the EU internally unmanageable have delayed the first, and will almost certainly delay the second, round of enlargement. Changes in the decision-making process are now at the top of the EU agenda, but governments are hesitant because enlargement can redistribute the balance of power and influence within the EU in unpredictable ways.

A 'hard' frontier was, until recently, considered a basic necessity for a security community. Nation state frontiers were, first and foremost, barriers, which enclosed a 'security community' (Deutsch et al. 1957). They were sealed and defended against external military threats. Frontiers were also seen as a security against certain forms of crime. Although it is the existence of such frontiers which creates certain forms of crime, such as people trafficking, this is not a popular, widespread perception. There has, in recent years, been a security discourse linking transfrontier crime such as terrorism, organised crime and illegal migration. When problems occur with those on the outside, a recurring reflex is to seek as much closure as possible. Yet, closed borders are no longer an option either for states or the EU (Amato and Batt 1999: 61).

There is no close parallel, as yet, between the EU and the state as a security community, and the frontiers of states are no longer the clear limits of a security community. There is no European army (or only an embryonic one) to defend it; the Western European Union has been integrated into the EU structure but it does not have an integrated military command structure like NATO; a European director of external and security policy, a Mr PESC (Javier Solana) has been appointed, but he is entirely dependent on the states for his authority. Policing is still a national remit (although regulated by Schengen rules for the policing of frontiers, and despite the establishment of an intelligence and information exchange in Europol); national criminal law jurisdictions remain distinct, even though influenced by European jurisprudence.

There is, moreover, a blurring of the old distinction between internal and external security. The whole area of security, comprising both internal and external dimensions, is one of overlapping circles. Membership of security arrangements, NATO, WEU, Europol and Schengen, does not coincide and is unlikely to coincide soon. Indeed, the phenomenon of overlapping circles may well become an even greater complicating factor in European security following the encouragement given in the 1997 Amsterdam Treaty and the 1999 Tampere Declaration for strengthened co-operation between two or more member states of the EU. New arrangements for internal security involving different combinations of states are a possibility.

There is also an eroding of the clearly defined security frontiers for policing purposes. Schengen, the export of Schengen to EU candidate members, and new technologies (of surveillance, tracking devices, etc.) support the blurring of boundaries and the re-establishment of border zones. Considerable emphasis is now placed on 'control in depth', a spatial approach reaching far beyond the frontier line, and involving international/European co-operation of the relevant control agencies. Moreover, one of the most important functions concentrated on the external frontier, identity checks on persons, are not, despite the aspiration to become so, uniform. Sensitivities about subsidiarity and sovereignty conserve marked differences in national practices concerning frontier control and especially 'control in depth', as well as influencing practices of cross-border co-operation at the internal as well as at the external frontiers of the EU.

The 1999 Tampere Declaration probably marks a move away from the priority given to repression of external criminal threats and preventing immigration, towards balancing measures against them, with the greater emphasis on the rule of law, human rights and the fair treatment of non-Europeans. These latter objectives are to be regarded as helpful to defend European security. The implication of this declaration is that security at the borders can best be guaranteed through co-operation rather than repression and exclusion. This will further erode the notion that a security community must have a 'hard' frontier.

IV

There is a crucial link between the perception of a frontier and a sense of identity. The openness and complexity of the external frontier suggest that the emerging European identity will be more pluralistic, less intensely felt, than national identities. This may contribute either to stability or produce a new form of disorder. Such disorder would be related to a general decline in the effectiveness of public authority, related to an increasingly globalised economy and confusion about the division of responsibilities between different levels of government.

The EU external frontier as a marker of a strong sense of European identity confronts two problems – it is neither sufficiently high nor sufficiently clear as a barrier to the outside. It is a frontier only for some purposes, a tariff frontier, the delimitation of an area for certain common policies, a legal territory for economic law and a means to control movement of persons. Many important matters are reserved to the states and limited to their territory. In addition, external frontiers coincide with frontiers of member states. Except in terms of identity checks, the distinction between internal and external frontiers is very obvious in the minds of citizens. Moreover, the external frontier is a ragged edge to the EU because of the microstates, the dependent and associated territories of the member states, and the variable geometry of the EU itself. An important state, the United Kingdom, is semi-detached for some purposes – frontier controls of persons, the single currency and jurisdiction of the European Court of Justice in third pillar conventions. This tears a hole in the integrity of the police, currency and legal frontiers of the EU. Finally, the external frontier is also a moving frontier as a result of successive EU enlargements.

The concentration of functions on the linear frontier, a feature of the old sovereign state, is impractical for the EU external frontier. This is due in part to the nature of the process of European integration. But the image, and sometimes the reality, of frontiers dissolving across the world under the influence of globalisation makes it difficult to establish the external frontier as exclusive:

> ... the edges of societies and markets are eroding and are less easy to draw on a map. New boundaries are needed; new ways of dividing the tasks of government; new ways of relating the diverse interests and concerns of citizens. ... These boundaries are not just a question of an organising principle but a principle of legitimacy (Horsman and Marshall 1995: 266–7).

Many functions frontiers used to have, cannot – or at least only in a restricted sense – be maintained under the pressures of globalisation, however that term is defined. The EU is obliged to interact, as a region with global connections, with the rest of the world. A project to construct an external frontier which would be analogous to the frontier of the old nation state is almost bound to lead to failure.

The external frontier therefore is, and will remain, different in kind from the old inter-state frontier which has played such a central role in the creation of national identities and international rivalries. The construction of a common external frontier under the Schengen regime – which brought the EU closer to what could be described as 'statehood' – has frequently been interpreted as the installation of an exclusionary regime directed against non-EU citizens. Member states have sought to exclude immigrants and asylum seekers as far as practical and compatible with their international obligations. This is creating a sense, thought regrettable by some, of 'we' Europeans as against 'them', particularly 'them' from Africa and Asia. This is replicating in a shadowy form the process of nation building. But it is a weak replica because, for large populations, foreigners are also those people who speak a different language.

The core policy issue is whether the external frontier can be conceived in a way which is non-exclusive, neither intended nor perceived to divide friend from foe, 'us' from 'them', those who enjoy rights from those who do not. This is achievable because of many factors – internal diversity of the EU, the importance which citizens and governments continue to attribute to the frontiers of the states, the non-coincidence of many forms and institutions of co-operation with the external frontier, uncertainty about where, in future, that frontier will be located, all the multiform expressions of interdependence, and international informational and political networks transcending frontiers, will help to keep the EU's frontier an open one.

Frontiers across the whole territory of the EU are, as this book has illustrated, being shaped by general European and global forces. But there is a kaleidoscopic variety of local problems and local perceptions. Frontiers can have high salience to those living near to them, but people living far in the interior of the same country may be only intermittently, if at all, conscious of frontier issues. In some places, particular migratory pressures or crime problems affect the perception of the frontier, in other places they are of scant importance. Differences in local economic and social conditions can result in the frontier with the same neighbouring country seeming to pose, as in a region like Alsace, very different problems within short distances. Some internal EU frontiers are becoming relatively more important as cultural lines of defence and means of defending identities, as their other functions decline. Close contact between populations divided by an internal frontier seldom appears to erode a sense of difference, and the frontier remains a clear line. In other places (and at the macro-European level), notions of marches, of a *limes* or of frontier regions are beginning to prevail over perceptions of frontiers as clearly defined limits or lines. General European and national perspectives on frontiers coexist with highly complex local realities.

The complexity of European frontiers means that 'the frontier' in Europe can never play the same role as it did in nineteenth-century America. It may be the destiny of the EU external frontier to shift eastwards until it encloses most of geographical Europe, and even Asia Minor. But this expansion cannot be a 'manifest destiny' as it was in the American case because there can be no simple understanding of what is expanding, why and to what end. The existence and displacement of this external frontier are changing and will change European societies and values. But there can be no arresting hypothesis about the relationship of the frontier to these changes, along the lines of the one proposed by Frederick Jackson Turner which provided the basis of a lively debate for three-quarters of a century and still forms an essential background to discussions of the expansion of America. The European frontier is a subject worthy of a great debate. Unfortunately, such a debate will inevitably be a disorderly one and carry with it the risk of disintegration into highly specialised discussions.

Notes

1 Introduction

1. The Channel Tunnel provides a fixed link between England and France and has some of the characteristics of a land frontier. For example, there are joint police stations at both ends of the tunnel. But, unlike land frontiers, it is what frontier police call a 'choke point', in that all people and goods have to pass through a narrow and, in principle, easy to control port of entry.
2. The China–Korea frontier consisted of a band of territory between 50 and 90 km across which, although it had one time been settled and cultivated, was forbidden to both Koreans and Chinese. Death was the penalty for settling in this zone, although vagabonds, outlaws and itinerants were occasionally to be found there; it achieved its purpose of dividing Chinese and Koreans. This separation was a deliberate attempt to put an end to the interminable wars between the two peoples who, according to Richthofen, had as a result become so distant from another that they had no accurate image of the appearance of the other – in the frontier region of China, Chinese people thought that Richthofen might be Korean.
3. This accords with a certain interpretation of nationalism – nationalism creates nations (and their territories), as part of a modernisation process, where they did not previously exist or existed only in an embryonic form (Gellner 1983, 1997).
4. Articles by French authors cover, more briefly, the same subject from a different perspective (particularly Foucher 1998, Moreau Deforges 1995).
5. Culture and language require, for a fuller exploration, anthropological approaches. Some of the most illuminating recent work on boundaries and identities has been written by anthropologists – see particularly Cohen (1998), Delamont (1995), Macdonald (1993) and Wilson and Donnan (1998).
6. The extraordinary success of Vivian Forrester's book (1997) *L'Horreur Economique* (Paris: Flammarion), which developed similar themes and which remained at the top of the French best-seller list for several weeks, is an example of this millenarian gloom.

2 Theory

1. Thorsten Malmberg has surveyed theories of human territoriality without reaching a convincing synthesis (Malmberg 1980). Most human and historical geographers and social scientists are critical of attempts at socio-biological theories of territories and adopt the position of Robert Sack that all territories are 'socially constructed' (Sack 1986) or, to use the older, less problematic, formulation of Jean Gottman, that the significance of territories is seen to lie in the uses to which it is put (Gottman 1973).

2. A large number of publications on sovereignty have been published since the publication of the second edition of Hinsley's classic text (Hinsley 1986). Notable contributions are James (1986), Jackson (1990), Camilleri and Falk (1992), Hedetoft (1994), Weber (1995), Lyons and Mastanduno (1995), Biersteker and Weber (1996), Bellamy and Castiglione (1997), Badie (1999) and MacCormick (1999).
3. But see MacCormick (1999) who treats both sovereignty and European integration in a rigorous and scholarly manner.
4. Recent influential publications are Anderson, B. (1983), Gellner (1983, 1997), Nairn (1997), Smith (1986, 1995), Hedetoft (1995) and Schnapper (1998). See also Anderson, M. (2000).
5. Sometimes states accept responsibilities for the same things in the context of more than one organisation, which makes it very difficult to evade them. For example, WEU members undertook in 1992 to engage in humanitarian and rescue tasks, peacekeeping operations and tasks of combat forces in crisis management. NATO shortly afterwards declared its intention to perform such tasks. In 1997 the European Council in Amsterdam decided to make these tasks an EU treaty obligation.
6. See Zielonka (1991).
7. See, for example, Anderson, M. et al. (1995); see also Sheptycki (1995, 1996).
8. Nine articles in *International Affairs*, 7 (3) (1999) provide a comprehensive review of the arguments about global justice.
9. Not all agree that the internationalisation of justice is a desirable trend as the 1998–2000 case in Britain on the extradition to Spain of General Pinochet illustrated. 'Communitarians' hold that rights and questions of justice should be decided within bounded human communities (Walzer 1983).
10. The best contributions concern North American borders (McCallum 1995, Engel and Rogers 1996). European contributions tend to be non-technical and descriptive in approach (Vernier 1993, Menville 1996).
11. For example, British government officials acknowledged that no such analysis had taken place to establish the effects of maintaining frontier controls against EU nationals when the other members of the Union (excepting Ireland) were abolishing them. See particularly the evidence of Mr Boys Smith, House of Lords Select Committee on European Communities (1999: 28).
12. Kroeber and Kluckhohn (1952) listed 164 definitions of culture.
13. A more recent and more distinguished book – Davies (1996) – has successfully rectified the balance and given full weight to Central and Eastern Europe.
14. However, the manufacturing function may be largely cut off from the country of origin. Fiat, for example, launched a new 'world car' in 1997 to be manufactured in Poland, Russia, India, Turkey, Brazil, Venezuela, Argentina, Vietnam, South Africa and Morocco, with sales of 1 million envisaged in 2000 (only 60 000 within the EU).
15. There are positions between these two extremes such as that of Samir Amin (Amin 1997) in which globalisation commenced around 1500 in a mercantilist form but was transformed into the free trade model, then a period between 1945 and 1990 in which there was an industrialisation of the periphery and, since 1990, a triumphalist proclamation of inevitable globalisation.

16. However, defending their interests through global negotiations is subject to the severe limitation of the absence of the ability to regulate capital flows. See Kahler (1998) and Griffith-Jones (1998).
17. For a review of diverse international regimes see Buck (1998). For reviews of the 'new internationalism' of multiple alternative social movements and over transfrontier advocacy networks see Keck and Sikkink (1998) and Waterman (1998).
18. The 'engulfing' of local cultures can be exaggerated and usually results in reactions. For a recent discussion see Jameson and Miyoshi (1998).
19. The most persuasive recent theoretical and empirical study of the role of EU member states is Moravcsik (1998).
20. The French decision to maintain controls on its frontier between Belgium and Luxembourg from 1995 to the present and to prevent entry of British beef to France in 1999 despite an EU decision to the contrary are examples of this continuing belief. These can be interpreted as symbolism or forms of pressure or as delaying tactics.

3   Internal Frontier Issues

1. The important exception, because it bedevils all negotiations on justice and home affairs within the EU, is the Anglo-Spanish dispute over Gibraltar (Morris and Haigh 1991, Gold 1994). See Chapter 5 for a more extended discussion of territories associated with EU member states.
2. The current demand for equality of status of German as one of the working languages of the EU may be an exception. It is a reasonable demand in that German is the mother tongue of more people than any other EU language but it is little spoken outside the German-speaking area, whereas English and French are widely disseminated.
3. A study commissioned by the European Commission estimated that frontier controls at the internal frontiers before 1993 could have cost traders 7.5 billion ECU or 1 per cent of the total value of trade. Complying with the EC VAT and statistical requirements remained costly, particularly in the initial stage of setting up the new system, so that the savings were estimated to be of the order of 5 billion ECU net. The savings per consignment of goods were greatest for the Mediterranean countries and least in the northern states, and when trade volumes were taken into account Germany, Italy and Spain were the main beneficiaries (European Commission 1997). Caution must be used in evaluating these estimates because of the sampling and estimating methodology used.
4. Differences between the police powers of Customs services inhibits some forms of direct co-operation between them. Criminal investigation powers were not normally part of the competences of southern European Customs. French Customs, for example, did not acquire criminal investigation powers until 1999.
5. See House of Lords (1998). The dispute between Britain and Spain over Gibraltar (Britain considered it inside and Spain outside the common external frontier) delayed the integration into Pillar I of part of the Schengen

acquis, concerning free movement, immigration and asylum, and the publication of the whole of the *acquis*. The result is considerable legal uncertainty and obscurity (den Boer 1998, den Boer and Carrado forthcoming).

6. Schengen currently consists of 13 signatory states and 10 which have fully implemented Schengen (with Denmark and Sweden on the threshold), while Greece was connected with the Schengen Information System in December 1997, and entry permits to the country have since then been dealt with according to the Schengen visa requirements (Nikolopoulos 1998: 107). At a meeting of Ministers of the Interior of all 12 Schengen states in Berlin in December 1998, it was decided that control of persons would remain in place at Greece's frontiers which had not passed the efficiency test of the Schengen inspection group.

7. In June 1998, the Schengen Executive Committee decided that certain Schengen documents should remain confidential. These included some decisions and declarations of the Executive Committee, some declarations of the Central Control Group, three annexes to the Common Visa Instructions, the SIRENE manual, three documents on the controlled delivery of drugs as well as the external frontier guidelines. These moves concerning official secrecy marks an important step towards the development of state-like characteristics in the EU.

8. There are six kinds of common visa – a 90-day visitors' visa valid for the whole of the Schengen area for nationalities on an agreed list, a 90-day visa for one or a restricted group of Schengen countries, a transit visa with a maximum of five days within the area, an airport transit visa for certain specified nationalities, a short-stay (15 days) common visa delivered at the frontier. Visas for longer than 90 days remain the responsibility of the states.

9. Data protection is an area which threatened to raise 'virtual' frontiers in Europe because, with the advent of large data banks in the 1980s, certain countries, particularly Germany, passed stringent data protection laws. This severely circumscribed the possibility of transferring personal data, even for law enforcement purposes, to other countries which did not have similar rules. The European Commission responded by initiating a data protection directive but legislation by the states was required. Italy, for example, had no data protection until two laws were passed in December 1996 (*Gazetta Ufficiale* 1997).

10. The European Parliament's Committee on Civil Liberties produced a number of critical reports. See particularly the Report of 2 October 1992 debated in December 1992.

11. Denmark has a different kind of opt-out: it is a member of Schengen but retains the sovereign right to decide whether to accept decisions agreed within the Schengen framework. The Scandinavian non-members of the EU, Norway and Iceland, have association agreements with Schengen in order to preserve the long-standing Nordic free movement area.

12. Like all the previous hesitations, this is subject to varying interpretations. The view inside the Ministry of the Interior was that the delay was proposed because the joint police stations – four with Germany and four with Spain – were not in place. The more political interpretation is that the French government did not have confidence in the measures taken by other

countries and that this proposed delay was intended as a warning to France's partners.

13. Parliamentary committees have produced a series of critical reports on Schengen. See particularly République Française – Sénat (1997), Sénat (1997a).

14. Anderson (1983), Cappelin and Batey (1993) Groß and Schmitt-Egner (1994), von Malchus (1975), Scott (1989), Ganster et al. (1997).

15. For an organisation chart of the Euroregion see Scott (1997: 123).

16. For a classification of forms of transfrontier co-operation see Schmitt-Egner (1996). Ratti (1996) theorises co-operation. Perkmann (1999) provides a recent general assessment of it.

17. Different layers of overlapping organisations are a feature of the French, German, Luxembourg and Swiss frontiers on the Rhine (*Coopération transfrontalière dans l'espace Saar-Lor-Lux* 1996). The proliferation of organisations and institutions sometimes causes frustration and occasional attempts are made to impose one co-ordinator for transfrontier co-operation. The Baden-Württemberg government decided to operate primarily, if not exclusively, through the Grenzlandreferat (set up in 1986 to replace an older unit) in Freiburg, a government office directly accountable to the Stuttgart government. The Grenzlandreferat was to be informed of all matters concerning the border and cross-border activities, and has to be consulted in all these matters (Schneider interview).

18. Arnold (1977), Arnold-Plassière (1979); for general studies see Guichonnet and Raffestin (1970: 166–218), von Malchus (1975), Baumert (1969) and Roth (1981).

19. With groups such as Hendaye-Bidassoa Environnement (established 1975), the Collectif des Associations de Défense de l'Environnement (1991) and Txinguderien Aldeko Koordinadora (1989). Although the ecologist groups presented themselves as transfrontier associations, the main impetus and direction tend to be predominantly inspired from one or the other side of a frontier.

20. This is not always the case. One example of continual bickering is centred on the Mont Blanc massif. In 1987, the association Mountain Wilderness France proposed that Switzerland, France and Italy should create an international park around Mont Blanc. The idea attracted the support of all environmental groups in the region, and the support of the *conseil général* of Haute Savoie. In June 1989, the French government announced a study for a national park 'with an international vocation' for the massif. This would initially comprise all the land above 2000 metres (which had been a protected area since 1951) and several mountain areas to the north, running along the Swiss border, with the possibility eventually of extending as far as Lake Geneva.

This scheme provoked a chorus of criticism. The mayor of Chamonix, Michel Charlet, regarded the park as 'negative protection, without any positive social project'. In 1991 the local authorities proposed their own plan – the 'Conférence Transfrontalière Mont Blanc', the presidency of which would alternate between the canton of Vaud, the autonomous region of Valle d'Aosta and a *syndicat intercommunal* 'Espace Nature Mont Blanc' which federated 13 communes of the *départements* of Savoie and Haute

Savoie. The transfrontier association set itself four general objectives – the support of mountain agriculture, protection of nature and landscapes, the development of 'integrated tourism' and the reduction of the impact of transport and its infrastructure.

The regional director of the French Ministry of the Environment, Alain Pialat, responded that the local authorities were incapable of carrying out any large-scale project. Charlet riposted that the local authorities, after carrying through their pilot projects, had obtained the financial backing of the Rhône–Alpes region and were now ready to implement their scheme (*Le Monde*, 5 August 1997). The environmental groups, which organised themselves into a transfrontier association, considered that both the states and the local authorities had evaded the genuine issues – the overexploitation of the massif, especially with the building of new tourist facilities and the decline in environmental protection in the area. Although some, such as Mountain Wilderness France, suggested a compromise, no consensus emerged. The saga continues.

21. For example, in Germany the 1949 Basic Law (article 32, 3e) permits the *Länder* to conclude treaties with foreign authorities within the areas of their legislative competence. If the Federal government enters into agreements which fall within the legislative competence of the *Länder* it must consult them. In Austria, another federal system, constitutional change had to be initiated in the 1980s. A 1988 constitutional amendment authorised the *Länder*, in their areas of competence, to enter into treaties with neighbouring states or with their regional authorities. *Bundes-Verfassungsgesetz*, Art. 16 paras. 1–3.

22. The Mediterranean countries were, with certain exceptions in north-east Italy, slower to embark on transfrontier co-operation but, stimulated by EU programmes, much progress has been made since 1990 (Ndiaye 1996, Ouyahia 1996, Alliès 1995, Covas 1995).

23. Kent County Council co-operates with Nord–Pas de Calais, Wallonia, Flanders and the Brussels region to exploit the opportunities provided by the Channel Tunnel; Sussex and Kent are members of the Transmanche region development programme funded by INTERREG; other forms of co-operation are Transmanche Metropole (Southampton, Portsmouth, Bournemouth, Poole, Caen, Le Havre, Rouen), Transmanche Euroregion (Kent, Nord, Sussex, Pas de Calais, Wallonia, Brussels, Flanders) and an association of East Sussex with neighbouring French *départements* (Church and Reid 1995).

24. There is an enormous disparity in budgets even of rich regions. In the 'four motors' association of the most dynamic French, Spanish, Italian and German regions – Rhône–Alpes had a budget in 1997 of ECU 1bn, compared with 9bn for Lombardy and 30bn for Baden-Württemberg.

25. Council of Europe's Committee of European Municipalities and Regions claims 100 000 members (for full list see European Parliament 1994).

26. Transfrontier maps and guides have been one of the most significant developments in terms of breaking down the image of national territories as enclosed and separate entities. An ambitious and specialised atlas of the upper Rhine was produced by the Regio Basiliensis, followed by maps of other transfrontier regions for a wider public. These maps partly meet a practical demand from tourists and travellers and partly are a symbolic

effacement of the frontiers of states. This is also the case for travel guides such as the Michelin Green Guide for the Rhineland and the *Grand Guide des Pyrénées* (1995).

27. As a consequence, in the literature on the associations so far, agendas for further research are more common than well-supported arguments and clear conclusions (see Aykaç 1994, Brown 1997, Blatter 1996, Hansen 1983, Hansen et al. 1996). In the most recent work there are signs of change (see particularly Groß and Schmitt-Egner 1994, Leresche and Levy 1995, Saez et al. 1997, Perkmann 1999).

28. But see Tannam (1995) for a pessimistic assessment of EU influence on promoting transfrontier co-operation in the difficult context of the Northern Ireland border.

4 The Case of French Frontiers

1. The total length of the frontier is 7660 km, with almost 900 road crossings, 4 tunnels, 64 international airports, and a maritime frontier of 4720 km with numerous seaports. The 2940 km of land frontiers are composed of the Franco-Belgian (630 km), Spanish (690 km), Swiss (550 km), Italian (500 km), German (435 km), Luxembourg (75 km) and Andorra (60 km) frontiers.

2. Despite this boost, Valenciennes remained the town with the highest level of unemployment in France – 22 per cent in the middle of 1997.

3. The INTERREG programme covered the *département* of the Ardennes in France and the *arrondissements* of Thuin, Philippeville, Dinant, Neufchâteau and Virton in Belgium, and totals 28 million ECUs – 12.45 per cent from the EU, the rest from central and local government. The programme covers assistance to local administrations and firms to co-operate to train in traditional crafts, to enhance the region as a tourist destination and for environmental protection programmes.

4. The total number of frontier workers crossing into Luxembourg and Germany from Lorraine increased from 7000 in 1968 to 31 000 in 1990, 42 000 in 1993 and an estimated 50 000 in 1998.

5. An Alsatian schoolmaster, born in the 1860s, changed his nationality four times, from French to German in 1871, German to French in 1919, French to German between 1940 and 1944; then, returning to French, left an interesting set of diaries (Husser 1989).

6. By contrast with the northern frontier, the north-eastern has one of the lowest unemployment rates in France, in part because workers from Lorraine, Alsace and Franche-Comté can find employment in Luxembourg, Germany and Switzerland (INSEE 1998).

7. Targeted efforts ensure that the availability of sub-contractors in specialised fields is known on the other side of the border, including the 'Salon of Sub-Contracting' in Freiburg, established on the initiative of Colmar. Among other examples are the Management Centre in Colmar (initiated by the Comité d'Expansion du Haut Rhin (CAHR) which has trilingual programme for managers, and the Metz ESIDC Ecole de Commerce (management school) in which two years, out of the three-year programme, are spent in another country (Perrin and Prétat interviews).

8. Söhlingen–Mulhouse is a partial exception, but other attempts such as Lahr–Strasbourg and, in south-west France, Biarritz–Bilboa have not succeeded.

9. Swiss attitudes towards transfrontier co-operation depend very much on the region and language group. The Italian-speaking Swiss are reserved about it, and the Tessin–Lombardy association, the Regio Insubrica, does not command much support. The *Tessinois* also voted 90 per cent against Swiss membership of the EC. Both reactions can be explained by the vulnerability of the Tessin to Italy. There is no large city like Basel, Zurich and Geneva, and the *Tessinois* feel they would inevitably be drawn into the orbit of Milan. The smallest (but one) of the language groups feels that its specificity would be threatened, and the *Tessinois* do not share the reaction found among the *Suisses Romandes* that we might as well be governed from Brussels as by Berne (Rossi interview). Europe signifies different things in different regions (Eugster interview).

10. This agreement, negotiated within the framework of the 1981 Madrid Convention, essentially comprises three elements: first, the definition of the territorial scope of the agreement (territorial collectivities adjacent – within 25 km of the frontier – to the land frontier and Corsica, together with bodies established by them); second, a comprehensive list of areas in which co-operation is permissible; third, the legal limits of co-operation – respect for national legislation and the competences of the territorial collectivities (the states are not responsible for the co-operative actions and their consequences).

11. For example, the Nicomède protocol between the universities of Nice, Turin and Genoa, together with the towns of Cuneo, Nice, Mondovi, Menton and Ventimiglia. One of the interesting outcomes is the technical college (opened in 1998) at Menton which draws both students and teaching staff from both sides of the frontier.

12. An outline convention, EURAZUR, co-signed by DG V of the European Commission, has been negotiated (but not yet implemented) by PACA, Liguria, the French and Italian Ministers of Labour, the employment exchanges and the main French and Italian trade unions, in order to establish a genuine transfrontier labour market.

13. A survey of 900 pre-adolescent schoolchildren in Menton showed that the frontier was a 'veritable deforming filter which separates two cultures'. These are based on very different sources on which understandings of the world are based – school and media being the most important (Dumont 1998).

14. The traffic on the Pyrenees has, by contrast with other frontiers, been very carefully monitored on the basis of ten observation points and published by the regional office of Midi Pyrénées (Direction Régionale de l'Equipement 1997).

15. Founded in April 1983 (three French regions, four Spanish autonomies and Andorra, with no central government participation, although a DATAR representative is sometimes present for meetings. DATAR created, in 1974, a commissariat for each mountain massif – a small administration to assist the development of areas in difficulty with small but significant resources, unlike the Working Committee, at its disposal (about £4 million a year in the 1990s to support projects in the Pyrenees). DATAR prepared detailed

plans and incorporated these in national plans (see DATAR 1992; LACE Magazine 1997–98).

16. About 100 French firms in the Spanish Basque country employ some 11 000 people, with the majority (52 per cent) in Vizcaya around Bilbao. But firms from the French border region and Aquitaine are not amongst them. By contrast, Spanish Basque firms are strongly represented in Pyrénées Atlantiques (CCI pour le Nord de l'Espagne 1997).

17. For example, a Price Waterhouse and the government of Navarre study of the impact of the single market in 1992 (Gobierno de Navarra 1992, 1992a) found that in all sectors but one (electrical wires and cables) the impact was either neutral or positive on Spanish production in the region. Publishing statistics and circulating of information about industrial structure are done with the help of the INTERREG programme (e.g. BEGIRA-Observatoire Economique du Pays Basque, EUSTAT-Vittoria, Insituto de Estadistica-Navarra 1998).

18. Published statistics suggest a strong association of immigrants and crime throughout the EU: between the late 1980s and early 1990s, the number of foreigners in jail rose by 297 per cent in Spain, 118 per cent in Portugal and 102 per cent in Luxembourg (Tomasevski 1992, 1994). In France, the proportion of foreigners in jail in 1975 was 18 per cent, and 31 per cent in 1993 (Gallo 1995). In Britain, the number of people in jail under immigration legislation tripled between 1992 and 1993 (Gallo 1995). There are serious problems of interpretation of crime statistics, and they have to be subject to critical scrutiny.

19. In 1997, DICCILEC registered 46 366 non-admissions and readmissions, an increase of almost 6 per cent over 1996. The largest groups were, in descending order of importance, Iraqis (mainly Kurds), Moroccans, Turks, former Yugoslavs. Iraqis were mainly apprehended at the Belgian frontier; Moroccans at the Belgian, Italian and Swiss frontiers; Turks at the Belgian and Swiss frontiers; former Yugoslavs at the Swiss and Italian frontiers; Algerians at the Spanish and Belgian frontiers.

20. French Customs have an elaborate system of risk analysis carried out at the national, interregional and regional levels by the Direction Nationale du Renseignement et de la Documentation (DRD), Centrale Interrégionale du Renseignement (CIR) and the Centre du Renseignement, d'Orientation et de Contrôle (CERDOC). In addition, there is an Observatoire des Echanges Intracommunautaires to analyse the risks arising from trade within the EU. Risk is analysed in seven phases; analyses at each level are subject to an evaluation, and are integrated into manual and cumputerised management tools. The French Customs insist that the results are not used in a mechanical way, but each operational service must use, in addition, initiative and judgement.

21. These were established by the Baden-Baden agreement of 7 September 1995 which 'officialised' the three stations, Strasbourg/Pont de l'Europe, Saarbrücken, Ottmarsheim/Neunburg, and created a fourth, Lauterbourg/Bienwald; and the Paris agreement of 3 June 1996 which officialised the existing Perthus/La Junquera station and created three others: Melles/Pont du Roy, Biratou/Irun, Canfranc/Somport. The two on the Italian frontier have not yet been officialised – Ventimiglia station, which has operated

since 26 June 1960, and Modane, which was opened on 17 November 1997. All these will be eventually transformed into Centres de Coopération Policière et Douanière for which agreements have been signed with Italy (the Chambéry agreement of 3 October 1997) and with Germany (the Mondorf agreement of 9 October 1997).

22. For Customs see Derrac (1996).
23. Such as SOFI for computerised Customs clearance, SCENT, developed by the European Commission as an on-line facility for rapid communication of Customs data, and SID, which is a project to link Customs data bases of EU member states.
24. A maximum of around 100 000 people in both cases. The actual number is probably lower, but a careful survey of the Pyrénées claimed that a third of the population (120 000) claimed to speak Catalan. The number who claimed to speak it well and use it regularly declined in the 1990s (Region Languedoc Roussillon 1993, 1998).
25. One indicator which illustrates a change in French central government culture is that DATAR (the French Land Use Planning Agency), formerly with a strong centralising outlook, was sceptical about INTERREG in the early 1990s. It became an enterprising promoter of transfrontier co-operation at the end of the decade (DATAR 1997, 1998).

5   The External Frontier of the European Union

1. Bilateral police co-operation is often easier between Switzerland and Germany than between France and Germany, because both have decentralised police organisations (Schneider interview).
2. TACIS: Technical Assistance for the Commonwealth of Independent States, i.e. the countries of the former USSR. PHARE: Poland and Hungary Assistance for Economic Recovery (subsequently extended to the Czech Republic, Bosnia-Herzegovina, Albania and Macedonia). ECOS/OUVERTURE is a European Commission Programme for external interregional co-operation, promoting co-operation between regions and cities in the EU and their counterparts in Central and Eastern Europe, the New Independent States and the Mediterranean non-member countries. The present and possible future eastern frontier of the EU will be further examined in Chapter 6.
3. In August 1999, San Marino restricted the entry of female domestic helpers to women over 50 'to protect its male citizens from ... voluptuous foreign women ensnaring them by marriage'. According to the report in the *Guardian*, a spokesman for the San Marino Foreign Ministry declared: 'It's a question of sovereignty and of the measures that a small state takes to protect itself' (Willan 1999).
4. Greenland, the world's largest island (2.18 million square kilometres, with a population of 55 000, mostly Inuit), obtained home rule from Denmark in 1979. Greenland joined the European Community with Denmark in 1973 but voted in a referendum in 1984 to leave the EC.
5. While the Finno-Russian border zone is very thinly populated, the population of the St Petersburg area is larger than that of the whole of Finland,

'one of the reasons why this frontier is the European Union's window on Russia' (Veijalainen 1998: 102).

6. In practice, they have to accept light controls because of lack of resources. In the Basel sector of the frontier in 1998 there were not enough personnel (about 270 officials) for adequate night cover, minor roads were unguarded and video cameras cannot be placed on them for data protection reasons, 200–300 trains every month are not controlled, 60 000 daily crossings are not properly controlled, the extraterritorial corridor from the airport to the city can be penetrated, and access to the international motorway cannot be rigorously controlled without unacceptable traffic delays (Keller interview).

7. In addition to human rights issues, this is another reason why particularly representatives of the German CDU and CSU have been critical of the EU candidate status offered to Turkey at the Helsinki summit of December 1999. See also Fritz-Vannahme (2000).

8. Montanari and Cortese (1993) were first to apply the Rio Grande comparison. Jean-Christophe Rufin alluded to the Rio Grande in 1991, when he stressed the 'demographic danger' originating in the southern Mediterranean states. The gap between the shores of the Mediterranean, he wrote, is far more precipitous than that between the banks of the Rio Grande (Rufin 1991). The Rio Grande comparison has become common currency. 'The widening wealth gap', Robert Fox wrote in *The European*, 'is fast turning the Mediterranean into Europe's Rio Grande – the frontier river swum by destitute "wetbacks" escaping their native Mexico to seek work, wealth and happiness in the United States to the north' (Fox 1997).

9. In 2000, of the 439 million Mediterraneans, 284 million live on the southern shores; by 2015, the figure is supposed to rise to 520 million, of whom 364 million (or 70 per cent) will live in the south (Tlili 1999: 70).

10. For example, in 1992, the European Parliament blocked aid packages to Syria and Morocco on human rights grounds.

11. For a background on frontier issues concerning Malta, see E. W. Anderson (1992).

12. The first major step was the Mediterranean Action Plan, initiated at Barcelona in 1976, which has subsequently been reinforced by conventions and protocols aiming at co-operation of all nations in the Mediterranean to clean up the sea by improving port facilities for the management of waste and ballast water, and by equipping coastal towns with sewage treatment plants. The Barcelona Convention of 25 July 1977 (pollution through dumping from ships and aircraft) was amended by Protocols in 1981 (pollution by oil and other harmful substances), 1983 (pollution from land-based sources) and 1984 (specially protected areas). A revised and updated text of the Barcelona Convention and Protocol was approved at a Conference held in Barcelona in June 1995.

13. There is a split responsibility for frontier control – the Guardia Civil for surveillance and the police for control of persons. Customs can arrest people on the high seas, but when landed, they have to be handed over to the judicial police; on land, Customs have jurisdiction only over goods.

14. Morocco has agreements with Spain, and now with Italy, to police illegal immigration but these agreements are of the nature of statements of good intent. The immigration authorities in Spain are sceptical of both the tech-

nical capacity and will of the Moroccan frontier police to control emigration from Morocco. Italy has also signed an agreement with Morocco to ensure that Moroccan patrol boats will try and stop illegal crossings from Morocco and is currently in the more difficult process of negotiating a similar agreement with Tunisia.
15. With the Lockerbie trial under way, and talks between Gaddafi and the Italian Premier d'Alema resulting in Libya's denunciation of terrorism, relations between the EU and Libya seemed to be improving since 1999.
16. Airport controls at Athens switched to the Schengen system on 1 December 1997.
17. Vigipirate was reinforced against football hooliganism before and during the World Cup of 1998.

6   The Case of the Eastern Frontier of the European Union

1. Changes may nevertheless occur on the other frontiers. If circumstances change, a northern enlargement, taking in Norway, Iceland and the Faroe Isles could happen. The southern frontier will be modified. The Mediterranean islands of Malta and Cyprus are first-tier candidates and Turkey is a longer-term candidate for membership. However, only the acceptance of Turkey would have a major impact on the EU.
2. Copenhagen established three criteria for membership: (1) institutional stability, democracy and rule of law, respect for human rights and protection of minorities; (2) a functioning market economy and sufficient competitiveness; and (3) acceptance of the *acquis communautaire*, including the goals of political union and economic and currency union (Tebbe 1998: 21). These criteria were repeated in the EU's 'Agenda 2000' document of July 1997 (Croft et al. 1999: 62, Mannin 1999: 41–50).
3. Average monthly wages in Central and Eastern European states varied, in 1994, between \$200 in the Czech Republic and \$10–15 in the Ukraine (*Business Central Europe*, March 1994: 73).
4. In Poland, they are still state-owned; in the Czech Republic they are in the hands of investment groups controlled by non-privatised banks (Tebbe 1998: 25).
5. This did not mean the end of territorial disputes in Eastern Europe. The delimitation of the German (GDR)–Polish frontier on the mouth of the Oder was only agreed, finally, in the summer of 1989, a few months before the fall of the Berlin Wall (Schultz and Nothnagle 1996).
6. Within the Soviet bloc, frontiers remained highly policed. For example, the border between Poland and Germany (GDR) was a border strictly policed and controlled until 1972, and again between 1980 and 1991 (Krämer 1999: 19).
7. The inner-German frontier is almost effaced from the landscape (Grimm 1995: 12), but it remains a psychological frontier, a 'wall in the heads' (Harvie 1996). Even in Berlin, where there are only very few physical remnants of the Wall being kept as memorials to the divided city, and an enormous retail and commercial centre is under construction, this division remains. Different unemployment levels, social behaviour and voting

> patterns still mark a divide in Germany, a 'relic boundary', even after monetary transfers from West to East Germany far in excess of £700 billion over the past ten years.

8. For a short sketch on the meaning of the terms *Mitteleuropa* and 'Central Europe', see Klemencic (1997: 15–17), Schubert (1993) and Busek and Wilfinger (1986).
9. See also Busch (1992).
10. Russian and Italian mafia organisations are repeatedly mentioned in the context of nuclear smuggling (*Die Welt* 15 June 1998, 21 July 1999). Yet, apart from the undercover operation by the German secret service, in which 363 g of plutonium were smuggled from Moscow to Munich on 10 August 1994, there is little evidence of trafficking in nuclear materials. Of 158 cases of weapons smuggling reported by the BKA in Germany in 1992, 18 involved radioactive material. On the other hand, 'reports suggest that 23 warheads went missing from a depot in Komsomolsk-na-Amure in March 1992'. However, 'it is hard to see where there is a credible and reliable market' for illegal nuclear material (Galeotti 1995: 8). For a balanced assessment, see Cameron (2000).
11. Remark made at the Colloquium 'Schengen Still Going Strong: Evaluation and Update', at Maastricht, 5 February 1999.
12. Not all refugees from ex-Yugoslavia headed west – by the autumn of 1998, more than 300 000 ethnic Hungarians had fled Serbia and moved across the border into Hungary (Long 1998).
13. 178 000 (1996), 134 419 (1997), 103 080 (1998) and 104 916 (1999).
14. The new 1993 international frontier between the Czech Republic and Slovakia was at first credited with the temporary decline (Bort 1996: 61–2) but the Department of Migration in Prague now considers the effects of the drastic tightening of the German asylum laws in 1993 as the main reason for the temporary decline (Mrkvica interview).
15. Nikitin was cleared of charges of espionage in December 1999 after receiving widespread international support. This vindication may show an unusual degree of judicial independence rather than a change in Russian official opinion.
16. Particularly in the Czech Republic where, in 1992, surface coal was still the source of 65 per cent of primary energy (Hilz 1998: 132).
17. Poland and the Czech Republic lead the table of *Waldsterben* with, in 1995, 54.9 and 59.7 per cent of their forests affected – the German level of 24.4 per cent was also above the European average (Hilz 1998: 133).
18. Austria increased its border guards' strength from 4566 in January 1977 to 5551 by 1 July 1997.
19. Marek Bienkowski, director of the Polish border guards, announced the building of 15 new border crossings on the eastern frontier by 2001, along with an increase of the number of border guards and the installation, aided by EU PHARE money, of electronic passport-reading equipment at border checkpoints. The EU is supporting the modernisation of Polish frontier surveillance technology with a subsidy of nearly £30 million. Using European PHARE money, Hungary has undertaken to open three new border crossings on its Romanian border, two on its Ukrainian border, one on the Slovene border, as well as upgrading Rajika on the Slovak border as a motorway crossing.

20. Border crossings between Germany and Poland increased by 40 per cent between 1990 and 1991; nearly 300 million people crossed the Polish borders in 1995; in 1996, 1.75 million lorries, 45 million cars and 122 million people crossed the Polish–German frontier (Kalek, Piwowarski and Brochwicz interviews; Hilz 1998: 135); at the German–Czech border the number of persons crossing the frontier rose from 59 to 98 million between 1991 and 1995, the number of cars from 17 to 30 million (Schwarz and Mrkvica interviews).

21. German politicians, like the Saxon Minister for the Interior (*Süddeutsche Zeitung* 24 November 1997), supported the wish of applicant states in East and Central European countries to participate in the Schengen Information System and maintained that a full link to the Strasbourg-based computer system was possible by mid-1999. Yet, the SIS computer cannot cope with the Scandinavian enlargement of Schengen, let alone extension to the east. The date expected for the introduction of the new upgraded system is around 2003.

22. Allegations that Italian organised crime was investing in Slovenian casino and tourist developments had little to do with border controls except insofar as most of the clients for the casinos come from Italy and would be discouraged by stringent checks. The different regulatory regime in Slovenia facilitates these investments.

23. Minority counting is notoriously difficult. Paul Gillespie (1999a) uses that figure for Romania; Romanian sources, citing the census of 1992, estimate 1.62 million Hungarians living in Romania. Nowak also gives the figure of *c.*570 000 Hungarians in Slovakia, according to the census of 1991 (Nowak 1994: 135). See also Stewart (1992), Schöpflin (1993) and Dunay (1997).

24. Liaison officers from Germany have been sent to Turkey and ten other states in Central and Eastern Europe. British and French liaison officers are also, to a lesser degree, present in Eastern Europe.

25. The EU has been much less present than the United States. For example, the US State Department has invested more than $8 millon into police training in Hungary, and the FBI has an office in Budapest.

26. The project has four general modules (police ethics, management, police co-operation in Europe, and training), and is subdivided into 13 specific modules covering control of migration flows, drug trafficking, financial crime and money laundering, stolen art, car theft, trade in human beings, trafficking in weapons and radioactive materials, environmental crime, methods of technical crime investigation, prevention of criminality, maintaining public order, policing a multicultural society, and dealing with extreme phenomena.

27. The Polish leader of the Christian-National Union, Ryszard Czarnecki, criticised the foundation of the Carpathian Euroregion in 1993 as an example of a supranational organisation leading to loss of national and cultural identity (*Grasshopper*, 1).

28. Main objectives are the 'Via Baltica' motorway link and an upgraded railway from the Polish–Lithuanian border to Kaunas.

29. Covering the borderlands of Germany, Poland and the Czech Republic, with 1.7 million inhabitants (Heffner 1998: 60), involving 40 communes of the Jelenia Gora voivodeship, and two communal unions on the German

and Czech side. Due to particular environmental problems (air pollution by power plants, damage caused by opencast mining), environmental issues are a priority for this Euroregion (Gruchman and Walk 1997: 182–3).

30. Eighteen towns and communities of the Zielona Góra voivodeship on the Polish side, and the German districts of Cottbus, Forst, Guben, Spremberg and Eisenhüttenstadt-Land, centred on the twin cities of Guben/Gubin (Heffner 1998: 60, Gruchman and Walk 1997: 183).

31. With *c*.800 000 inhabitants (450 000 on the German side, 350 000 in Poland). The secretariats are situated in Frankfurt/Oder and Slubice (Heffner 1998: 60). The centrepiece is the European University Viadrina at Frankfurt/Oder, founded in 1991. One-third of the *c*.3000 students are recruited from Poland. The university is complemented by the 'Collegium Polonicum' (opened in 1998), a cross-border research and teaching institute on the bank of the Oder in Slubice, run jointly by the Viadrina and the Adam-Mickiewicz-University of Poznan. The Pomerania Euroregion includes 54 communes and towns of the Szczecin voivodeship, nine districts and towns from Brandenburg on the German side; it covers over 17 000 square miles and a population of approximately 1.5 million (Gruchman and Walk 1997: 183).

32. Including the Szczecin industrial centre, the island of Bornholm/Denmark, and Sweden. It was formally established in December 1995 as a pilot project for Baltic Sea partnership.

33. The quadrilateral agreement establishing the Euroregion 'Niemen' was signed on 9 February 1996 by Poland, Lithuania, Belarus and Russia (Kaliningrad) (Euroregion Niemen, 1996: 4). Russian (Kaliningrad) co-operation lagged behind; and reluctance on the part of Belarus meant that little progress was made beyond statements of intent (Kokscharow 1997).

34. An example of environmental co-operation is the Sewage Project Bärenstein/Vejprty in the borderlands of Saxony and the Czech Republic opened in 1996. PHARE/CBC and INTERREG II provided capital grants for the project. This pilot project is embedded in a wider strategy of the Saxon State Ministry for the Environment and State Development, 'Cross-border Sewage and Drinking Water Solutions on the Oder', supported by the EU LIFE programme (Freistaat Sachsen 1997). In the Euroregion Spree–Neisse–Bober, a similar sewage plant at Guben/Gubin was built with support from INTERREG II.

35. Peripheral zones often have unspoiled resources, which provide a basis for sustainable, environmentally friendly tourism. For example, the Danube national park, between Austria and Hungary, was agreed in October 1996.

36. Examples include Czech, Bavarian and Austrian borderlands, as illustrated by *Glas ohne Grenzen*, a guide to the glass museums and collections in the Bayerischer Wald, Böhmerwald and Mühlviertel (Arbeitsgruppe der Glasmuseen 1994). There are cultural festivals like *Mitte Europa*, or Bavarian–Bohemian *Kulturtage* in Weiden, as well as programmes for the stocking of Czech libraries with the literature from across the border (Freistaat Bayern 1995: 34), or the provision of German–Czech one-year school exchanges and financial support for Czech language courses in German adult education centres (Euregio Egrensis).

37. See Euregio Bayerischer Wald-Böhmerwald (n.d.) and Euregio Egrensis (n.d.).
38. Among the few concrete German–Polish joint ventures in the Polish borderlands are the Volkswagen investments in Gorzów Wielkopolski (Landsberg) where cables and leads are manufactured, and Poznan where VW built a car factory.
39. Unemployment rates vary widely on the German–Polish and German–Czech borders. In the Euroregion Pomerania there is 25 per cent unemployment on the German (rural) side, only 6.3 per cent around Szczecin; in the Euroregion Elbe–Labe the figures are 14.5 per cent (German) and 5.5 per cent (Czech).
40. Differences in 'national character' and different wage and wealth levels came second and third; among secondary obstacles, historical legacy replaced language as the main issue of concern (Jerábek 1998: 96).
41. Euroregions are promoting the mutual learning of languages, as in the 'Sptkania' project of the Euroregion Spree–Neiße–Bober, involving seven elementary schools in Poland and Germany, respectively (Euroregion Spree–Neiße–Bober 1997: 10).
42. Yet, close encounters with wealth and wage differences or with phenomena like street prostitution can also have a negative effect on the perception of 'the other' (Neuss et al. 1998: 161).
43. This is also the case for universities along the Baltic coast, in Szczecin, Greifswald and Rostock (Gruchman and Walk 1997).

Bibliography

Ágh, A. (1998) *The Politics of Central Europe*, London: Sage.

Alcock, A. (1970) *The History of the South Tyrol Question*, London: Michael Joseph.

Algieri, F. (1996) 'In Need of a Comprehensive Approach: the European Union and Possible External Security Challenges', in Algieri, F., Janning, J., Rumberg, D. (eds), *Managing Security in Europe: the European Union and the Challenge of Enlargement*, Gütersloh: Bertelsmann.

Aliboni, R. (1991) *European Security Across the Mediterranean*, Paris: Institute for Security Studies/Western European Union (Chaillot Papers, 2).

Alliès, P. (1995) 'Les Régions du Sud et les Programmes Méditerranéens de l'Union Européenne', *Pôle Sud*, 2, 141–6.

Almond, G. A., Verba, S. (1963, new edn 1989) *The Civic Culture*, London: Sage.

Almond, G. A., Verba, S. (eds) (1981) *The Civic Culture Re-Visited*, London: Sage.

Amato, G., Batt, J. (1999) *The Long-Term Implications of EU-Enlargement: the Nature of the New Border*, Florence: European University Institute.

Amin, S. (1997) *Capitalism in the Age of Globalization*, London and New Jersey: Zed.

Ancel, J. (1938) *Géographie des frontières*, Paris: Gallimard.

Anderson, B. (1983) *Imagined Communities: Reflections on the Rise and Spread of Nationalism*, London: Verso.

Anderson, B. (1991) *Imagined Communities: Reflexions on the Origin and Spread of Nationalism*, London: Verso.

Anderson, E. W. (1992) 'Malta: Boundaries, Threats, Risks', *Boundary Bulletin*, 4, 21–4.

Anderson, M. (1982) 'Scenarios for Conflict in Frontier Regions', in Strassoldo, R., Delli Zotti, G. (eds) *Co-operation and Conflict in Border Areas*, Milano: Angeli, 145–78.

Anderson, M. (ed.) (1983) *Frontier Regions in Western Europe*, London: Frank Cass.

Anderson, M. (1983a) 'The Political Problems of Frontier Regions' in Anderson, M. (ed.), 1–17.

Anderson, M. (1996) *Frontiers: Territory and State Formation in the Modern World*, Cambridge: Polity.

Anderson, M. (1998) 'Transfrontier Co-operation – History and Theory', in Brunn, G., Schmitt-Egner, P. (eds), 78–97.

Anderson, M. (2000) *Border Regimes and Security in an Enlarged European Community*, Florence: European University Institute Working Paper.

Anderson, M. (2000a) 'Control of Immigration and Exclusion', *Scottish Affairs*, 30, 16–27.

Anderson, M., Bort, E. (eds) (1996) *Boundaries and Identities: the Eastern Frontier of the European Union*, Edinburgh: ISSI.

Anderson, M., Bort, E. (eds) (1997) *Schengen and EU Enlargement: Security and Co-operation at the Eastern Frontier of the European Union*, Edinburgh: ISSI.

Anderson M., Bort, E. (eds) (1998) *The Frontiers of Europe*, London: Pinter.

Anderson M., Bort, E. (eds) (1998a) *Schengen and the Southern Frontier of the European Union*, Edinburgh: ISSI.

Anderson, M., den Boer, M., Cullen, P., Gilmore, W., Raab, C., Walker, N. (1995) *Policing the European Union: Theory, Law and Practice*, Oxford: Clarendon Press.

Anderson, P. (1999) 'A Ripple of the Polonaise', *London Review of Books*, 21(23), 3–10.

Angouras, V. (1998) 'Greece's Northern Frontier', in Bort, E. (ed.), 121–39.

Archibugi, D., Held, D. (eds) (1995) *Cosmopolitan Democracy*, Cambridge: Polity.

Arnold, M. (1977) *La Coordination des schémas d'aménagement des régions frontalières: le cas de l'Alsace, de la Rhénanie-Palatinat, du Pays de Bade et de la Suisse du Nord-Est*, Strasbourg: Council of Europe.

Arnold-Plassière, M. (1979) 'La Coopération régionale en matière de l'aménagement du territoire: l'étude du cas de la vallée du Rhin', Thesis Strasbourg.

Arthur, P. (1999) 'Anglo-Irish Relations in the New Dispensation: Towards a Post-Nationalist Framework', in Anderson, M., Bort, E. (eds) *The Irish Border: History, Politics, Culture*, Liverpool: Liverpool University Press.

Ash, T. G. (1999) *History of the Present: Essays, Sketches and Despatches from Europe in the Nineties*, London: Allen Lane.

Asiwaju, A. I. (1996) 'Public Policy for Overcoming Marginalisation: Borderlands in Africa, North America and Western Europe' in Nolutchungu, S. (ed.) *Margins of Insecurity: Minorities and International Security*, Rochester: Rochester University Press, 251–84.

Association Randonnées Pyrénéennes (1995) *Grand Guide des Pyrénées France, Espagne, Andorre*, Editions Milan.

Auffermann, B. (1992) 'Finnland: Neuorientierung nach dem Kalten Krieg', *Aus Politik und Zeitgeschichte*, B43, 36–47.

Aykaç, A. (1994) *Transborder Regionalisation*, Sindelfingen: Libertas (Libertas Paper 13).

Badie, R. (1995) *Fin des Territoires*, Paris: Fayard.

Badie, B. (1999) *Un Monde sans Souveraineté: les Etats entre Ruse et Responsabilité*, Paris: Fayard.

Baettig, M., Ricci, C. (1995) 'L'Europe des Régions: de la Collaboration Franco-Italo-Suisse à la coopération avec les Pays de l'Est', in Haegi, C. (ed.).

Balme, R., Barbosa, C., Burbaud, F. (1997) 'La Coopération entre Aquitaine et Euskadi: convergences et divergences', in J. Palard (ed.), 119–30.

Balta, P. (ed.) (1992) *La Méditerranée: Réalités et espoirs de la coopération*, Paris: La Découverte/Fondation René Seydoux.

Banos, K. (1998) 'Cyprus: What Does the Green Line Actually Divide?' in Bort, E. (ed.), 141–52.

Barker E., Clark G., Vaucher, P. (eds) (1952) *The European Inheritance*, Oxford: Oxford University Press.

Barrat, J. (1997) *Géopolitique de la francophonie*, Paris: Presses Universitaires de France.

Bartlett, R., Mackay, A. (eds) (1989) *Medieval Frontier Societies*, Oxford: Clarendon Press.

Baumert, R. (1969) *La 'Regio'*, Paris: Dalloz.

Beck, U. (1999) 'Beyond the Nation State', *New Statesman*, 6 December.

Becker, P. (1998) 'Der Nutzen der Osterweiterung für die Europäische Union', *Integration*, 4, 225–37.

Bellamy, R. P., Castiglione, D. (1997) 'Building the Union: the Nature of Sovereignty in the Political Architecture of Europe', *Law and Philosophy*, 16, 421–45.

Belorgey, J. M. (1991) *La Police au Rapport*, Nancy: Presses Universitaires de Nancy.

Bergdoll, U., Oldag, A. (1999) 'SZ-Interview mit EU-Erweiterungskommissar Verheugen', *Süddeutsche Zeitung*, 29 September.

Berger, M. (1997) 'Die Bratislava Connection', *Kurier*, 20 April.

Beyerlin, U. (1998) 'Neue rechtliche Entwicklungen der regionalen und grenz-überschreitenden lokalen Zusammenarbeit', in Brunn, G., Schmitt-Egner, P. (eds), 118–34.

Bhabha, H. K. (1994) *The Location of Culture*, London: Routledge.

Biersteker T. J., Weber, C. (eds) (1996) *State Sovereignty as Social Construct*, Cambridge: Cambridge University Press.

Bigo, D. (1996) *Les Polices en Réseaux. L'Expérience Européenne*, Paris: Presses de Sciences Po.

Bigo, D. (1998) 'Frontiers and Security in the European Union: the Illusion of Migration Control', in Anderson, M. Bort, E. (eds), 148–64.

Bigo, D. (1999) 'The Landscape of Police Co-operation', in Bort, E. and Keat, R. (eds), 59–74.

Billig, M. (1995) *Banal Nationalism*, London: Sage.

Blake, G., Pratt, M., Schofield, C., Lin Sien, C., Grundy-Warr, C. (eds) (1997) *Environmental Boundaries and Environmental Security: Frameworks for Regional Cooperation*, The Hague: Kluwer Law International.

Blatter, J. (1996) 'Political Co-operation in Cross-Border Regions: Two Explanatory Approaches', Zurich: ESRA.

Blechschmidt, P. (1999) Interview with Peter Schatzer, *Süddeutsche Zeitung*, 15 November.

Blechschmidt, P. (1999a) 'Luxusschleusung für 40 000 Mark', *Süddeutsche Zeitung*, 15 November.

Bonnino, E., King, A. and others (1997) *How Much Popular Support is there for the EU*, Brussels: Philip Morris Institute.

Borja, A. (1997) 'Escenarios estratégicos para Euskal Herria: cooperación trans-fronteriza entre las regiones vascas?' Bilbao: *Jornados de Cooperación Transfronteriza*, Euskadi-Aquitania.

Borja, A., Letamendia, F., Sodupe, K. (1998) *La Construccion del Espacio Vasco-Aquitano. Un Estudio Multidisciplinar*, Bilbao: Universidad del País Vasco.

Bort, E. (1996) 'Coping with a New Situation', in Anderson, M., Bort, E. (eds), 61–2.

Bort, E. (1997) 'Boundaries and Identities: Cross-Border Co-operation and the Eastern Frontier of the European Union', in Svob-Dokic, N. (ed.), The *Cultural Identity of Central Europe*, Zagreb: Europe House, 133–44.

Bort, E. (1997a) 'Crossing the EU Frontier: Eastern Enlargement of the EU, Cross-Border Regionalism and State Sovereignty', *Interregiones*, 6, 20–31.

Bort, E. (1998) '*Mitteleuropa*: the Difficult Frontier', in Anderson, M., Bort, E. (eds), 91–108.

Bort, E. (ed.) (1998a) *Borders and Borderlands in Europe*, Edinburgh: ISSI.

Bort, E. (2000) 'The 1998 Belfast Agreement: Peace for a "Troubled" Region?', in Bort, E., Evans, N. (eds), 429–61.

Bort, E., Evans, N. (eds) (2000) *Networking Europe: Essays on Regionalism and Social Democracy*, Liverpool: Liverpool University Press.

Bort, E. and Keat, R. (eds) (1999) *The Boundaries of Understanding*, Edinburgh: ISSI.

Bourdieu, P. (1993) *Invitation to Sociology*, London: Sage.

Boure, R. (1996) 'Régions Frontalières, Télévision et Communication Electronique', *Sciences de Société*, 37, 111–29.

Bourret, C. (1995) *Les Pyrénées Centrales du IXe au XIXe siècle: la formation progressive d'une frontière*, Aspet: Pyrégraph.

Brandes, D. (1995) 'Die Zerstörung der deutsch–tschechischen Konfliktgemeinschaft 1938–1947', Niedersächsische Landeszentrale für politische Bildung (ed.), *Tschechen, Slowaken, Deutsche: Nachbarn in Europa*, Bonn: Bundeszentrale für politische Bildung.

Braudel, F. (1973) *The Mediterranean World in the Age of Philip II*, Vol. 2, London: Collins.

Brem, S., Bruno, S. (1997) *Managing Local Conflicts through Transnational Co-operation: the Example of the Alpine Convention*, Berne: ECPR Wokshop 9.

Brennock, M. (1999) 'Ahern backs Hungary's EU Entry, and Irish Success', *The Irish Times*, 4 November.

Bretherton, C. (1999) 'Security Issues in the Wider Europe: the Role of EU-CEEC Relations', in M. Mannin (ed.), 183–213.

Breuilly, J. (1998) 'Sovereignty, Citizenship and Nationality. Reflections on the Case of Germany', in Anderson, M., Bort, E. (eds), 36–67.

Briner, H. (1996) 'Das Europa der Regionen – die Perspektive des 21. Jahrhunderts', in Anderson, M., Bort, E. (eds), 39–46.

Brown, C. (1997) 'Two Heads are Better than One: Why Border Regions Collaborate', Åre-Meråker: ERSA.

Brunn, G., Schmitt-Egner, P. (eds) *Grenzüberschreitende Zusammenarbeit in Europa: Theorie – Empirie – Praxis*, Baden-Baden: Nomos.

Brunn, G., Schmitt-Egner, P., Cappelin, R., Batey, P. W. J. (eds) (1993) *Regional Networks, Border Regions and European Integration*, London: Pion.

Buck, S. J. (1998) *The Global Commons: an Introduction*, London: Earthscan.

Burke, I. (1998) 'The Sea and Land Borders of Portugal and the Euro Med Partnership', in Anderson, M., Bort, E. (eds) (1998a), 93–107.

Burke-Kennedy, D. (1999) 'An Island Still Torn by the Forces of Conflict', *The Irish Times*, 6 December.

Burleigh, M., Wipperman, B. (1991) *The Racial State: Germany 1933–1945*, Cambridge: Cambridge University Press.

Burnett Tylor, E. (1871) *Primitive Culture: Researches into the Development of Mythology, Philosophy, Religion, Art and Custom*, London: Murray.

Busch, H. (1992) 'Organisierte Kriminalität: Vom Nutzen eines unklaren Begriffs', *Demokratie und Recht*, 20, 374–95.

Busek, E., Wilfinger, G. (eds) (1986) *Aufbruch nach Mitteleuropa: Rekonstruktion eines versunkenen Kontinents*, Vienna: Edition Atelier.

Buttsworth, M. (1995) 'Globalisation: What's New? Gunpowder, Genghiz and Henry the Navigator' in Phillimore, J. (ed.) *Local Matters: Perspectives on the*

Globalisation of Technology, Institute of Science and Technology, Murdoch University, 182–86.

Buzan, B. (1991) *People, States and Fear: an Agenda for International Security Studies in the Post-Cold War Era*, London: Harvester Wheatsheaf.

Buzan, B. (1997) 'Re-thinking Security after the Cold War', *Cooperation and Conflict*, 32(1), 5–28.

Caluori, J. (1994) 'Die Überwachung der "grünen Grenze" ist wichtig und anspruchsvoll', in *Das Grenzwachtkorps* (excerpts from a special edition of *Zoll-Rundschau*), 32–7.

Cambot, P. (1998) 'Commentaire du Traité de Bayonne du 10 mars 1995 relatif à la coopération frontalière entre collectivités territoriales', in Lafourcade, M. (ed.) *La Frontière des Origines à nos jours*, Bordeaux: Presses Universitaires de Bordeaux.

Cameron, G. (2000) *Nuclear Terrorism: a Threat Assessment for the Twenty-first Century*, London: Macmillan.

Camillera, J. A., Falk, J. (1992) *The End of Sovereignty? Politics in a Shrinking World*, Aldershot: Elgar.

Caplan, R., Feffer, J. (eds) (1996) *Europe's New Nationalism: States and Minorities in Conflict*, Oxford: Oxford University Press.

Cappelin, R., Batey, P. W. J. (eds) (1993) *Regional Networks, Border Regions and European Integration*, London: Pion.

Casadevante Romani, C. F. de (1985) *La Frontera Hispano-Francesa de Vecindad* (Especial referencia al sector frontizero del País Vasco), Bilbao: Universidad del País Vasco.

Chaussier, J. -D. (1997) 'Scènes du débat politique au Pays Basque français; recomposition ou simulacre?' in J. Palard (ed.), 71–92.

Church, A., Reid, P. (1995) 'Transfrontier Co-operation, Spatial Development Strategies and the Emergence of a New Scale of Regulation: the Anglo-French Border', *Regional Studies*, 29(3), 297–316.

Cohen, A. P. (1994) *Self-Consciousness: an Alternative Anthropology of Identity*, London: Routledge.

Cohen, A. P. (1998) 'Boundaries and Boundary Consciousness', in Anderson, M., Bort, E. (eds) (1998), 22–35.

Cole, J. W., Wolfe, E. R. (1974) *The Hidden Frontier*, New York: Academic Press.

Colley, L. (1992) *Britons: the Forging of the Nation 1707–1837*, New Haven: Yale University Press.

Connolly, K. (1998) 'Hundreds Held in Border Logjam', *The Guardian*, 9 October.

'Coopération Transfrontalière – Europe du Sud', *Pôle Sud*, 3.

Coulter, C. (1998) 'No "Flood" of Refugees in Europe', *The Irish Times*, 2 December.

Covas, A. (1995) 'La Coopération transfrontalière entre régions sous développées. Le cas d'Alentjo (Portugal) et d'Extramadura (Espagne)', *Pôle Sud*, 3, 72–8.

Croft, S., Redmond, J., Wyn Rees, G., Webber, M. (1999) *The Enlargement of Europe*, Manchester: Manchester University Press.

Cullen, P. J. (1997) *Crime and Policing in Germany in the 90s*, Institute of German Studies Discussion Paper series (IGS), 13, Birmingham: University of Birmingham.

Curtin, D., Meijers, H. (1995) 'The Principle of Open Government in Schengen and the European Union: Democratic Retrogression?', *Common Market Law Review*, 32, 391–442.

Cvjeticanin, B. (ed.) (1999) *The Mediterranean: Cultural Identity and Intercultural Dialogue*, Zagreb: Institute for International Relations/Culturelink.

Czaban, L. (1999) 'Hungarian Economic Transformation: Gradual Progress towards Accession?', in Mannin, M. (ed.), 276–94.

Czachór, Z. (1998) 'Polen in Europa: Zentrum oder Peripherie?', in Neuss, B., Jurczek, P., Hilz, W. (eds), 32–47.

Darré, A. (1997) 'France–Espagne Aquitaine–Euskadi. Images croisées et relations transnationales', in Palard, J. (ed.), 31–50.

Dauderstädt, M. (1996) 'Ostmitteleuropas Demokratien im Spannungsfeld von Transformation und Integration', *Integration*, 4, 208–23.

Davies, N. (1996) *Europe: a History*, Oxford: Oxford University Press.

De Castro Ruano, J. L. (1997) 'La Coopération transfrontalière entre le Pays Basque et l'Aquitaine' in Palard, J. (ed.), 103–18.

Delamont, S. (1995) *Appetites and Identities: an Introduction to the Social Anthropology of Western Europe*, London: Routledge.

Demangeon, A., Febvre, L. (1997, first edn 1935) *Le Rhin. Problèmes d'histoire et d'économie*, Paris: Perrin.

Den Boer, M. (ed.) (1998) *Schengen's Final Days. The Incorporation of Schengen into the New TEU, External Borders and Information Systems*, Maastricht: EIPA.

Den Boer, M., Corrado, L. (forthcoming) 'For the Record or Off the Record: Comments about the Incorporation of Schengen into the EU', *European Journal of Migration and Law*, 4.

Deniau, X. (1995) *La Francophonie*, Paris: Presses Universitaires de France.

Derrac, M. (1996) 'L'Adaptation de la douane au nouveau contexte international et communautaire', *Revue Française de Finances Publiques*, no. 54.

Deutsch, K. W. et al. (1957) *Political Community and the North Atlantic Area*, Princeton: Princeton University Press.

Dinan, D. (1994) *Ever Closer Union?: An Introduction to the European Community*, Basingstoke and London: Macmillan.

Dion, R. (1947) *Les Frontières de la France*, Paris: Hachette.

Djian, J. -M. (1996) *La Politique culturelle*, Paris: le Monde Editions.

Douglas, W. A. (1998) 'A Western Perspective on an Eastern Interpretation of where North meets South: Pyrenean Borderland Cultures', in Wilson, T. M., Donnan, H. (eds), *Border Identities: Nation and State at International Frontiers*, Cambridge: Cambridge University Press.

Doukupil, J. (1998) 'Entwicklung und Zusammenarbeit im tschechisch–deutschen Grenzgebiet', in Neuss, B. et al. (eds), 82–7.

Dumont, G.-F. (1998) 'La Coopération transfrontalière de proximité', in *La Coopération Transfrontalière Franco-Italienne*, Nice: Institut du Droit de la Paix et le Dévéloppement, 75–86.

Dunay, P. (1997) 'Whence the Threat to Peace in Europe?', in Gambles, I. (ed.), 40–60.

Dupuy, P.-M. (1983) 'Legal Aspects of Transfrontier Co-operation', in Anderson, M. (ed.), 50–63.

Duroselle, J.-B. (1991) *Europe: a History of its Peoples*, London: Viking.

Dyson, K., Wilks, S. (1983) *Industrial Crisis*, Oxford: Martin Robertson.

Eco, U. (1987) 'Reports from the Global Village' in *Travels in Hyperreality*, London: Pan, 135–57.

Eco, U. (ed.) (1988) *Meaning and Mental Representations*, Bloomington: Indiana University Press.

Éger, G., Langer, J. (eds) (1996) *Border, Region and Ethnicity in Central Europe*, Klagenfurt: Norea.

Engel, C., Rogers, J. H. (1996) 'How Wide is the Border?', *American Economic Review*, 86(5), 1112–25.

Esposito, J. (1994) 'Political Islam: Beyond the Green Menace', *Current History*, 93(579).

Fabre, T. (1997) 'Frontiers and Passages', *Rive (Review of Mediterranean Politics and Culture)*, 2, 8–15.

Febvre, L. (with Demangeon, A.) (1935) *Le Rhin. Problèmes d'histoire et d'économie*, Paris: Colin.

Febvre, L. (1997) ed. Schüttler, P. *Le Rhin: Histoire, mythes et réalités*, Paris: Perrin.

Fink, O. (1996) *La Coopération décentralisée des collectivitiés locales: l'exemple alsacien*, Strasbourg: Hirlé.

Fitzgerald, G., Gillespie, P. (1996) 'Ireland's British Question', *Prospect*, October.

Fitzmaurice, J. (1993) 'Regional Cooperation in Central Europe', *West European Politics*, 16(3), 380–400.

Foucher, M. (1998) 'The Geopolitics of European Frontiers', in Anderson M., Bort, E. (eds), 235–50.

Foucher, M. (1999) 'Europe and its Long-lasting Variable Geography', in Bort, E., Keat, R. (eds), 163–9.

Fox, R. (1997) 'Europe's Rio Grande Widens', *The European*, 20 November.

Francis, A. (1999) 'Poland: the Return to Europe', in Manning, M. (ed.), 295–317.

Fritz-Vannahme, J. (2000) 'Spiel ohne Grenzen', *Die Zeit*, 20 January.

Funk, A. (1994) *Control Myths: the Eastern Border of the Federal Republic of Germany before and after 1989*, Madrid: ECPR Working Paper.

Galeotti, M. (1995) *Cross-Border Crime and the Former Soviet Union (Boundary & Territory Briefing, 1, 5)*, Durham: International Boundaries Research Unit.

Gallo, E. (1995) 'The Penal System in France: From Correctionalism to Managerialism', in Ruggiero, V., Ryan, M., and Sim, J. (eds) *West European Penal Systems: a Critical Anatomy*, London: Sage.

Gambles, I. (ed.) (1995) *A Lasting Peace in Central Europe? The Expansion of the European Security-community*, Paris: WEU/Institute for Security Studies (Challiot Paper 20).

Gamillscheg, H. (1999) 'Finland Aims to Draw EU's Attention to Russia', *Frankfurter Rundschau* (English web edition), 10 November.

Gandiaga, R. (1998) L'Espace Bayonne-Saint Sebastien, lieu d'échanges trans-frontaliers. Un territoire en cours d'intégration'. Thesis Université Montesquieu–Bordeaux IV.

Ganster, P. et al. (eds) (1997) *Borders and Border Regions in Europe and North America*, San Diego: San Diego State University Press.

Gasperlin, M. (1997) 'Schengen Needs Modification: a Slovenian Perspective', in Anderson, M., Bort, E. (eds), 102–3.

Gellner, E. (1983) *Nations and Nationalism*, Oxford: Blackwell.

Gellner, E. (1997) *Nationalism*, London: Weidenfeld and Nicolson.

Gerner, K. (1997) 'The Evolving Political Role of Borders and Border Regions in Central Europe' , in Ganster, P. et al. (eds), 141–62.

Giannoni, R. (1998) 'La Coopération transfrontalière de proximité', in *La Coopération Transfrontalière Franco-Italienne*, Nice: Institut du Droit de la Paix et le Développement, 63–8.

Gillespie, P. (1999), 'Not Much Success as Czechs Find Fruits of Democracy Sour', *The Irish Times*, 9 January.

Gillespie, P. (1999a) 'Hungary Presses Reluctant EU for Accession Date', *The Irish Times*, 16 January.

Giulianotti, R., Williams, J. (eds) (1994) *Game Without Frontiers: Football, Identity and Modernity*, Aldershot: Arena.

Glassner, M. A. (1993) *Political Geography*, New York: Wiley.

Gold, P. (1994) *A Stone in Spain's Shoe: the Search for a Solution to the Problem of Gibraltar*, Liverpool: Liverpool University Press.

Gómez-Matarán, N. (1998) 'Cross-Border Co-operation in Southern Europe: the Catalunya/Languedoc Roussillon/Midi Pyrenees Euroregion', in Brunn, G., Schmitt-Egner, P. (eds), 162–71.

Gottman, J. (1973) *The Significance of Territory*, Charlottesville: University of Virginia Press.

Grabbe, H., Hughes, K. (1998) *Enlarging the EU Eastwards*, London: Chatham House Papers, Royal Institute of International Affairs.

Gray, J. (1998) *False Dawn: the Delusion of Global Capitalism*, London: Granta.

Griffith-Jones, S. (1998) *Global Capital Flows: Should they be Regulated?* Basingstoke: Macmillan.

Grimm, F.-D. (1995) 'Veränderte Grenzen und Grenzregionen, veränderte Grenzbewertungen in Deutschland und Europa', in Grimm, F. -D. (ed.), 1–16.

Grimm, F.-D. (ed.) (1995a) *Regionen an deutschen Grenzen: Strukturwandel an der ehemaligen innerdeutschen Grenze und an der deutschen Ostgrenze*, Leipzig: Institut für Länderkunde.

Groß, B., Schmitt-Egner, P. (1994) *Europas kooperierende Regionen: Rahmenbedingungen und Praxis grenzüberschreitender Zusammenarbeit deutscher Grenzregionen in Europa*, Baden-Baden: Nomos.

Gruchman, B., Walk, F. (1997) 'Transboundary Cooperation in the Polish–German Border Region', in Ganster, P. et al. (eds), 177–91.

Gruša, J. (1996) '"Ich will die Grenze loben": Gedanken zur Kultur der Grenze', in Anderson, M., Bort, E. (eds), 3–32.

Guibernau, M. (1999) *Nations without States: Political Communities in a Global Age*, Cambridge: Polity.

Guichonnet, P., Raffestin, C. (1970) *Géographie des frontières*, Paris: Presses Universitaires de France.

Guizzi, V. (1997) 'The European Union between Widening and Strengthening', *The European Union Review*, 2(1), 49–59.

Habermas, J. (1992) 'Citizenship and National Identity: Some Reflections on the Future of Europe', *Praxis International*, 12(1), 1–19.

Haegi, C. (1995) 'The Regions in the Face of Europe', *Regions of Europe*, 10, 70–3.

Hall, E. T. (1977) *Beyond Culture*, New York: Anchor.

Handl, V. (1998) 'Die deutsch–tschechische Erklärung von 1997: Politisches Ende eines schwierigen historischen Kapitels?', *Welttrends*, 22, 9–26.

Hansen, N. (1983) 'International Co-operation in Border Regions: an Overview and Research Agenda', *International Regional Science Review*, 8(3), 255–70.

Hansen, N., Church, A., Reid, P. (1996) 'Urban Power International Networks and Competition. The Example of Cross Border Cooperation', *Urban Studies*, 33(8), 1297–318.

Harvie, C. (1996) *The Walls in the Head*, Edinburgh: ISSI.

Heberlein, H. (1996) 'Die Euregio Egrensis: Grenzüberschreitende Zusammenarbeit im deutsch–tschechischen Grenzraum', in Anderson, M., Bort, E. (eds), 47–56.

Heberlein, H. (1997) 'Das Karlsruher Übereinkommen mit Frankreich, Luxemburg und der Schweiz über die grenzüberschreitende Zusammenarbeit', *Bayerische Verwaltungsblätter*, 737–42.

Hedetoft, U. (1994) 'The State of Sovereignty in Europe: Political Concept or Cultural Self-Image', in Zetterholm, S. (ed.) *National Cultures and European Integration*, Oxford: Berg.

Hedetoft, U. (1995) *Signs of Nations: Studies in the Political Semiotics of Self and Other in Contemporary European Nationalism*, Aldershot: Dartmouth.

Heffner, K. (1998) 'Entwicklung und Zusammenarbeit im deutsch–polnischen Grenzraum', in Neuss, B. et al. (eds), 48–70.

Held, D. et al. (1999) *Global Transformations: Politics, Economics and Culture*, Cambridge: Polity.

Hilpold, P. (1996) 'Wirtschaftlicher Regionalismus – Koordination und Wettbewerb der Integrationszonen', *Integration*, 4, 224–35.

Hilz, W. (1998) 'Sicherheitspolitische Kooperation zwischen Deutschland, Polen und der Tschechischen Republik', in Neuss, B. et al. (eds), 123–43.

Hinsley, F. H. (1986) *Sovereignty*, 2nd edn, Cambridge: Cambridge University Press.

Hitchens, C. (1990) 'The Island Stranded in Time: Cyprus', in Eyre, R. et al., *Frontiers*, London, BBC Books, 116–41.

Hobsbawm, E (1997) *On History*, London: Weidenfeld and Nicolson.

Hoffet, F. (1951) *Psychoanalyse de l'Alsace*, Paris: Flammarion.

Hoffman, J. (1999) *Sovereignty*, Buckingham: Open University Press.

Holmes, L. (1998) 'Europe's Changing Boundaries and the "Clash of Civilisations" Thesis', in Murray, P., Holmes, L. (eds), 19–42.

Holmes, L. (forthcoming) 'Crime, Corruption and Politics: International and Transnational Factors', in Zielonka, J., Pravda, A. (eds) *Democratic Consolidation in Eastern Europe: International and Transnational Factors*.

Horn, J. (1997) *Auf dem Weg zur 'Euro-Stadt'? Die deutsch–polnische Zusammenarbeit in den an der Oder und Neiße geteilten Städten*, Berlin: Bundesinstitut für ostwissenschaftliche und internationale Studien.

Horsman, M., Marshall, A. (1995) *After the Nation-State: Citizens, Tribalism and New World Disorder*, London: HarperCollins.

Howells, J. Wood, M. (1993) *The Globalisation of Production and Technology*, London: Belhaven.

Huntington, S. P. (1996) *The Clash of Civilizations?*, New York: Simon and Schuster.

Hurst, P., Thompson, G. (1996) *Globalization in Question*, Oxford: Blackwell.

Husser, P. (1989) *Un Instituteur alsacien: entre France et Allemagne. Journal de Philippe Husser 1914–1951*, Paris: Hachette.

Hutchings, K., Dannreuther, R. (eds) (1998) *Cosmopolitan Citizenship*, Basingstoke: Macmillan.

Huysmans, J. (1995) 'Migrants as a Security Problem: Dangers of "Securitizing" Societal Issues', in Miles, R., Thränhardt, D. (eds).

Huysmans, J. (1998) 'Dire et écrire la sécurité: le dilemme normatif des études de sécurité', *Cultures et Conflits*, 27(2), 177–204.

Illés, I. (1996) *The Carpathian Euroregion*, Tübingen: Europäisches Zentrum für Föderalismus-Forschung.

Ilves, T. H. (1997) 'Try Listening to the Opinion of East and Central Europeans', *International Herald Tribune*, 17 April.

Jackson, R. (1990) *Quasi-States: Sovereignty, International Relations and the Third World*, Cambridge: Cambridge University Press.

Jaedicke, W., Schwab, O. (1999) 'Brücke oder Bedrohung? Haltungen zur Kooperation in deutsch–polnischen Grenzregionen', *Welttrends*, 22, 27–43.

Jajesniak, D., Stoklosa, K. (1999) *Geteilte Städte an der Oder und Neiße*, Potsdam: Verlag für Berlin Brandenburg.

James, A. (1986) *Sovereign Statehood: the Basis of International Society*, London: Allen & Unwin.

Jameson, F., Miyoshi, M. (eds) (1998) *The Cultures of Globalisation*, London: Duke University Press.

Jennings, I. (1956) *The Approach to Self-Government*, Cambridge: Cambridge University Press.

Jerábek, M. (1998) 'Regionalentwicklung und grenzüberschreitende Zusammenarbeit im tschechisch–deutschen Grenzraum, in Anderson, M., Bort, E. (eds), 88–89.

Joenniemi, P. (1997) 'Interregional Cooperation and a New Regionalist Paradigm', in Ganster, P. et al. (eds), 65–79.

Joppke, C. (1999) *Immigration and the Nation State: the United States, Germany and Great Britain*, Oxford: Oxford University Press.

Jurczek, P. (1997) 'Zwischenbilanz der grenzübergreifenden Zusammenarbeit in den deutsch–tschechischen Euroregionen, dargestellt am Beispiel der EUREGIO EGRENSIS', *Schriften zur Raumordnung und Landesplanung* (special issue).

Kahler, M. (ed.) (1998) *Capital Flows and Financial Crises*, Ithaca: Cornell University Press.

Kaltenborn, O. (1997) 'Die neue Todesgrenze an der Neiße', *Süddeutsche Zeitung*, 12 June.

Keating, M. (1998) *The New Regionalism in Western Europe: Territorial Re-structuring and Political Change*, Cheltenham: Elgar.

Keck, M. E., Sikkink, K. (1998) *Activists beyond Borders: Advocacy Networks in International Relations*, Ithaca: Cornell University Press.

Kennard, A. (1997) 'A Perspective on German–Polish Cross-Border Co-operation and European Integration', in Anderson, M., Bort, E. (eds), 53–60.

Khader, B. (ed.) (1994) *L'Europe et la Méditerranée: géopolitique de Proximité*, Paris: Harmattan.

King, R. (1998) 'The Mediterranean: Europe's Rio Grande', in Anderson, M., Bort, E. (eds), 109–34.

Klemencic, M. (1997) 'The Changing Shape of Central Europe', in Svob-Dokic, N. (ed.), 15–17.

Knight, R. (1997) *Austrian Identities: National, Ethnic and Provincial*, Berne: ECPR Workshop 26.

Koepke, W., Schmelz, B. (eds) (1999) *Das gemeinsame Haus Europa: Handbuch zur europäischen Kulturgeschichte*, Munich: Deutscher Taschenbuch Verlag.

Koivumaa, K. (1998) 'Europe: Several Identities, or One Single Identity?', *Perspectives*, 10, 21–37.

Kokscharow, A. (1997) 'Euroregio Neman: Das Projekt steht. Nun muß es realisiert werden', *W & U*, 3.

Konrád, G. (1985) *Antipolitik: Mitteleuropäische Meditationen*, Frankfurt: Suhrkamp.

Kopstein, J. (1998) 'Die Politik der nationalen Aussöhnung: Erinnerung und Institutionen in den deutsch–tschechischen Beziehungen seit 1989', *Welttrends*, 22, 49–66.

Kräfke, S., Heeg, S., Stein, R. (1997) *Regionen im Umbruch*, Frankfurt am Main: Campus.

Krämer, R. (1997) *Grenzen der Europäischen Union*, Potsdam: Brandenburgische Landeszentrale für Politische Bildung.

Krämer, R. (1999) 'Zwischen Kooperation und Abgrenzung – Die Ostgrenzen der Europäischen Union', *Welttrends*, 22, 9–26.

Kroeber, A. L., Kluckhohn, C. (1952, 2nd edn 1964) *Culture: a Critical Review of Concepts and Definitions*, Cambridge, Mass: Museum Papers col. 47.

Kuhnle, S. (1992) 'Norwegen', *Aus Politik und Zeitgeschichte*, B43/92, 12–21.

Kuisel, R. F. (1993) *Seducing the French: the Dilemma of Americanization*, University of California Press.

Kundera, M. (1984) 'A Kidnapped West or Culture Bows Out', *Granta*, 11, 93–119.

Kurcz, Z. (1999) 'Polnische Grenzregionen im Vergleich', *Welttrends*, 19, 63–74.

Langer, J. (1996) 'The Meanings of the Border in Central Europe', in Éger, G., Langer, J. (eds), 49–67.

Leo, R. (1998) 'Schengen and its Daily Practice on the Borders: the Particular Situation of the Borders in Friuli Venezia Giulia', in Anderson, M., Bort, E. (eds), 109–12.

Leonard, M. (1999) 'A World without Children', *New Statesman*, 11 October.

Leonardi, R. (1992) 'The Role of Sub-National Institutions in European Integration', *Regional Politics and Policy*, 2(1–2), 1–14.

Lepesant, G. (1996) 'Géopolitique des frontières orientales de l'Allemagne dans la perspective d'un élargissement de l'Union Européenne et de l'OTAN', Thesis, 2 vols, Lyon II.

Lepesant, G. (1998) *Géopolitique des Frontières orientales de l'Allemagne*, Paris: Harmattan.

Leresche, J. -P. (1995) 'Enclavement et désenclavement: la Suisse et la coopération régionale transfrontalière', *Revue Internationale de Politique Comparée*, 2(3), 485–504.

Leresche, J. -P. (1996) 'La Suisse au risque de la coopération transfrontalière? Recomposition des espaces régionaux et redefinition du fédéralisme', in Baulme, R. (ed.) *Les Politiques du néo-régionalisme*, Paris: Economica.

Leresche, J. Levy, R. (eds) (1995) *La Suisse et la coopération transfrontalière: repli ou redéploiement?* Zurich: Seismo.

Lesch, M. (1998) 'Die Eltern ließen ihr totes Kind zurück', *Die Welt*, 14 January.

Letamendia, F. (1997) 'Basque Nationalism and Cross-Border Co-operation between the Southern and Northern Basque Counties', *Regional and Federal Studies*, 7(2), 25–41.

Letamendia, F. (1997a) 'Régime institutionnel et coopération transfrontalière. La Comparaison entre le Nord et le Sud est-elle possible?' in Palard, J. (ed.), 51–70.

Lloyd, J. (1999) 'The Velvet Revolution with Material Failings', *Scotland on Sunday*, 14 November.

Long, A. (1998) 'NATO Membership Point of No Return for Hungary', *The Irish Times*, 7 October.

Loose, H. -W. (1998) 'Schmuggelware Mensch', *Die Welt*, 8 September.

Loughlin, J. (1993) 'Federalism, Regionalism and the European Union', *Politics*, 23(1), 9–16.

Loughlin, J. (1995) 'Regional Policy in the European Union', in Morgan, R., Stavridis, S. (eds) *EU Regional Policies in the 1990s*, Aldershot: Dartmouth.

Loughlin, J. (1996) 'Nation, State and Region in Western Europe', in L. Beckmans (ed.) *Culture: the Building-Stone of Europe 2002*, Brussels: Inter-University Press.

Loughlin, J. (1997) '"L'Europe des Régions" et la fédéralisation de l'Europe', in Palard, J. (ed.), 15–30.

Lukes, S. (1974) *Power: a Radical View*, London: Macmillan.

Luverà, B. (1996) *Oltre il confine. Regionalismo europeo e nuovi nazionlismi in Trentino-Alto Adige*, Bologna: Il Mulino.

Lyons, G. M., Mastanduno, M. (eds) (1995) *Beyond Westphalia? State Sovereignty and International Intervention*, Baltimore: Johns Hopkins University Press.

McCallum, J. (1995) 'National Borders Matter: Canada–U.S. Regional Trade Patterns', *American Economic Review*, 85(3), 615–23.

MacCormick, N. (1993) 'Beyond the Sovereign State', *Modern Law Review*, 56, 1–18.

MacCormick, N. (1999) *Questioning Sovereignty: Law, State and Nation in the European Commonwealth*, Oxford: Clarendon Press.

McCrone, D. (1998) *The Sociology of Nationalism*, London: Routledge.

Macdonald, S. (ed.) (1993) *Inside European Identities*, Oxford: Berg.

Machowicz, S. (1997) 'Euroregion Pomerania: Perspectives of a Quadruple Cross-Border Co-operation around the Baltic Sea, in Anderson, M., Bort, E. (eds), 99–101.

Malmberg, T. (1980) *Human Territoriality: a Survey of Behavioural Territories in Man with Preliminary Analysis and Discussion of Meaning*, Paris: Mouton.

Mann, M. (1993) 'Nation States in Europe and Other Continents: Diversifying, Developing, not Dying', *Daedalus*, 122(3), 115–40.

Mannin, M. (ed.) (1999) *Pushing the Boundaries: the European Union and Central and Eastern Europe*, Manchester: Manchester University Press.

Mannin, M. (1999a) 'EU–CEE relations: an overview', in Mannin, M. (ed.), 3–30.

Mannin, M. (1999b) 'Policies towards CEEC', in Mannin, M. (ed.), 31–69.

Marengo, F. D. (1998) 'The Mediterranean Boundaries of the European Union', in Murray, P., Holmes, L. (eds), *Europe: Rethinking the Boundaries*, Aldershot: Ashgate, 93–104.

Marks, G., Hooghe, L., Blank, K. (1994) 'European Integration from the 1980s: State-Centric vs Multi-Level Governance', *Journal of Common Market Studies*, 32, 3.

Martinez, O. J. (1994) 'The Dynamics of Border Integration: New Approaches to Border Analysis', in Schofield, H. (ed.) *Global Boundaries*, London: Routledge, 1–15.

Menville, J. (1996) 'Frontières et Capital-Risque Régional', *Sciences de la Société*, 37, 97–109.

Miles, R., Thränhardt, D. (eds) (1995) *Migration and European Integration: the Dynamics of Inclusion and Exclusion*, London: Pinter.

Miller, D. (1995) *On Nationality*, Oxford: Clarendon Press.

Molle, P. (1996) 'External Borders Pilot Project', *Placement Report*, Strasbourg: Centre des Études Européennes.

Montanari, A., Cortese, A. (1993) 'South to North Migration in a Mediterranean Perspective', in King, R. (ed.), *Mass Migrations in Europe: the Legacy and the Future*, London: Belhaven Press, 212–33.

Morata, F. (1995) 'L'Europe et le Réseau C-6: l'Emergence du Suprarégionalisme en Europe du Sud', *Pôle Sud*, 2, 117–27.

Moravcsik, A. (1998) *The Choice for Europe: Social Purpose and State Power from Messina to Maastricht*, Ithaca: Cornell University Press.

Moreau Deforges, P. (1995) 'Quelles Frontières pour l'Union Européenne', *RAMSES*, July, 261–7.

Moritz, M. (1993) 'Alte und neue Regionen', in *Régions, régionalismes et conscience régionale face à l'intégration européenne*, Cracow: Centre International de la Culture, 63–80.

Morris, D. S., Haigh, R. H. (1991) *Britain, Spain and Gibraltar*, London: Routledge.

Müller-Graff, P.-C. (1998) 'Whose Responsibilities are Frontiers?', in Anderson, M., Bort, E. (eds), 11–21.

Murphy, A. B. (1996) 'The Sovereign State as a Political–Territorial Ideal', in Biersteker T. J., Weber, C. (eds) *State Sovereignty as Social Construct*, Cambridge: Cambridge University Press.

Murray, P., Holmes, L. (eds) (1998) *Europe: Rethinking the Boundaries*, Aldershot: Ashgate.

Nairn, T. (1997) *Faces of Nationalism: Janus Revisited*, London: Verso.

Nairn, T. (1998) 'After Brobdingnag: Micro-states and their Future', in Anderson, M., Bort, E. (eds), 135–47.

Nairn, T. (2000) 'Interstitial Sovereignty, or Fleas and Elephants: Micro-sovereignty in the New World Order' in Bort, E., Evans, N. (eds), 101–8.

Ndiaye, P. (1996) 'La Coopération transfrontalière des collectivités décentralisées sur l'arc méditerranéen', *Sciences de la Société*, 37(2), 151–71.

Neubauer, M. (1997) 'Verflechtungen bis zur Tatra und zum Bug', *Franken Post*, 26 January.

Neuss, B., Jurczek, P., Hilz, W. (eds) (1998) *Grenzübergreifende Kooperation im östlichen Mitteleuropa*, Tübingen: Europäisches Zentrum für Föderalismus-Forschung.

Newton, B., Walsh, L. (1999) 'The Czech Republic: the Economic Road to Transformation', in Mannin, M. (ed.), 217–49.

Nicolas, J. (1991) 'Half Truths about Half Europe', *The Guardian*, 25 October.

Nikolopoulos, G. P. (1998) 'Security Arrangements at the External Borders of Schengen: a View from Greece', in den Boer, M. (ed.), 105–11.

Nobles, G. H. (1998) *American Frontiers: Cultural Encounters and Continental Conquest*, London: Penguin.

Nordman, D. (1998) *Frontières de France: de l'espace au territoire, XVIe–XIXe siècle*, Paris: Gallimard.

Nowak, J. (1994) *Europas Krisenherde*, Reinbek bei Hamburg: Rowohlt.

Ochmann, C. (1998) 'Auf dem Weg in die Europäische Union: Die politische Integrationsfähigkeit der Beitrittskandidaten', in Neuss, B. et al. (eds), 7–18.

Offe, C. (1996) 'Capitalism by Design? Democratic Theory Facing the Triple Transition in Eastern Europe', *Social Research*, 58(2), 3–13.

Ohmae, K. (1994) *The Borderless World*, London: HarperCollins.

O'Reilly, G. (1999) 'Gibraltar: Sovereignty Disputes and Territorial Waters', *Boundary and Security Bulletin*, 7(1), 67–81.

Ouyahia, E. (1996) 'Régions Transfrontalières et Environnement sur l'Arc Méditerranéen', *Sciences de la Société*, 37, 173–88.

Palard, J. (ed.) (1997) *L'Europe aux frontières: la coopération transfrontalière entre régions d'Espagne et de France*, Paris: Presses Universitaires de France.

Palidda, S. (ed.) (1996) *Immigrant Delinquency: the Social Construction of Deviant Behaviour and Criminality of Immigrants in Europe*, Brussels: European Community.

Perkmann, M. (1999) 'Building Governance Institutions Across European Borders', *Regional Studies*, 33(7), 657–67.

Perrin, B. (1996) 'Coopération transfrontalière des collectivités locales: Contenu et limites de l'accord de Karlsruhe', *Revue Adminstrative*, 27(2), 177–204.

Pfeiffer, F. (1999) 'Schleuserbande vor Gericht', *Süddeutsche Zeitung*, 13 January.

Pisani, E. (1992) 'En quête d'un avenir', in Balta, P. (ed.).

Plaschke, H. (1994) 'National Economic Cultures', in Zetterholm, S. (ed.) *National Cultures and European Integration*, Oxford: Berg.

Platzöder, R. and Verlaan, P. (eds) (1997) *The Baltic Sea: New Developments in National Politics and International Cooperation*, The Hague: Kluwer Law International.

Poalini, A. J., Jarvis, A. P., Reus-Smit, C. (1998) *Between Sovereignty and Global Governance: the United Nations, the State and Civil Society*, Basingstoke: Macmillan.

Prantl, H. (1998) 'Europa verschließt sich Flüchtlingen', *Süddeutsche Zeitung*, 3 September.

Prantl, H. (1999) 'Wieviel Nachzug?', *Süddeutsche Zeitung*, 22 January.

Raento, P. (1997) 'Together and Apart: the Changing Context of the Basque Borderland', in Landgren, L. -F., Hyrynen, M. (eds) *The Dividing Line: Borders and National Peripheries*, Renvall Institute Publications 9, 241–8.

Raento, P. (1997a) 'Political Mobilisation and Place-specificity: Radical Nationalist Street Campaigning in the Basque Country', *Space and Polity*, 2(1), 191–204.

Raith, W. (1995) *Organisierte Kriminalität*, Reinbek bei Hamburg: Rowohlt Taschenbuch Verlag.

Ratti, R. (1996) 'Problématique de la Frontière et du Développement des Régions-Frontières', *Sciences de la Société*, 37, 37–48.

Ratti, R., Reichmen, S. (eds) (1993) *Theory and Practice of Transborder Cooperation*, Basel: Helbing & Lichtenhahn.

Reinecke, W. H. (1998) *Global Public Policy: Governing without Government?*, Washington DC: Brookings Institution.

Richardson, J. (ed.) (1996) *European Union: Power and Policy Making*, London: Routledge.

Richter-Malabotta, M. (1998) 'Some Aspects of Regional and Transfrontier Co-operation in a Changing Europe', in Anderson, M., Bort, E. (eds) (1998b), 41–72.

Rippert, L. (1998) 'Sicherung der Außengrenzen der Bundesrepublik Deutschland', in den Boer, M. (ed.), 93–9.

Rizk, M. (1997) *Sarreguemines: une ville au cœur de la dynamique européenne*, Paris: Mémoire Institut des Etudes Politiques de Paris.

Roch, I. (1999) 'Grenzüberschreitende Regionalentwicklung – Basis europäischer Integration?' *Welttrends*, 22, 44–62.

Rohrlich, P. E. (1987) 'Economic Culture and Foreign Policy: the Cognitive Analysis of Economic Policy Making', *International Organisation*, 41, 1.

Roth, V. (1981) 'Analyse und Evaluation bestehender Kooperationsmodelle im Raume Basel,' in Biucchi, B., Gauderd, G. (eds) *Régions Frontalières*, Saint Saphorin: Editions Georgi.

Rufin, J.-C. (1991) *L'Empire et les nouveaux barbares*, Paris: Editions Jean-Claude Lattès.

Ruggie, J. R. (1993) 'Territoriality and Beyond: Problematizing Modernity', *International Organisation*, 47(1), 139–74.

Sack, R. D. (1986) *Human Territoriality: its Theory and History*, Cambridge: Cambridge University Press.

Saez, G., Leresche, J. -P., Bassand, M. (1997) *Gouvernance métropolitaine et transfrontalière*, Paris: Harmattan.

Sahlins, P. (1989) *Boundaries: the Making of France and Spain in the Pyrenees*, Berkeley: University of California Press.

Said, E. (1993) *Culture and Imperialism*, London: Chatto & Windus.

Scherer, P. (1998) 'Geheimdienste schlagen Alarm', *Die Welt*, 21 August.

Schmidt-Häuer, C. (1999) 'In der Warteschlange', *Die Zeit*, 21 October.

Schmitt-Egner, P. (1994) *Europas kooperiende Regionen*, Baden-Baden: Nomos.

Schmitt-Egner, P. (1996) 'Die "Europäische Kompetenz" von Regionen – ein Paradigma für den Transnationalen Regionalismus', *Interegiones*, 5, 7–56.

Schnapper, D. (1998) *Community of Citizenship; on the Modern Idea of Nationality*, London: Transaction Publishers.

Schneider, J. (1998) 'Spezialisten für Grenzfälle', *Süddeutsche Zeitung*, 3 September.

Schöpflin, G. (1993) 'Hungary and its Neighbours', *Chaillot Papers*, 7, Paris: Institute for Security Studies of WEU.

Schöttler, P. (1997) Presentation of Febvre, L., *Le Rhin: histoire, mythes et réalités*, Paris: Perrin.

Schubert, M. (1993) *Die Mitteleuropa-Konzeption Friedrich Naumann und die Mitteleuropa-Debatte der 80er Jahre*, Sindelfingen: Libertas.

Schuler, M. et al. (1997) *Strukturatlas der Schweiz*, Zurich: Bundesamt für Statistik.

Schultz, H., Nothnagle, A. (eds) (1996) *Grenze der Hoffnung: Geschichte und Perspektiven der Grenzregion an der Oder*, Potsdam: Verlag für Berlin-Brandenburg.

Schwennicke, C. (1997) 'Abwehrmauer an den Ostgrenzen', *Süddeutsche Zeitung*, 3 January.

Scott, J. (1989) 'Transborder Cooperation, Regional Initiatives, and Sovereignty: Conflicts in the Upper Rhine Valley', *Publius*, 19.

Scott, J. (1997) 'Dutch German Euroregions: a Model for Transboundary Cooperation', in Ganster, P. et al. (eds), 107–40.

Severin, K. (1997) 'Illegale Einreise und internationale Schleuserkriminalität: Hintergründe, Beispiele und Maßnahmen', *Aus Politik und Zeitgeschichte*, B46.

Sheptycki, J. (1995) 'Transnational Policing and the Makings of a Postmodern State', *British Journal of Criminology*, 35(4) (Autumn), 613–35.

Sheptycki, J. (1996) 'Law Enforcement, Justice and Democracy in the Transnational Arena: Reflections on the War on Drugs', *International Journal of the Sociology of Law*, 24, 61–75.

Sheptycki, J. (1998) 'Police Co-operation in the English Channel Region 1968–1996', *European Journal of Crime, Criminal Law and Criminal Justice*, 6(3), 216–35.

Sheridan, K. (1999) 'Czechs give President a Warm Welcome', *The Irish Times*, 20 October.

Skok, M. (1998) 'Selective Integration? Schengen Restrictions and the Dynamic of Transborder Connections between Slovenia and Italy', in Anderson, M., Bort, E. (eds) (1998b), 73–91.

Smart, V. (1995) 'Europol Warning on Eastern Mafias', *The European*, 31 August.

Smith, A. D. (1986) *The Ethnic Origins of Nations*, Oxford: Blackwell.

Smith, A. D. (1992) 'National Identity and the Idea of European Unity', *International Affairs*, 68(1), 55–76.

Smith, A. D. (1995) *Nations and Nationalism in the Global Era*, Cambridge: Polity.

Staunton, D. (1999) 'Saturday Profile: Jörg Haider', *The Irish Times*, 9 October.

Stewart, A. (1992) *Migrants, Minorities and Security in Europe*, London: Research Institute for the Study of Conflict and Terrorism.

Stokke, O. S., Tunander, O. (1994) *The Barents Region: Co-operation in Arctic Europe*, London: Sage.

Strassoldo, R. (1972) *Sviluppo Regionale e Difensa Nazionale*, Trieste: Lint.

Strassoldo, R. (1973) 'Regional Development and National Defense: a Conflict of Values and Power in a Frontier Region', in Strassoldo, R. (ed.) *Boundaries and Regions*, Trieste: Lint.

Strassoldo, R. (1998) 'Perspectives on Frontiers: the Case of Alpe-Adria', in Anderson, M., Bort, E. (eds) (1998a), 75–90.

Strassoldo, R. (1999) 'Studying Borders in the Gorizia Area', in Bort, E., Keat, R. (eds), 129–38.

Sultana, R. G. (1999) 'Towards Increased Collaboration in the South: the Mediterranean Education Project', in Cvjeticanin, B. (ed.), 179–85.

Szász, J. A. (1997), 'The Role of Folklore in the Identity of Minorities: Mother Country and Region, Cultural Interaction and Co-operation', in Svob-Doka, N. (ed.), 45–58.

Tannam, E. (1995) 'EU Regional Policy and the Northern Ireland Cross-Border Administrative Relationship', *Regional and Federal Studies*, 5(1), 67–93.

Tapia, C. (1997) *Les Jeunes face à l'Europe. Représentations, Valeurs, Idéologies*, Paris: Presses Universitaires de France.

Tebbe, G. (1998) 'Wirtschaftliche Voraussetzungen der EU-Mitgliedschaft: Polen und Tschechien', in Neuss, B. et al. (eds), 19–31.

Tikkanen, V., Käkönen, J. (1997) 'The Evolution of Cooperation in the Kuhmo-Kostamuksha Region of the Finnish–Russian Border', in Ganster, P. et al. (eds), 163–75.

Tlili, R. (1999) 'Culture et géopolitique en Méditerranée', in Cvjeticanin, B. (ed.), 65–70.

Tomasevski, K. (1992) *Prison Health*, Helsinki: Helsinki Institute for Crime Prevention and Control.

Tomasevski, K. (1994) *Foreigners in Prison*, Helsinki: Helsinki Institute for Crime Prevention and Control.

Tovias, A. (1997) 'The EU and Mediteranean Countries', *Marmara Journal of European Studies*, 5(1–2), 119–32.

Traynor, I. (1998) 'Fortress Europe shuts Window to the East', *The Guardian*, 9 February.

Turner, F. J. (1953, first published 1894) *The Frontier in American History*, London: Holt.

Urban, T. (1999) 'Heute gestohlen, morgen in Polen', *Süddeutsche Zeitung*, 18 December.

Usher, J. (1998) 'Languages and the European Union', in Anderson, M., Bort, E. (eds), 222–34.

Vasconcelos, A. (1996) 'General Frameworks and Concepts', in Faria, F., Vasconcelos, A. (eds) *Security in Northern Africa: Ambiguity and Reality*, Paris: Institute for Security Studies/Western European Union (Chaillot Paper 25).

Veijalainen, R. (1998) 'Security Arrangements at the External Borders of Schengen: a View from Finland', in den Boer, M. (ed.), 101–11.

Vernier, A. (1993) 'Problèmes posés aux Régions Frontalières', *Revue de l'Institut de Recherches Economiques et Sociales*, 2, 65–92.

Von Lampe, K. (1995) 'Understanding Organized Crime: a German View', paper presented at the Annual Meeting of the Academy of Criminal Justice Sciences, Boston, Mass., 7–11 March (extended version).

Von Malchus, V. (1975) *Partnerschaft an europäischen Grenzen: Integration durch grenzüberschreitende Zusammenarbeit*, Bonn: Europa Union Verlag.

Von Richthofen, F. (ed. Petersen, K. D.) (1984) *Entdeckungsreisen in China: 1868–1872: Die Ersterforschung des Reiches der Mitte*, Darmstadt: Wissenschaftliche Buchgesellschaft.

Vidal de la Blache, P. (1917) *La France de l'Est*, Paris: Colin.

Vrbetic, M. (1995) *European Union and its Neighbors in the East and the South*, Zagreb: Institute for International Relations (Euroscope Reports 1).

Waever, O. (1996) 'European Security Identities', *Journal of Common Market Studies*, 34(1), 103–32.

Waever, O., Kelstrup, M. (1993) 'Europe and its Nations: Political and Cultural Identities', in Wæver, O. et al., 61–92.

Waever, O., Buzan, B., Kelstrup, M., Lemaitre, P. (1993) *Identity, Migration and the New Security Agenda in Europe*, London: Pinter.

Wallace, C., Chmouliar, O., Sidorenko, E. (1997) *The Eastern Frontier of Western Europe: Mobility in the Buffer Zone*, Vienna: Institute for Advanced Studies.

Wallace, H., Wallace, W. (eds) (1996) *Policy Making in the European Union*, Oxford: Oxford University Press.

Wallace, W. (1983) 'Less than a Federation – More than a Regime: the Community as a Political System' in Wallace, H. et al. (eds) *Policy Making in the European Union*, Chichester: Wiley.

Wallace, W. (1991) *The Transformation of Western Europe*, London: Pinter.

Walzer, M. (1983) *Spheres of Justice*, Oxford: Blackwell.

Ward, I. (1996) *The Margins of European Law*, Basingstoke and London: Macmillan.

Waterman, P. (1998) *Globalization, Social Movements and the New Internationalism*, London: Mansell.

Weber, C. (1995) *Simulating Sovereignty: Intervention, the State and Symbolic Exchange*, Cambridge: Cambridge University Press.

Weber, E. (1977) *Peasants into Frenchmen: the Modernisation of Rural France*, London: Chatto & Windus.

Weiner, M. (1995) *The Global Migration Crisis: Challenges to States and to Human Rights*, New York: HarperCollins.

Weissman, O. (1997) 'Arbeitsgemeinschaft Donauländer: Multi-Regional Co-operation for a Common Europe', in Anderson, M. Bort, E. (eds), 85–90.

Wiberg, U. (1993) 'Transborder Co-operation between Universities', in Ratti, R., Reichman, S. (eds), 331–45.

Widgren, J. (1990) 'International Migration and Regional Stability', *International Affairs*, 66(4), 749–66.

Willan, P. (1999) 'Hands off Our Menfolk, Says Miniature State', *The Guardian*, 24 August.

Wils, L. (1996) *Histoire des Nations Belges*, Ottignies: Quorum.

Wilson, T. M., Donnan H. (eds) (1998) *Border Identities: Nation and State at International Frontiers*, Cambridge: Cambridge University Press.

Wösendorfer, H. (1997) 'Hainburg–Gabcikovo–Nagymaros: Symbols of Conflict in the 1980s and '90s', in Anderson, M., Bort, E. (eds), 91–8.

Zanettin, M. -P. (1997) 'La Conurbation Bayonne/Saint Sebastien à l'épreuve de l'Acte Unique: les frontières de la mythologie européenne', in Palard, J. (ed.), 155–68.

Zetterholm, S. (ed.) (1994) *National Cultures and European Integration*, Oxford: Berg.

Zielonka, J. (1991) 'Europe's Security: a Great Confusion', *International Affairs*, 67(1), 127–37.

Documents

Accord entre le Ministère de l'Economie et des Finances de la République Française et le Ministère Fédéral d'Allemagne sur la Coopération des Administrations Douanières dans les Régions Frontalières Communes, Lyon 12 March 1997.

AEBR/European Commission (eds) (1997, 2nd edn.) *Practical Guide to Cross-border Cooperation*, Gronau: AEBR (Association of European Border Regions).

AEBR/LACE (Linkage Assistance and Cooperation for the European Border Regions) (1993) *Grenzüberschreitende Zusammenarbeit in der Praxis: Infrastruktur und Planung in grenzüberschreitenden Regionen (Anhang 1)*, Gronau: AEBR.

Apeilor – Association pour l'Expansion Industrielle de la Lorraine (1997) *La Lorraine: une économie ouverte sur le monde*, Metz.

Arbeitsgruppe der Glasmuseen und Glassammlungen/Euregio Böhmerwald-Bayerischer Wald (eds) (1994) *Glas ohne Grenzen/Sklo bez Hranic*, Deggendorf: Weiss.

Association des Élus pour un département Pays Basque (1997) *Pourquoi un département Pays Basque*, Bayonne.

Aubert (1993) 'Rapport de la Commission d'Enquête sur les moyens de lutter contre les tentatives de pénétration de la Mafia en France', *Journal Officiel de la République Française*, Assemblée Nationale, 28 January, Document no. 3251.

Bayonne–San Sebastián (1997) *Note Technique sur le montage opérationnel et financier de l'observatoire transfrontalier Bayonne/San Sebastián*, Diputatiòn foral de Guipuzkoa: District Bayonne-Anglet-Biarritz.

BEGIRA–Observatoire Economique du Pays Basque, EUSTAT-Vittoria, Insituto de Estadistica-Navarra (1998) *L'Industrie en Aquitaine-C.A. Euskadi-Navarre CEMR (1995)*

Bundesministerium für Raumordnung, Bauwesen und Städtebau (ed.) (1995) *Raumordnerische Leitbilder für den Raum entlang der deutsch–polnischen Grenze*, Bonn.

Chambre de Commerce et de l'Industrie (CCI) de la Moselle (1996) *La Coopération Transfrontalière dans l'Espace Sar-Lor-Lux Metz*.

CCI de Perpignan et des Pyrénées Orientales (1994) *Regards sur l'Economie des Pyrénées Orientales*, Perpignan.

CCI de Perpignan et des Pyrénées Orientales (1997) *Les Pyrénées Orientales territoire frontalier: concurrence et coopération Saillagouse*.

CCI pour le Nord de l'Espagne (1997) *Implantations transfrontalières*.

Collège Européen de Technologie (1997) *Rapport d'Activités 1997*, Longlaville.

Colmar, Direction des Affaires Economiques et de l'Emploi (1998) *Coopération Transfrontalière*, Colmar–Freiburg 22 January.

Communauté de Travail des Pyrénées (1994) *Charte d'Action*, Prades 6–7 May 1993, Jaca.

Conseil du Léman (1997) *Résultats de l'étude sur la conscience lémanique*, Geneva.

Convention de coopération en vue de la création d'un groupement local de coopération transfrontalière, Centre Hardt-Rhin Supérieur du 5 novembre 1997, Freiburg im Breisgau.

Convention Tripartite: Collège Européen de Technologie – France, Belgium, Luxembourg, Athus 22 April 1991.

Co-operation in the Baltic Region (1996), compiled by Stalvant, C. -E., Baltic Sea States Summit, Visby 3–4 May 1996.

Coopération transfrontalière dans l'espace Saar-Lor-Lux (1996), Metz: Chambre de Commerce et d'Industrie.

COPEF (n.d.) *Etudes des échanges économiques des régions du territoire de la COPEF*, Blagnac.

Council of the Baltic States (1994) *'BSS Monitor' for III Ministerial Session*, Tallinn.

Council of Europe (1983) *European Outline Convention on Transfrontier Co-operation between Territorial Communities or Authorities*.

Council of European Municipalities and Regions, Reference Book 1995/6, London: Kensington Publications.

DATAR (1992) *Projet Pyrénées de l'Etat pour le XIème Plan*, 3 vols, Toulouse: Commissariat à l'Aménagement des Pyrénées.

DATAR (1997) *Espaces transfrontaliers. La Lettre de la Mission Opérationnelle Transfrontalière*, Paris: Ministère de l'Équipement.

DATAR (1998) *Les Projets transfrontaliers. Colloque le 15 et le 16 janvier 1998 à Strasbourg*, Paris: Ministère de l'Aménagement du Territoire et de l'Environnement.

Déclaration Commune pour un Pôle Européen de Développement par la République Française, le Grand Duché de Luxembourg et le Royaume de Belgique, Luxembourg 19 July 1985.

Département de l'Ariège (1995) *La Clientèle Espagnole à Bonsacre*, Winter 94/95 Comité départemental du tourisme: Foix.

Direcció General de la Planificació i Acció Territorial (1993) *Euregió: Eurorégion. Midi Pyrénées, Languedoc-Roussillon, Catalunya*, Barcelona.

Direction Régionale de l'Équipement: Midi Pyrénées (1997) *Liaisons transpyrénéennes trafics*.

EUREFI (Europe–Régions–Financement) (1996) *Fonds Transfrontalier de Développement*, Arlon: Longlaville.

European Commission (1997) *L'Expérience RECITE I. Rapport d'évaluation du Recite Office. Première génération de projets: 1900–1995*, Brussels.

European Commission (n.d.) *ECOS-Ouverture: a European Commission Programme for External Interregional Co-operation*, Brussels.

European Communities (1997) *Single Market Review*, vol. 3 no. 3 'Customs and Fiscal Formalities at Frontiers', prepared by Price Waterhouse, Luxembourg: Official Publications of the European Communities.

European Communities (1997a) *Single Market Review*, vol. 5 'Road Freight Transport', prepared by NEA Transport Research and Training, Luxembourg: Official Publications of the European Communities.

European Parliament (1994) *Organisations Representing Regional and Local Authorities at the European Level*, Strasbourg.

European Treaty Series 106 (1980) *European Conventions and Agreements*, Vol. IV *1975–1982*, Strasbourg: Council of Europe.

Euregio Bayerischer Wald–Böhmerwald (ed.) (n.d.) *Der Weg in die gemeinsame Zukunft*, Freyung.

Euregio Bayerischer Wald–Böhmerwald (ed.) *Euregio-Post: Informationsblatt*, Freyung.

Euregio Egrensis (ed.) (n.d.) *Willkommen im Herzen Europas*, Plauen.

Euregió: Eurorégion, Midi Pyrénées, Languedoc-Roussillon, Catalunya. (1993), Barcelona: Direcció General de la Planificació i Acció Territorial.

Europa-Universität Viadrina (n.d.) *Studieren an der Europa-Universität Viadrina*, Frankfurt/Oder.

Euroregion Elbe–Labe (ed.) (1995) *Kultur- und Sportkalender*, Pirna.

Euroregion Niemen (ed.) (1996) *A Project of Establishing of [sic] the Trans-Border Union of Euroregion 'Niemen'*, Suwalki.

Euroregion Pro Europa Viadrina (n.d.) *Die Euroregion Pro Europa Viadrina stellt sich vor*, Frankfurt/Oder.

Euroregion Spree–Neiße–Bober (ed.) (1997) *Auf dem Weg nach Europa*, Guben.

Freistaat Bayern/Kommission der Europäischen Gemeinschaften (1995) *INTERREG II Gemeinschaftsinitiative zur Förderung grenzüberschreitender Zusammenarbeit im bayerisch–tschechischen Grenzraum (Operationelles Programm 1995–1999)*, Munich.

Freistaat Sachsen (1997) *Abwasserentsorgung über Grenzen hinweg*, Leipzig: Staatsministerium für Umwelt und Landesentwicklung.

Gazetta Ufficiale della Repubblica Italiana (1997) *Legge 31 dicembre 1996*, n. 675, n. 676 Rome 8 January 1997.

Generalitat de Catalunya (1998) *El Libre Verd de les Energies Renovables a l'Euregio/LE Livre Vert des énergies renouvables de l'Euroregion*, Barcelona.

Gobierno de Navarra (1992) *Impacto del mercado. nico europeo en la empresa industrial navarra*, Pamplona.

Gobierno de Navarra (1992a) *Las comarcas fronterizas de Navarra ante el mercado nico*, Pamplona.

Groupe de Travail Intercommunal dans l'espace Sarro-Lorraine (1994) *Projets pour un avenir commun en Europe*, Interreg II, Sarreguemines.

Groupe de Travail Intercommunal 'SarreMoselle Avenir' (1997) *Etude sur la question du statut juridique de 'SarreMoselle Avenir' et les diverses possibilités de créer un organisme de coopération transfrontalière*, directed by Eckly, P., Seiter, N., Académie de la Coopération Transfrontalière, Blaesheim.

House of Lords, Select Committee on the European Communities (1998) Session 1997–98, 31st Report, *Incorporating the Schengen Acquis into the European Union*, London: Stationery Office.

House of Lords, Select Committee on European Communities (1999) Session 1998–99, 7th Report, *Schengen and the United Kingdom's Border Controls*, London: Stationery Office.

INFOBEST (1996, 1997) *Rapport d'Activités*, Vogelgrun-Breisach.

INSEE (1998) 'Le Chômage par zones d'emploi', INSEE Première 577.

Internationale Bodenseekonferenz (ed.) (1995) *Bodenseeleitbild*, Konstanz.

Kommunalgemeinschaft Europaregion Pomerania e.V. (ed.) (1996) *Die Pomerania: Eine Euroregion stellt sich vor*, Löcknitz.

Kommunalgemeinschaft Europaregion Pomerania e.V. (n.d.) *Eine Präsentation*, Löcknitz.

LACE (1997) *Fiches Info*.

LACE Magazine (1997–98) *Les Pyrénées et leurs Régions*, 1, 17–23.

Landesamtsdirektion-Öffentlichkeitsarbeit/Niederösterreichische Landesregierung (ed.) (1993) *Die ARGE Donauländer* (Niederösterreichische Schriften 67), Vienna.

Ministère de l'Économie, des Finances et de l'Industrie (1998) *L'Action de la Douane en 1997, le 23 mars 1998*, Paris: Direction de la Communication.

Ministère de l'Intérieur – Direction Générale de la Police Nationale (1997) *Plan d'Action pour la Direction Centrale du Contrôle de l'Immigration et de la Lutte contre l'Emploi des Clandestins de 1997 à 2000*, June 1997.

OECD (1979) *The Protection of the Environment in Frontier Regions*, Paris: OECD.

OECD (1997) *Outlook for Employment*, Paris, OECD.

PAMINA (Palatinat, Mittelerer Oberrhein, Nord Alsace) (1995) *Comportements socio-économiques de la population dans l'espace PAMINA 1994*, Karlsruhe.

Pays d'Ariège (n.d.) *Journal du Conseil Général de l'Ariège*, no. 27. Dossier Ariège Catalogne.

PED 10 ans, un Espace nouveau, un avenir partagé Pôle Européen de Développement IDELUX, Longlaville 1995.

Préfecture de la Région Lorraine, *Revue de la Presse Transfrontalière*, 6 issues a year.

Prefet de Région Midi-Pyrénées (1995) *Fonds Structurels 1994/1999.*

Programme Pyréne, Toulouse: Commissariat à l'Amènagement des Pyrénées.

Protocol (1991) between the Government of the United Kingdom and the Government of the French Republic, Concerning Frontier Controls and Policing, Co-operation in Criminal Justice, Public Safety and Mutual Assistance Relating to the Channel Fixed Link, Sangatte, 25 November, London: HMSO.

Regio-Büro-Bodensee (ed.) (1996) *Grenzübergreifende kooperative Aktivitäten in der Regio Bodensee*, Konstanz.

Région Languedoc Roussillon (1998) *Panorama du Languedoc Roussillon*, Montpellier.

Région Languedoc Roussillon (1993, 1998) *Catalan – Pratiques et Représentations dans les Pyrénées Orientales*, Sondage – Résultats et Analyses, Montpellier.

République Française (1993) Journal Officiel 6 January 1996, 227, *L'Accord entre le gouvernement de la République française et le gouvernement de la République italienne concernant la coopération transfrontalière entre collectivités territoriales, signé à Rome le 26 novembre 1993.*

République Française – Assemblée Nationale (1994) *Rapport d'information déposé par la délégation de l'Assemblée Nationale pour les Communautés Européennes sur les propositions de la Commission Européenne relatives au franchissement des frontières extérieures et à la politique des visas*, Paris, 1 June.

République Française, Ministère de l'Intérieur (1997) *Plan d'Action pour la Direction Centrale du Contrôle de l'Immigration et de la Lutte contre l'Emploi des Clandestins de 1997 à l'an 2000*, Paris, June.

République Française – Sénat (1997) *Session Extraordinaire de 1996–1997, annexe au procès-verbal de la séance du 24 septembre 1997, Rapport fait au nom de la commission des Affaires étrangères* (on the abolition of frontier controls and the entry of Italy and Greece into Schengen).

République Française – Sénat (1997a) *Session Ordinaire de 1997–1998, annexe au procès-verbal de la séance du 18 octobre 1997, Rapport d'information sur l'intégration de Schengen dans l'Union Européenne.*

Résolution du Comité d'Accompagnement Politique sur les Orientations Futures du Pôle Européen de Développement, Pétange 1 July.

Résolution Commune du 29 octobre 1993 relative à l'agglomération du Pôle Européen de Développement par la Région Wallone, le Gouvernement Français et le Grand Duché de Luxembourg, Longwy 1993.

Saar Moselle Avenir (1997) *Assemblée Générale Constitutive 25 Nov. 1997*, Sarreguemines.

Schmitt-Egner, P. (1994) *Report submitted for Europa 2000*: 'Développement des régions frontalières et de la coopération transfrontalière dans une démarche d'intégration: éléments d'analyse et de proposition', Section 3.

Statuts du groupement local de coopération transfrontalière 'Centre Hardt-Rhin Supérieur' du 27 novembre 1997, Bad Krozingen.

Transpireneus (1994) 'Programme coprésenté par le département de l'Ariège et les collectivités locales des Pyrénées espagnoles', Foix: duplicated.

Ueberschlag, J. Député du Haut Rhin (1996) *La Coopération Transfrontalière, Rapport à Monsieur le Premier Ministre*, Paris: Ministère de l'Équipement.

Vernier, A. (1993) *Rapport sur l'aménagement du territoire dans les régions frontalières*, Paris: Confédération Française des Travailleurs Chrétiens, Institut des Recherches Economiques et Sociales.

Ville de Menton, Città de Ventimiglia (1991) *Protocole d'Intention. Coopération Transfrontalière de Proximité*, 22 April.

Interviews

Ellen Ahnfelt, Norwegian Ministry of Justice, September 1996.
Gil Arias Fernández, Head of Asylum, Frontiers and Immigration, Spanish National Police, November 1997.
Peter auf der Maur, Chief of Police, Basel, July 1997.
René Basset, Customs, Sarreguemines, January 1998.
Regierungsdirektor Johann Bauer, Main Customs Office, Weiden, March 1996.
Colonel Wosjack Brochwicz, Deputy Commander-in-Chief of the Polish Border Police, June 1996.
Llibert Cuatrecasas, Comisionat per a Actuaciones Exteriors, Generalitat de Catalunya, September 1996.
Françoise Delcasso, Chambre de Commerce et d'Industrie de Perpignan et des Pyrénées Orientales, Antenne de Saillagouse, June 1998.
Pedro Diaz-Pintado Moraleda, Sub-Director of the General Directorate of the Spanish National Police, November 1997.
Jean-Paul Durieux, Mayor of Longwy, January 1995.
Jean Dussourd, Préfet des Hautes-Pyrénées, December 1995.
Jens Eikas, Norwegian Ministry of Foreign Affairs, September 1996.
Robert Eugster, Assistant Director Swiss Federal Aliens Office, July 1997.
Rémy Festhauer, Caisse Primaire d'Assurance Maladie, Sarreguemines, January 1998.
Raymond Gantz, maire of Kunheim, President of SIVOM Hardt-Nord, January 1998.
Marko Gasperlin, Head of the Bureau for State Border Security and Aliens, Slovenian Ministry of the Interior, November 1996, March 1998.
Marian Kalek, Head of Border Station, Olszyna/Forst, March 1996.
Franz Kauper, Polizeioberrat, Border Police, Furth im Wald, March 1996.
Eva Kettis, Council of the Baltic Sea States, Swedish Ministry for Foreign Affairs, September 1996.
Catherine Kunegel, Secretary General, Pole Européen de Développement, Longwy, January 1998.
Joseph Lauter, Collège Européen de Technologie, Longlaville, January 1995.
Christian Masson, Affaires Economiques et de l'Emploi, Colmar, January 1998.
Robert Mauchoffe, Caisse Primaire d'Assurance Maladie, Sarreguemines, January 1998.
Daniel Meyer, Député-Maire, Colmar, January 1998.
Christoph Moschberger, Infobest, Vogelgrun Breisach, January 1998.
Milos Mrkvica, Head of Migration Division, Foreign and Border Police, Prague, March 1996, September 1998.
José Maria Muñoa, Director External Affairs, Basque Autonomous Government, October 1996.
Per Nuder MP, Swedish Parliament, September 1996.
Jean Perrin, CCI de Colmar et du Centre-Alsace, Colmar, January 1998.
Colonel Jerzy Piwowarski, Head of Border Security, Olszyna/Forst, March 1996.

Michel Prétat, CCI de la Moselle, January 1998.

Manuel Prieto Montero, Commissioner for Aliens and Documentation, Spanish National Police, November 1997.

Jean-Marc Risse, Secretary General, Mairie, Sarreguemines, January 1998.

Michele Rossi, Political and Institutional Section, Swiss Federal Department of Foreign Affairs, July 1997.

Pascal Royer, Chambre de Commerce de Perpignan et des Pyrénées Orientales, June 1998.

Claude Salgues, Chambre de Commerce de Perpignan et des Pyrénées Orientales, June 1998.

Regierungsdirektor Schneider, Grenzlandbüro, Regierungspräsidium Freiburg, November 1995, July 1998.

Ivo Schwarz, Director of Foreign and Border Police, Plzen, March 1996.

Corrado Scivoletto, Prefect, Commissioner Extraordinary of the Italian Government for Immigration, March 1997.

Jutta Seidel, State Chancellery, Free State of Saxony, May 1996.

Jean-Marius Solano, Maire adjoint de Bayonne, Relations Transfrontalières, District Bayonne Anglet Biarritz, June 1998.

Colonel Jacques Strahm, Swiss Frontier Guards, Region III, July 1997.

Michel R. Théraulaz, Chief of Cantonal Police, Geneva, July 1997.

Adelin Thomas, Collège Européen de Technologie, Longlaville, January 1998.

Stein Ulrich, Chief of Police, Ski, Norway, September 1996.

M. R. C. van Ginderen, Euregio Maas-Rhein, September 1997.